W9-CHL-548

PLACE IN RETURN BOX to remove this checkout from your record.
TO AVOID FINES return on or before date due.
MAY BE RECALLED with earlier due date if requested.

DATE DUE	DATE DUE	DATE DUE
MAR 3 0 2003	MAY 1 0 2004	
07 27 05		
JAN 2 1 2006		
SEP 0 2 2007		
NOV 2 9 2007		

6/01 c:/CIRC/DateDue.p65-p.15

THE AMERICAN
WAR AND PEACE
1860-1877

THE AMERICAN WAR AND PEACE, 1860-1877

Emory M. Thomas
University of Georgia

PRENTICE-HALL, INC., *Englewood Cliffs, New Jersey*

Library of Congress Cataloging in Publication Data

Thomas, Emory M.
   The American war and peace, 1860–1877.

   Bibliography:
   1. United States—History—1849–1877.   2. United
States—History—Civil War.   3. Reconstruction.
I. Title.
E415.7.T48   973.7   72–12609
ISBN 0–13–211417–8
ISBN 0–13–211409–7 (pbk)

© 1973 by Prentice-Hall, Inc.
Englewood Cliffs, New Jersey

Printed in the United States of America

10   9   8   7   6   5   4   3   2   1

Prentice-Hall International, Inc., *London*
Prentice-Hall of Australia, Pty. Ltd., *Sydney*
Prentice-Hall of Canada, Ltd., *Toronto*
Prentice-Hall of India Private Limited, *New Delhi*
Prentice-Hall of Japan, Inc., *Tokyo*

For My Mother and Father
and
for Mary Pollard Thomas

CONTENTS

PREFACE

The title of this book is a pedantic double entendre which I hope expresses the significance of what happened to Americans between 1860 and 1877. This was *The* American war; this conflict and the peace settlement of Reconstruction defined much of the American experience before 1860 and conditioned much of American life after 1877. This was the American *War and Peace* in the same sense that Leo Tolstoy perceived Russia's epic struggle against Napoleon. Perhaps Gettysburg was the American Borodino.

The events of this era lend themselves to dramatic narrative, and here I have tried within an informal narrative approach to preserve some of the drama of the times. Because no history, narrative or otherwise, can be void of the historian's preconceptions and biases, I have abandoned subtlety and openly advocated an interpretation centering upon ideologies—a clash of ideologies or world views which made war a possibility, then defined the combatants' response to the conflict, and finally conditioned the peace.

In addition to a narrative and an interpretation, I have also attempted a synthesis of recent scholarship about the period. Consequently my greatest debts are owed to those scholars whose labors have aided and inspired my own. Among a host of others, I especially appreciate the works and words of Professors Frank E. Vandiver, Bell I. Wiley, Raimondo Luraghi, Eugene D. Genovese, and Eric Foner. Naturally these gentlemen bear no responsibility for what I have done with their ideas; in most cases they were thoroughly unaware of their influence.

My gratitude extends more directly to Milton Kaplan of the Library of Congress, to Charles B. Hodges, Jr., of the University of Georgia, and to Robert P. Fenyo and Helen S. Harris of Prentice-Hall. I must also thank a number of anonymous readers who read all or part of the manuscript for Prentice-Hall; their constructive criticism has been invaluable.

Emory M. Thomas

THE 1
LATE
UNPLEASANTNESS

Some time between 3:00 and 3:20 on the morning of April 12, 1861, Colonel James Chesnut decided to begin the Civil War within an hour and a half. Chesnut made his decision reluctantly. The forty-six-year-old South Carolinian had been until recently a United States Senator. When continued union between South and North seemed intolerable to him, Chesnut accepted secession and the Southern Confederacy. On that fateful morning he was serving the Confederacy as aide to General P. G. T. Beauregard. A reasonable man, Chesnut realized that his new nation hardly needed war. Yet when called upon to decide between peace and war, Chesnut chose war. Under the circumstances, he felt he could do nothing else.

The circumstances in which Chesnut and his country found themselves were these. For some months the seven Confederate States of

America had asserted independence from the United States. The government in Washington had tried to ignore this assertion and conduct business as usual. But a portion of this business involved maintaining military installations within seceded states. Fort Sumter was such an installation, built upon an island which commanded the entrance to Charleston Harbor and garrisoned by the United States Army. Near Pensacola, Florida, on the Gulf Coast, the United States still held Fort Pickens, held it more firmly in fact than Sumter.

Possession of these forts became a cause célèbre. In his inaugural address back in March, Abraham Lincoln had insisted that he intended to retain Pickens and Sumter. To him surrender of government property was tantamount to surrender of governmental authority over the Southern states.

That "other" President, Jefferson Davis the Confederate, was also adamant about Pickens and Sumter. The Confederate States could not abide potentially hostile foreign forts upon Southern soil. Davis had seriously considered an overt assault upon Pickens and then abandoned the scheme as too risky. Ultimately, by early April both Davis and Lincoln focused their attention upon Fort Sumter. Both presidents sought a "showdown," an end to the tension which had been building for months. Davis believed (rightly) that his chances of winning a "showdown" were better at Sumter. Lincoln soon saw that his best opportunity to avoid losing the "showdown" was at Sumter. The fortress in Charleston Harbor was running out of food; Lincoln would have to act quickly.

Once the island fortress had attracted attention, neither side could break the impasse gracefully. General Beauregard's army could not "sneak" across open water and evict the garrison peaceably. Nor could the Confederates use the 47 guns they had trained on the fort without committing an overt act of war. On the other hand, Federal troops on the island could not get off without attracting attention and making the surrender look exactly like what it was.

Finally, hunger was the only hope of preserving the stalemate and a semblance of peace. Sumter's commander Major Robert Anderson would not surrender the fort; but he would evacuate it to save his men from starvation. Anderson was a good soldier; his orders were to stay, and he would follow those orders. Still, Anderson was from Kentucky; he shared the agonies of border-state men. He believed in union, yet he knew that Southerners were not ogres. Anderson dreaded the thought of civil war, and he dreaded even more the prospect that he might have a hand in starting that war. During the early days of April, Anderson continued to prepare Fort Sumter for war. He also kept a careful watch on his dwindling food supply and hoped that the war, if there had to be one, would begin somewhere else.

Then on April 8 President Lincoln, responding to the larger cause of union, dashed Anderson's hopes and sent a relief expedition to Sumter by sea. When the relief ship arrived, Anderson would be resupplied with food and could no longer abandon his post with honor. And Anderson was an honorable man.

President Davis and the Confederate government at Montgomery, Alabama, in turn responded to the Southern cause and to Lincoln's move. President Jefferson Davis determined to have Sumter and reasoned that Beauregard's army should capture the fort before the supplies arrived. Lincoln had given curt assurance that the ship contained only provisions; but Davis was not sure he could trust the man. Resupply, Davis reasoned, was an act of war. It was time to have the "showdown."

At 2:00 P.M. on April 11, Beauregard sent Chesnut to demand Anderson's surrender. Anderson refused. Neither man knew quite what to do next. Anderson asked if Confederate guns would open on the fort without further warning. Chesnut did not know; he thought not; he was sure there would be warning. The men shook hands, and just as Chesnut was preparing to leave Anderson remarked that unless the relief ship arrived very soon he would be "starved out." On the way back to Charleston and Beauregard's headquarters, Chesnut pondered Anderson's parting words. He repeated them to Beauregard and discussed the possibility that Anderson would have to evacuate Sumter before he was resupplied. It was a slender straw; but the Southerners grasped for it.

Shortly before 1:00 on the morning of April 12, Chesnut and three other Beauregard aides returned to Sumter in a rowboat. After Anderson greeted his visitors, Chesnut handed him a note from Beauregard requesting the precise day and hour on which Anderson would agree to evacuate the fort. Chesnut, as senior officer among the Confederates present, had authority to accept or reject Anderson's reply and so to decide between peace and war, then and there. The Federal commander asked for time to consider the matter and roused his fellow officers. While Anderson and his staff debated their reply, Chesnut and two other aides waited. They waited nearly two hours.

With Chesnut were Captain Stephen D. Lee and Lieutenant A. R. Chisolm. One other aide to Beauregard had rowed out to the fort with them. Roger A. Pryor was an aggressive, "fire-eating" newspaper editor from Virginia. A day or so earlier Pryor had been exhorting South Carolinians to "strike a blow." Since Virginia was still in the Union and since the purpose of the mission was peace instead of war, Pryor discreetly waited outside the fort.

While the Southerners waited, Anderson agonized. He sought to reconcile his orders and his emotions and finally decided in favor of his orders. Just after 3:00 in the morning Anderson returned to Chesnut and handed him a note. In it Anderson stated that he would leave Fort Sumter at noon on April 15, if he received no further instructions from Washington, if he were not resupplied, and if no hostile act were committed against him or his flag in the interim.

Chesnut read the note and retired to a casemate with Lee and Chisolm. The three men considered Anderson's note for only a few minutes. Lee and Chisolm concurred with Chesnut that Anderson had insisted upon too many conditions. The relief ship from Washington was expected at any time. It was almost sure to arrive before noon on the fifteenth, and if it did, one or more of Anderson's conditions would be inconsistent with Beauregard's orders to take the fort. Thus Chesnut did the only thing he felt he could do. He decided to begin a war. At 3:20 A.M. Chesnut returned to Anderson. Lee sat down with pen and paper and wrote the sentence Chesnut dictated.

> Sir: By authority of Brigadier General Beauregard, commanding the provisional forces of the Confederate States, we have the honor to notify you that he will open the fire of his batteries on Fort Sumter in one hour from this time.

Then the Southerners bid Anderson farewell. Anderson responded in kind and told Chesnut that should he not see him again in this world, he hoped to see him in the next. Chesnut nodded and returned to his boat.

That early morning was dark and raw on the waters of Charleston Harbor. An easterly storm thrashed the coast. No doubt the Confederates huddled low in their small boat and relied upon their excitement to warm them. Their destination was Fort Johnson, a bit more than a mile due west of Sumter. With the easterly wind aiding its six oars, the boat reached Fort Johnson around 4:00. Chesnut summoned Captain George S. James who commanded the Confederate batteries and ordered him to open fire at 4:30 A.M. James's first shot would signal the other shore batteries to commence the general bombardment.

Captain James hesitated a moment after hearing Chesnut's order. He stared at Roger Pryor whom he much admired. Would Pryor like to fire the first shot, "strike a blow" as he had long urged others to do? James told Pryor, "You are the only man to whom I would give up the honor of firing the first gun of the war."

Then it was Pryor's turn to hesitate. Speeches about war and war itself were two entirely different matters. In a voice choked with emotion he answered, "I could not fire the first gun of the war."

Their mission fulfilled, Chesnut's party went again to their boat and headed for Beauregard's headquarters to make their report. As 4:30 neared they stayed the oarsmen and stared back toward Fort Johnson. The boat drifted in the dark; wind and waves made the only sounds.

After long moments the sky to the south flashed as though lightning had struck Fort Johnson. Then came the deep boom from a ten-inch mortar. James had pulled the lanyard himself. From the boat Chesnut and the others followed the thin, red arc inscribed by the fuse of the shell. The missile exploded brilliantly about one hundred feet over the center of darkened Fort Sumter. All agreed it was a "capital shot."

Sumter and Civil War

What really happened at Fort Sumter? Captain James's shot began the Civil War; that much is fairly certain. Yet knowing *how* the war began does not necessarily mean we know *why*.

The participants in the Sumter crisis acted reluctantly within pre-scribed limits. Chesnut and Anderson did not cause the war. On the contrary, they merely acted out roles. It was as though two members of a theater audience had been suddenly taken onto the stage and cast as leads in the last scene of the last act of a tragic drama. Neither man had a script, but both had witnessed the preceding acts, and they played their parts in close accord with what had gone before. And we could say more or less the same thing about Lincoln and Davis. By April, 1861, Davis was committed to preserving the integrity of the Confederacy. Lincoln was just as committed to restoring the Southern states to the Union.

So we return to the question, *Why?* For more than a century Americans have attempted to answer this question—to say with precision what caused the Civil War. The answers given have often revealed more about those suggesting them than about the question. Nevertheless it will be helpful to survey briefly what Americans have said about the cause or causes of their Civil War.

Devils

Civil wars are usually bitter, and the American experience was no excep-tion. Thus during the strife and its immediate aftermath, people adopted what one historian has called the "devil theory" of causation. Depending upon which side one favored, the war originated as a plot hatched by "bad men." Unionists, both Southern and Northern, spoke of a "slave-holders' conspiracy." A small group of men to advance their selfish in-terests had spirited the South out of the Union and into war. This is the way one Pennsylvania preacher phrased it in March of 1865:

> There is one monster devil with which the nation is tortured which must be placed prominently as *the great evil* of these times. This is the SECESSION DEVIL.

> Other evil spirits give us great trouble, but this one the most of all, because he is the most obstinate, the most malignant, and the most destructive of them all.

The preacher went on to describe the "Secession Devil" as a "rebellious," "ambitious," "lying," "thieving," "cruel," "mean," and perversely "religious" devil. Advocates of the devil theory were seldom subtle.

There were Northern "devils" also. Many Southerners during and after the war blamed the conflict upon a vicious conspiracy of abolitionist hypocrites or upon self-serving Black Republicans. One ex-Confederate soldier portrayed the abolitionists and the Republican leaders as co-conspirators.

> [The abolitionists,]
> those raving fanatics continued their work of printing books, tracts, pamphlets, magazines and newspapers, and scattering them broadcast over the country. . . . They had, at last, found a "sectional issue" and a "social question" upon which they could vent all their fanatical rages, and enlist and combine all their powers and resources—hate-inspired falsehood and misrepresentations—to drive the South from a Union which they, themselves, had always hated. . . .

Then came the Republican conspirators and their evil genius William H. Seward, Lincoln's Secretary of State. Seward was full of "tremendous and bloody schemes" whose object was a "bloody and destructive war." This war would in turn produce a " 'strong government' with all the arbitrary powers of a Monarchy without its name." Thus the old soldier attempted to save in print the cause he had lost on the battlefield. Those Southerners who believed that the war began as a consipracy of Northern devils, not only made "damn" and "Yankee" one word; they also meant the construction quite literally.

State's Rights

If the war were not the doing of satanic men, perhaps it was the product of misguided men. Southerners especially have used the cause of State's rights to explain the war. The argument was most popular during the first quarter century after 1865; yet it lingers even now. No less an advocate than Jefferson Davis began his book *The Rise and Fall of the Confederate Government:*

> The object of this work has been from historical data to show that the Southern States had rightfully the power to withdraw from a Union into which they had, as sovereign communities, voluntarily entered; that the denial of that right was a violation of the letter and spirit of the compact between the States; and that the war waged by the Federal Government

against the seceding States was in disregard of the limitations of the Constitution, and destructive of the principles of the Declaration of Independence.

The war, said Davis and others, was about the right of secession. And the right of secession hinged upon an interpretation of the Union as a compact of sovereign states. If indeed the Southern states had the right to withdraw from the Union, then the actions of the Lincoln administration were unjust. "State's rights" as the cause of the Civil War offered Southerners the opportunity to discuss the war in unoffensive, legal abstractions, to justify their cause, and to avoid the unpleasant factor, their "peculiar institution."

Slavery

While Southerners explained the war with didactic prose about State's rights, most Americans accepted one word as the cause of the conflict—slavery. James Ford Rhodes in his *History of the United States from the Compromise of 1850* (1895) expressed it this way:

> Nothing in all history is plainer than that the ferment of which I have been speaking [secession and war] was due solely to the existence of slavery. That the North had been encroaching upon the South, that it had offered an indignity in the election of Lincoln, was for South Carolinians a feeling perfectly natural, and it was absolutely sincere. The President-elect believed that slavery should ultimately be done away with, while they were convinced that it was either a blessing, or else the only fit condition of the negro in contact with the white.

Rhodes and others were magnanimous. Slavery was evil; but Southerners were not to blame. They simply held slaves at that point in time when most of Christendom became convinced that slavery was wrong. Indeed Rhodes laid the blame for slavery not just on the South, but on the entire nation. And if everyone was wrong, no one could be guilty.

Of course not all Americans were as generous with their moral judgments as James Ford Rhodes. To say that slavery caused the Civil War implied in many minds blame for the slaveholders. Still this blame was more implied than expressed by historians during the two decades on either side of 1900.

Clashing Economies

During the nineteen-teens Americans and their historians "discovered" anew that men and nations are often motivated by their pocketbooks.

Charles A. Beard led many other scholars in an extensive reexamination of the nation's past in search of economic interpretations. For Beard and others the Civil War was really about economic systems; all else was incidental.

> [The war was] the social cataclysm in which the capitalists, laborers, and farmers of the North and West drove from power in the national government the planting aristocracy of the South. Viewed under the light of universal history, the fighting was a fleeting incident; the social revolution was the essential, portentous outcome.

Principles like State's rights and slavery were important only as slogans to obscure the real issue—power. Northerners sought power to extend a bourgeois empire of capital, industry, and free farms. Southerners tried to retain the power of a planting aristocracy against the encroachments of a rising middle class. Beard linked the American Civil War to interpretations of the English and French revolutions which stressed the fundamental bourgeois–landed aristocrat conflict. Hence the American event was part of a universal economic tide and was neither local nor unique.

Clashing Civilizations

One of the most significant American intellectual movements during the 1930s was the "Fugitive" or Southern Agrarian phenomenon. Led by a group of scholars at Vanderbilt University, the Southern Agrarians used the antebellum Southern past to chasten the 1930s present. The Agrarians resented the mass culture and industrial civilization which seemingly had produced only chaos, ugliness, and the Depression. They constructed an idealized image of the Old South and presented an "Agrarian South" as an alternative to the industrial present. Simple, neighborly, farming, folk stood in stark contrast to the crude, impersonal, industrial twentieth century.

The Civil War, then, was about the overthrow of this agrarian world of the South.

> This struggle between an agrarian and an industrial civilization, then, was the irrepressible conflict, the house divided against itself, which must become according to the doctrine of the industrial section all the one or all the other. It was the doctrine of intolerance, crusading, standardizing alike in industry and in life. The South had to be crushed out; it was in the way; it impeded the progress of the machine. So Juggernaut drove his car across the South.

Not all proponents of the "clashing civilizations" theory of Civil War causation were Southern Agrarians. Nor did all of the Agrarians carry their moral judgments to the Luddite proportions of the passage quoted above. For many historians, "clashing civilizations" was an explanation of the war which incorporated and expanded the "clashing economies" theory without incurring the onus of economic determinism. Still, "clashing civilizations" was so broad and abstract a phrase that it often covered everything but explained nothing.

Blundering Politicians

The so-called revisionist school of Civil War causation came into vogue during the 1930s and 1940s. Although revisionists differed widely among themselves, and some of them shifted their ground during the 1950s, a synopsis of their explanation for the war would go like this: War is a bad thing, and wars can be and have been prevented. In 1860–61 the mass of the American people neither wanted nor needed four years of bloodletting. None of the issues which supposedly caused the war were important enough to justify the conflict. Many revisionists held that slavery was dying out. Agricultural and industrial economies should complement each other. Why war? The war was caused by agitators and extremists and by politicians who allowed the clamor to get out of hand. Thus James G. Randall concluded,

> If one word or phrase were selected to account for the war, that word would not be slavery or state rights or diverse civilizations. It would have to be such a word as fanaticism (on both sides), or misunderstanding, or perhaps politics.

The revisionists reflected a pacifist bent of mind. They also revealed a Southern slant in their thinking. They played down slavery as a moral issue, and played up abolitionists as the arch-villains. Their heroes were moderates like Stephen A. Douglas. The war was, for revisionists, a Republican war, spurred on by abolitionist radicals and their pro-slave counterparts in the South and begun by an administration which could not or would not rise above sectional animosity.

Slavery Revisited

Critics of the revisionist explanation of the war have attacked all sides of the position. Yet the most persistent assault has been upon the revisionist's treatment of slavery. During the late 1950s and the 1960s, the trend among historians has been to reemphasize the moral issue of slavery as the cause of the war. As early as 1949, while revisionism was still in full flower, Arthur M. Schlesinger, Jr. wrote:

Nothing exists in history to assure us that the great moral dilemmas can be resolved without pain; we cannot therefore be relieved from the duty of moral judgement on issues so appalling and inescapable as those involved in human slavery; nor can we be consoled by sentimental theories about the needlessness of the Civil War into regarding our own struggles against evil as equally needless.

Besides reemphasizing slavery as the central issue in the war, post-revisionist historians have expanded their investigations of slavery to include considerations of race and racism. Slavery as a moral issue still persists. But the larger problem of "racial adjustment," as one historian phrased it, has rated more attention in recent years.

Where Are We Now?

When historians began to think of slavery as only one feature of the larger issue of racism, they also expanded the implicit moral indictment to include people other than just slaveholders. Evidence of racist attitudes and actions has come from all sections of the United States. Perhaps it has been this humbling realization that has conditioned recent attitudes about the causes of the Civil War. Scholars have of late been more reluctant to assess guilt or state one cause for the war. If racism was more important than slavery, and if racism was a national character trait, then it has become more difficult to lay blame. The issue of slavery still pervades thinking about the war. Slavery seemed so much a part of every sectional issue; but precisely because it was part of these issues it is maddening to try to isolate slavery as the cause of the conflict. Thus most people agree that slavery was important, but very few scholars can agree on how and why slavery was important. Was slavery the most brutal form of racism? If so then most Americans differed as racists only in matters of degree. Was slavery more important as part of the plantation economy? If so then are we really talking about "clashing economies" and not slavery per se?

Is it possible to find a cause for the American Civil War? To assert that slavery was the single cause of the war starts more arguments than it stops. People do not believe much in "devils" anymore. "State's rights" sounds like Southern apology. "Clashing civilizations" requires more definition than anyone has yet supplied. "Clashing economies" seems too simple or too deterministic. "Blundering politicians" overlooks too much. Maybe it is presumptuous even to attempt to ask what *caused* the war. Perhaps it would be better to ask "What was the war about?" or "What does the war mean?"

When we think in these terms we are dealing with more than just four years of war—more even than the war and Reconstruction, its essential aftermath. We are dealing with matters which transcend the mid-nineteenth century and the United States. We are asking questions about a national trauma which is still felt and about local events which had and have larger implications for what we call Western Civilization.

In recent years American historians have put aside the smug confidence which in times past allowed them to state that this event or that institution caused the Civil War. The trend in recent scholarship has been to explain more than to blame—to discuss conditions which made the war possible, rather than a cause which made the war inevitable—most important to deal with meaning rather than cause. In short, historians of the mid-twentieth century have abandoned many of their provincial preconceptions and are asking new questions in new ways.

However original they appear, these questions express or imply a debt to historians past. As an example, consider a recent review essay in which William W. Freehling has suggested that "monstrous fears feed on monstrous realities," and that the Republican Party employed "precisely the sly and diabolical methods Southerners expected the antislavery demon would use." Freehling is a superb historian, and he probably does not believe in devils. Yet he argues that the strong-willed, often devious, acts of clever men had much to do with the coming of the Civil War. If Freehling's contention is not a restatement of the "devil theory" (and it is not), then it certainly incorporates an assumption or two from the "devil theories."

Obviously one important function of this or any other textbook is that of summarizing recent scholarship about its topic. So the simplest answer to the question "Where are we now?" regarding explanation and meaning of the Civil War–Reconstruction experience is "read this book and find out."

But this book, like all books, has a point-of-view implied or expressed. And the interpretation expressed here will be a much metamorphosed version of the "clashing civilizations" explanation which seems to be at the leading edge of recent scholarship. In fact it is better said as a "clash of ideologies." The emphasis upon ideology draws especially upon recent works by Eugene D. Genovese (*The World the Slaveholders Made*) and Eric Foner (*Free Soil, Free Labor, Free Men*). Simply stated, these two historians suggest that the issue which divided North and South in 1860–61 was nothing less than opposing "world-views," or ideologies. Southerners seceded from the Union to protect their "world," and Northerners fought to prevent secession for the sake of their "world." Genovese and Foner may not recognize their ideas as they are filtered into this book; still they deserve credit, if not the blame, for the interpretation here.

To explain the world-views of Northerners and Southerners we must examine the respective worlds. This means we must now attempt a very difficult task. We must examine and try to summarize life in the United States before 1860. For without this background the events at Fort Sumter on April 12, 1861, have little or no meaning.

THE BEGINNING

James Chesnut, Jr.

Robert Anderson.

Ft. Sumter as seen from Ft. Johnson.

Jefferson Davis, Courtesy of the Virginia State Library.

Abraham Lincoln.

Artist's conception of the Battle of Ft. Sumter.

THE 2
OLD
NORTH

New York, February 29, 1848

Members of the Racket Court celebrated leap year in 1848 with a gala ball and supper. The committee on arrangements converted the court itself into a dancing saloon. Thirty-six hundred yards of muslin trimmed with gold galloon and artificial flowers covered the playing area to create the appearance of a grand tent. A 35-piece orchestra performed while "pretty girls, with pink dresses, were attended by beaux with black mustaches and white vests." In the gallery above the dancers "charming girls and agreeable cavaliers" looked on. Every room in the large building was festively and tastefully decorated for the "pleased and happy company." Abundant servants spread the supper on long tables in the bowling alley. In fact hundreds of "worthy people" were employed preparing and attending the decorations and epicurean supper fare. Approximately 300 members and subscribers of the Racket Court paid ten dollars each to put on the fete. And the committee on arrangements expended the entire amount on the evening. One discerning member pronounced the following verdict, "There has been nothing more *recherché*, nothing better arranged, and nothing attended with more complete success, since the last leap year."

Horse Creek, Spring, 1847

The celebration began spontaneously. A party of hunters and trappers happened upon another party of hunters and trappers camped at Horse Creek; old friends met and proclaimed a feast. The hosts were Creole French and French Canadian; the guests were mostly of Anglo-American extraction. Both groups were dressed in buckskin hunting shirts and pants which had not been completely removed from the time they were first put on. Caps of skins covered their bushy heads and full beards covered their faces. They carried knives, tomahawks, powder horns, and bullet pouches on their person most of the time. In short the "mountain men" looked colorful, smelled awful, and lived wild—in accommodation with the American wilderness.

The Indian squaws of the hosts came out of their skin-covered lodges to prepare the food. They stirred up cooking fires and readied pots and kettles. Then the squaws began entreating the youngest and plumpest of a pack of dogs to come within tomahawk range. Some dogs ran, and the women gave chase. Finally the mountain men brought down six fine canines with their rifles.

The result of these preparations was a sumptuous dog stew. Long into the night men sat around the pots talking and eating. At last the stew was gone, and all regretted that there was no more. Fortuitously a "wolfish-looking cur" stuck his head under the lodge skin. The closest hunter quickly slit the animal's throat and threw it to a squaw to skin and clean. In a short while the mountain men, asserting "meat's meat," resumed the feast.

The two celebrations just recorded happened within the same country at about the same time. Besides revealing a bit about the quality of life in the United States in the mid-nineteenth century, these events graphically demonstrate the diversity of the nation. And they underscore the difficulty of trying to summarize in a few pages these varied conditions of life.

We can, however, make five general statements about America (with emphasis upon the Northern states) during the three decades preceding the Civil War:

1. The United States experienced rapid and varied growth between 1830 and 1860.
2. The nation's economy grew also, changing form and becoming ever more industrial and more laissez-faire capitalistic.
3. A mounting feeling of nationalism influenced thought and action during the period.
4. The mid-nineteenth century was for Americans an age of romanticism.
5. From 1830 to 1860 many Americans were touched by a spirit of reform.

Growth, economic change, nationalism, romanticism, and reform—these characteristics offer a topical framework within which we can think about the country on the eve of its dissolution. Let us examine such topic separately.

Growth

National folklore and popular culture well record Americans' preoccupation with size and quantity—about everything from the number of oil wells in Texas to the size of a woman's breasts. Only recently have ecologists driven home the point that quantity often has a direct effect on quality in human life. This fact, so obvious that it is often overlooked, makes it important for us to consider size and numbers when describing American life, both now and in the past. And during the 1830s, 40s, and 50s, many things in the United States dramatically increased in size and number.

Between 1830 and 1860 the nation came close to doubling its land area. The war with Mexico, the Oregon settlement with Great Britain, and the Gadsden Purchase added 1,234,381 square miles. These new square miles affected the country in many ways. To cite just one example, the new land brought slavery again into the national political arena. The question was, would the newly acquired territory be open or closed to slavery; and this issue dominated American politics from the late 1840s through the 1850s.

The population of the country grew even faster than did the land area—from just under 13 million in 1830 to just over 31.5 million in 1860, three more people per square mile. Sheer numbers, of course, affected life and life styles in the United States. Even more important though were the sources and distribution of these numbers.

In 1860 nearly 13 out of every 100 Americans were foreign-born. Most of these immigrants came from Northern Europe; many were of German or Irish extraction. The vast majority of the immigrants lived north of Mason and Dixon's line, roughly 3.5 million out of the four million total, and many lived in urban rather than rural areas. The foreign-born Americans brought much to their adopted homeland—everything from Roman Catholicism to lager beer.

The most striking population increase between 1830 and 1860 occurred in the northern tier of states.

Section	Population in 1830	Population in 1860
Northeast	5.5 million	10.6 million
North Central	1.6 million	9.1 million
South	5.7 million	11.1 million

These figures are rounded off; but they give a precise enough indication of where Americans were multiplying most rapidly.

Also significant was the fact that urban population was increasing at a much faster rate than rural population. During the two decades prior to 1860 rural population (people living in communities of less than 2,500) grew 83 percent. In the same time period, however, the number of urbanites (people living in communities of more than 2,500) increased 345 percent. In 1860 about 6.2 million people lived in cities and towns and about 25.2 million in the countryside. The United States, then, was still a nation of farmers; however, their urban brethren were already significant in numbers and increasing geometrically.

Someone once said that there are three kinds of lies—"lies, damn lies, and statistics." The statistics given thus far hopefully reveal truth, not falsehood; nevertheless, out of deference to the quoted sage, let us now look at the truth which lay behind America's statistical growth.

Economic Change

Americans during the colonial and new nation periods devoted most of their economic energies to trade and agriculture. During the post-Civil War period the American economy was characterized by industrial capitalism. The period with which we are concerned—1830 to 1860—marked the transition—from agriculture to industry and from mercantilism to laissez faire. Exceptions abound to these generalizations. But if we accept the necessity to generalize, and recognize the limitations, then we may find these statements helpful.

In 1860, for the first time on record American industry produced goods and services worth more than American agriculture. What lay behind this highly significant economic shift? The principal thrust of the American economy changed because there were attendant changes in American economic minds, markets, movement, and methods.

Most Americans entered the nineteenth century committed to the economics of mercantilism. The heritage of British colonial policy, the influence of Alexander Hamilton, and the promises of Henry Clay's "American System" reinforced the idea that government should be in partnership with its constituent producers and traders. Just as British statesmen had tried to order an expanding empire to serve economic nationalism before 1776, so did Americans think of government in terms of expansion and protection for the common good. American mercantilism spoke in the first person plural, and it said things like National Bank, protective tariffs, internal improvements, and empire.

It would be impossible to say exactly when Americans changed their economic minds. By the 1830s, however, the doctrine of laissez faire was ascendant, and mercantilism was in decline. The Age of Jackson may or may not have been the age of the Common Man. It was certainly the age of the capitalist "on the make." By mid-century the national bank was dead, tariff duties were going down, internal improvements smelled of "grab bags," and "empire" had strong connotations of individual exploitation. Government still entered the marketplace; but after 1830 government's economic role was designed and used more to benefit interests and individuals than the common good.

An economic "mind" thinks about more than production and exchange. And capitalism is more than an economic system; it pervades culture as well as the marketplace. For Americans in the mid-nineteenth century, capitalism meant opportunity for all and promised wealth and power to those who worked hard and well. In the North especially, Americans assumed that work produced success and that merit was measured in the marketplace. These assumptions led some Northerners to the conclusion that Southern planters were idle degenerates and some Southerners to the conclusion that "Yankees" were crass, money-grubbers.

This transition of mind from mercantilism to laissez faire was at least partially in accommodation to some fast-changing economic realities. For one, American domestic and foreign markets were expanding. Those 18 million people added to the population between 1830 and 1860 demanded more goods and services. And they demanded that these goods and services be transported across those new square miles added to the country during the same period. In 1844 the United States received trade concessions from China. Ten years later Japan began to allow trade with Americans. In 1846 the free traders in England secured repeal of the Corn Laws. This abandonment of import duties on corn (wheat) symbolized the end of British protective markets and the beginning of free trade. As a result of these expanding world markets, American foreign trade (import and export) more than tripled between 1840 and 1860.

To serve these growing markets the United States underwent what one historian has termed a "transportation revolution." The nation built roads and canals and dredged rivers and harbors. Increasing numbers of steamboats plied American rivers in the "golden age" of the paddle and side wheelers. But most important for domestic commerce was the coming of railroads. In 1830 there were 23 miles of railroad track in the United States. Thirty years later there were 30,626 miles of track. By the 1850s government subsidies further speeded construction. A glance at a map of rail routes in 1860 reveals the significant fact that most of the longer lines ran east-west, tending to link the Northeast to the West. These advances in transportation meant that producers could expand to serve wider markets. Wider markets in turn allowed producers to specialize and produce a greater qauntity of the same item with greater efficiency.

The "transportation revolution" affected international as well as national movement. The 1850s were the years during which American-style clipper ships dominated ocean commerce. These ships had long, sleek hulls and carried a fantastic amount of sail. They combined size and speed; at their best clippers weighed 750 tons, could make just under 500 miles per day, and could sail from New York to Liverpool in just over 13 days. By the late 1850s, however, the age of steam had arrived. And along with the other members of the Atlantic community, Americans made the transition from sail to steam.

Markets for goods and the facilities with which to move goods were, of course, worthless without the goods themselves. During the second third of the nineteenth century Americans did increase their production of goods at a phenomenal rate. They did so in part because there were more of them in a larger land area. However, the most significant factor in the economic growth of the United States during this period was not the number of producing units (farms, factories and such), but rather the change in methods of production. Farmers and manufacturers, especially, took advantage of technological innovations and began a trend toward more specialized production for wider markets.

This is certainly not to imply that the age of assembly lines, mass production, and giant corporations began in the mid-nineteenth century. It did not. Most farms were family farms, specialized only in the sense that they produced more corn, for example, than anything else. Still, when a significant number of corn-producing general farms lay side by side, it is possible to imagine the origins of an American "corn belt." Such inventions as John Deere's steel plow and Cyrus McCormick's reaper made it possible for fewer workers to till larger tracts. Increased use of fertilizers and wiser use of the land (crop rotation, for example) added to production. And the "transportation revolution" made it possible to market the increased yields. Americans had been largely commercial, rather than subsistence, farmers before. During the 1830s, 40s and 50s, they simply became more so.

During the three decades prior to the Civil War, American industry expanded. Again, however, the words "industry expanded" should not trigger visions of the skyline of modern Pittsburgh. Most American factories in the period we are discussing were small units which processed locally grown produce (flour and lumber mills, breweries, distilleries, meat packers, and such). Still, if we avoid the temptation to overstate we can recognize that the United States by 1860 had essentially made the transition from a preindustrial nation to an industrial nation. Iron, machinery, and textiles formed a "heavy industry" base. In addition, Americans manufactured everything from needles and pins to Otis elevators and steamboats.

Those people actually doing this manufacturing, American labor, were among the first to feel the bad effects of industrialization. For the first time in the American experience, the mid-nineteenth century witnessed an excess of working men. This surplus manifested itself locally and sporadically; yet combined with the "bust" period of the business cycle, a labor surplus could and did yield "hard times." Before 1860 there had been periodic attempts on the part of American labor to organize. Still, unions and strikes were small, local, and few in number during the period. For the most part laboring men in the United States had little concept of class awareness. Indeed, they were reluctant to consign themselves to the confines of class in the European sense. American workingmen, as a whole, were protocapitalists. They believed in the work-ethic— that one day they would open their own shop and cease to be labor. Thus action taken in the interest of class might have implied that they were somehow outside of the American Dream. And this the majority of working people were unwilling to admit. Perhaps this attitude, even more than manufacturing statistics, best illustrates the fact of American industrial adolescence in 1860.

Nationalism

"Why, our people can turn their hands to a'most anything from whippin' the universe to stuffin' a mosquito." One American spoke these words to a British traveler in the 1840s; no doubt he voiced the sentiments of many, if not most, of his fellow countrymen.

Nationalism is a curious thing. The word usually describes the assertive actions and feelings of a group of people who share something in common. That something may be race, language, religion, territory, culture, heritage or some combination of these and other human elements. Any veteran of a survey course in "Western Civilization" can summarize the nineteenth century as an "age of nationalism," and most can give examples of the power of national identity in the political history of the period. These examples often include some from the American experience. Yet American nationalism (and perhaps all nationalisms) is and was unique. In the nineteenth century it was considerably more than the local symptom of a Western Civilization contagion.

Nationalism as manifested by the nineteenth century was a schizophrenic phenomenon. It was at the same time defensive and aggressive, concurrently altruistic and mean. Perhaps it all began with the American Revolution, perhaps with the Puritan colonists. Americans had self-interests and opportunities to assert these interests at the expense of others. But Americans also had their Revolution and their Declaration of Independence which implied for the nation a mission and a destiny. The United States began its national life small and weak. But the new nation increased rapidly in land, people, and power—so rapidly in fact that few men could say at any given time how powerful the country was in relation to other nations in Europe and the Americas.

Thus Americans practiced their nationalism in erratic bursts. They were so defensively proud of their stand against Great Britain in the War of 1812 that they rationalized their chaotic (and sometimes catastrophic) war effort and British magnanimity in the Peace of Ghent into a replay of David and Goliath. The "underdog" Americans by wit and skill had won a national victory over the conquerors of Napoleon. Jacksonian Americans by the late 1820s and 1830s, however, transformed the "underdog" image into something quite different. For example, George Frederick Bancroft (Polk's Secretary of the Navy and the Jacksonian era's "court" historian) projected a view of the United States as the agent of the Almighty. For Bancroft and other Jacksonians the American nation was God's way of bringing liberty and democracy to His people. And a chosen nation need not be humble or defensive in its thoughts or actions.

It was perhaps natural that the young nation saw itself variously as the international underdog and as God's agent of liberty and democracy. A deeper and more persistent dilemma was reconciling national self-interest (and sometimes downright greed) with the American sense of mission to export the Revolution and to share the blessings of democracy.

During the 1840s two words expressed the dichotomy—"Manifest Destiny." This phrase expressed the militant dream that the United States should and would extend from the Atlantic to the Pacific. The obvious question is, Why? Why should the nation span the continent, and more importantly why did Americans become excited enough about expansion to threaten war with England and fight a war with Mexico? Part of the answer was that it suited the self-interests of all or some Americans to expand in the name of Manifest Destiny. Expansion was a source of national pride. Land speculation had always been an important factor in the American economy. Southern politicians eyed the West as a source of future expansion of the slave-plantation system and thus of more Southern politicians. More land meant more resources and more wealth. And prevailing racial attitudes suggested that the Western land was being wasted in the hands of inferior Mexicans and savage Indians. Pride, speculation, slavery, wealth, and race—when many Americans said Manifest Destiny they meant one or some of these less exalted considerations.

All was not ignoble, though. When many Americans said Manifest Destiny, they meant "extension of the area of freedom." The United States, the great hope of democracy, needed to expand to fulfill its mission and destiny. In that sense the American expansion of the 1840s was a logical extension of the Revolution.

Must we decide between these motives and say whether American nationalism involved self-interest or ideals? No. It encompassed both motivations, and for our purposes this descriptive observation is sufficient. We do, however, need to observe this schizophrenic American nationalism in action during the 1850s.

During the decade before the Civil War nationalism remained significant in American thought and action. Rhetorically, Manifest Destiny yielded to Young America. The Young America movement involved a significant faction within the Democratic Party led by Stephen A. Douglas. In part the Young Americans hoped to smother the growing sectional strife with a broad and assertive nationalism. They urged American support of liberal movements everywhere, such as Louis Kossuth's revolution in Hungary. Many Young Americans also wished to continue the expansion of the United States into Cuba and Central America. These latter goals only served to make many people suspect that Young America was synonymous with slavery expansion.

While the Young America nationalists looked outward, many Americans expressed their nationalism by looking inward at their society. They saw among other things the increasing numbers of foreign-born Americans and became alarmed. The 1850s witnessed the first significant incidence of nativism within the United States. In the abstract, of course, it was preposterous for Americans, all of whom were descended from immigrants, to resent more recent arrivals. Yet nativism was a strong emotion. The popular stereotype of the drunken, brawling Irishman began during this period. And some nativism was more precisely anti-Catholicism in resentment of the large numbers of German and Irish Catholics who came to the United States in the 1840s and 1850s. Samuel F. B. Morse, inventor of the telegraph, even went so far as to allege a Popish Plot against American liberties. Nor was Morse alone in his fears and warnings. Myriad secret, "patriotic" societies sprang up, and in the 1850s these societies coalesced into the Know-Nothing Party which became the political expression of nativism. In the elections of 1856 Know-Nothing presidential candidate Millard Fillmore attracted a significant percentage of the popular vote, and numerous state candidates won office.

Nationalism in America, then, manifested itself in the best and worst ways. It called upon Americans to keep the Spirit of '76 and extend it. Nationalism also inspired or associated with racism, greed, and xenophobia. Whatever its character, nationalism was a strong emotion and motive force in the American mind. As we shall see nationalism affected the Southern mind also. However Southern nationalism ultimately confined itself to things Southern. Thus the Civil War period presents fascinating opportunities for the study of loyalty and nationalism. In 22 states American nationalism was sufficiently strong to be a motive force in a great war effort. Yet in 11 other states nationalism turned inward, became sectional loyalty, and as Confederate nationalism inspired an equally great war effort.

Romanticism

It is not too difficult to demonstrate the existence of a romantic spirit in the United States during the three or four decades before the Civil War. We need only to view the art of Thomas Cole or George Caleb Bingham, to recall the prose of James Fenimore Cooper or Herman Melville, to reflect upon the idealistic thought of Ralph Waldo Emerson or Henry David Thoreau, or to read the poetry of John Greenleaf Whittier or Henry Wadsworth Longfellow, to perceive the dominance of the romantic over the realistic. The difficulty with romanticism lies in defining it and in determining its impact upon American life in the mid-nineteenth century.

Essentially, romanticism is a way of perceiving or estimating reality which emphasizes the ideal. The romantic estimate of reality may or may not be true. Emerson, for example, may have been an astute observer of his time; but many who shared Emerson's romantic view generated from it nothing more than flabby sentimentalism. It may be pessimistic (like Melville) or optimistic (like Whittier). What distinguishes the romantic mind from the unromantic mind is not so much the truth of its perception or the temper of its mood, but rather the preoccupation of the romantic mind with ideals. The romantic may impose his ideal upon present reality (either like Thoreau to attempt to transform that reality, or like John

Pendleton Kennedy to attempt to glorify that reality). The romantic may identify himself with ideals he sees in the past (like Longfellow's *Paul Revere*) or in nature (like Cole's landscapes). Finally, the romantic mind is often characterized by a lack of discipline, by a flair for the dramatic, and by an emphasis upon emotion (Edgar Allen Poe is a good example here).

The preceding paragraph provides at least a loose definition of romanticism. We still need to see this nineteenth-century phenomenon in action. Perhaps, however, we have already observed one aspect of the romantic mind at work. In discussing nationalism, it may be that we were talking about a political expression of romanticism, at least to the extent that American nationalism stressed ideals like "expanding the area of freedom" and "Manifest Destiny." In later chapters we may find other examples. Without recalling the romantic commitment to ideals shared by many Americans in the mid-nineteenth century, it may be difficult for twentieth-century Americans to understand why so many of their ancestors were so passionately devoted to the abstraction, Union, to go to war for it. And the unreal attitude of many Americans toward war itself reflected the romantic mind at work. Too many found out the hard way that war was not the chivalrous adventure depicted in the novels of Sir Walter Scott.

Perhaps the best example of the romantic spirit at work in America was the Transcendental movement. Transcendentalism, as the word suggests, involved the fundamental assumption of a transcendence between the finite and infinite. God, or the "Oversoul" as some Transcendentalists phrased it, was in the world, in man and in nature. Conversely man was "in God" and could realize his godliness by following his conscience and by near mystical experiences in nature and in contemplation. If these things were so, then man, the Transcendentalists believed, was not the miserable creature that orthodox Christians kept insisting he was. Man had the capacity to transcend the temporal world and become an expression of the eternal.

Men who believe that they can speak with the voice of God can liken themselves to romantic heroes and also can be quite tenacious about their ideals. Such a man was Thoreau who not only wrote his famous essay "Civil Disobedience"; he also acted out his principles by going to jail rather than paying his taxes to support the Mexican War which Thoreau believed to be unjust. The point here is that Thoreau and his fellow Transcendentalists expressed the romantic spirit of the nineteenth century. They did so by rejecting many traditional institutions and mores and by attempting to live their ideals. In the process they exhibited romantic characteristics such as a concern for nature, a sometimes mystical, undisciplined turn of mind, and an acceptance of emotion, as well as reason, as a basis for action.

Transcendentalism was more than a romantic, intellectual movement; it was also a reform movement. Emerson said it most categorically, "What is man born for but to be a Reformer. . . ."

Reform

"Reform" is a pregnant word. Most Americans probably think of reform as meaning "the doing of some liberal good," and this definition often fits. Yet many reform movements in the American experience have pursued goals which were neither liberal nor good. Moreover, reformers have been among the most noble Americans; but reformers have also been "unreasoned and half-cracked." One historian has suggested substitution of the term "moral stewardship" to depict more accurately the nature of what we commonly call reform. The implication is that the common denominator of reform movements is the conviction on the part of the participants that they have a truth which they wish to share with or impose upon their fellows. This was true of mid-nineteenth century American reformers, whether they crusaded for free love or temperance or the abolition of slavery.

"Moral stewardship" may not supplant "reform" in popular usage. The term, however, does point up the limitations of "reform" as "the doing of some liberal good." And it may accurately describe the motives of the reformers or "moral stewards." Reform in the 1830s, 40s, and 50s began as a personal or corporate striving for perfection. This desire had mixed origins—some religious, some romantic, some democratic idealistic, and some intensely personal. Whatever their origins or nature, reform enthusiasms left their mark on nineteenth-century America.

One harassed American protested in 1838, "Matters have come to such a pass that a peaceable man can hardly venture to eat or drink, or to go to bed or to get up, to correct his children or to kiss his wife, without obtaining the permission and direction of some . . . society." Reform groups sought to improve the lot of prisoners and insane persons. Organizations crusaded for women's rights. Others attempted to outlaw "demon rum." Nativists sought to purify the country by getting rid of the foreign peril. Anti-Catholic crusaders insisted that the United States was in danger from Rome. Utopian bands tried to demonstrate that communities based upon socialism, or free love, or celibacy, or something else offered the closest approach to human perfection. Peace and public education inspired activist groups of reformers. In a sense laissez-faire capitalism was a reform in that its advocates believed that free marketplaces made better men. All these and other enthusiasms, too, competed for the attention and support of Americans. Yet none of these reformers matched the zeal and the capacity for arousing people of the abolitionists.

Concern about slavery was not new in nineteenth-century America. The roots of antislavery sentiment extended far into the colonial past, at least to 1754 when Quaker theologian John Woolman published a pamphlet *Some Considerations on the Keeping of Negroes* . . . indicating the practice. Unique about the antislavery movement of the mid-nineteenth century was its activist fervor. Abolitionism had ceased to be largely theological and passive and had become more political and active.

One reason for this change of emphasis and tactics among abolitionists was the change which took place within the community of slaveholders. Until about the 1820s many Americans believed that slavery was a temporary thing, at most a necessary evil, which would die of natural economic causes in the near future. Then came the cotton boom in the South. The "peculiar institution" breathed new economic life and blossomed anew instead of withering as expected. Moreover, the slaveholders especially in the South had begun to change their minds about slavery. They began to speak of slavery as a "positive good" instead of a "necessary evil." This revival of slavery and vigorous justification of slaveholding demanded from those opposed to the practice, not platitudes, but action. Add to this new circumstance the religious, romantic, idealistic, and personal motives for reform mentioned earlier, and the stage was set.

The abolitionist cast of characters was large and varied. Some were muddle-headed "do-gooders" who sought to wish slavery away. Others, recent studies indicate, were virulent racists who hoped that by abolishing slavery they could also abolish black people in their state or territory. Many well-meaning people and some highly placed people like Henry Clay and John Marshall supported the American Colonization Society and its efforts to send free black volunteers to Africa. Yet the American Colonization Society failed, either to transplant significant numbers of Afro-Americans or to face up to the possibilities of racial pluralism in the United States.

Some abolitionists such as Arthur and Lewis Tappan in New York formed well-organized, well financed groups. Others like Frederick Douglass were former slaves. Some like William Lloyd Garrison eschewed organizations and asked only an audience or readership for their message. Still others congregated in schools like Oberlin College to spread the word. Abolitionists were both inside and outside the church and established politics. They were black and white, male and female. They came from all sections of the country. Angelina and Sarah Grimke, for example, began writing antislavery pamphlets in Charleston, South Carolina, and Cassius M. Clay edited a militantly abolitionist newspaper in Lexington, Kentucky.

Abolitionists varied, too, in their method. Perhaps the American Colonization Society was the mildest form of antislavery action. At the opposite end of the spectrum were genuinely radical root-and-branchers like Garrison, Theodore Parker, Wendell Phillips and Gerritt Smith who sought immediate, uncompensated emancipation by any means. In between these poles were all shades and degrees of opinion as to method. Abraham Lincoln, for example, prior to 1860 proposed compensation to the slaveholders and voluntary colonization as the ultimate solution.

Understandably, the abolitionist movement made few friends in the South. Yet neither were abolitionists always well received north of Mason and Dixon's line. Mobs broke up meetings and presses, and in Alton, Illinois, a mob murdered abolitionist editor Elijah Lovejoy.

By the 1850s, however, the abolitionists had made their point in the North. Perhaps their diversity and disagreement about a common program was their greatest asset. For every American willing to admit the fundamental wrong of slavery, there was some wing of the abolitionist movement capable of attracting his support. That support might be in the form of a prayer, a vote, a contribution, a speech, or a violent act. And if no outlet for his particular temper or talent existed in his community, the abolitionist convert could always follow precedent and start his own splinter group.

Somewhere between the New York Racket Court and the "mountain men" on Horse Creek was *the* mid-nineteenth century American. Maybe he was a German immigrant living on land ceded by Mexico in 1848 who believed in laissez-faire economics and Manifest Destiny, owned railroad stock, operated a small manufacturing establishment, planned to move to a city, admired the works of Cole, Hawthorne, and Emerson, participated in the local antislavery society, and joined the Sons of Temperance. Of course no such person existed. The United States in the 1830s, 40s, and 50s, was a mixture of all those elements we have discussed and more. To portray *the* Americans of this period would require a very large composite photograph—about the size of Vermont. Perhaps, though, if we had such a photograph we might recognize the characteristics and conditions described in this chapter as dominant.

THE 3
OLD
SOUTH

What was it really like down there, back then? For many people the ante-bellum South was like *Gone with the Wind* with Scarlett O'Hara and barbecues and Tara and "po' white trash" and happy "darkeys." The Old South, of course, was not exactly like that or any of the "moonlight and magnolia" myths which abound about that time and place. Still, like most myths, the legend of the Old South contains a germ of truth. The dual challenge of describing the Old South is that of distinguishing between myth and reality *and* of summarizing conditions of life no less varied than those of the "Old North."

Perhaps we can begin with five general statements.

1. The Southern economy was largely agricultural.
2. The institution of racial slavery strongly influenced the Southern experience.

3. A unique form of planter aristocracy dominated the Southern social structure.
4. There was a definable "mind" in the Old South which by 1860 had become amazingly unified and dangerously closed.
5. By 1860 Southern sectionalism had become Southern nationalism.

Let us use these statements as a topical outline and examine each in turn.

The Southern Economy

The official song of the Confederacy "Bonnie Blue Flag" began with the words "We are a band of brothers /and native to the soil." The unofficial national anthem "Dixie" started, "I wish I was in the land ob Cotton." The South, then, was the "land ob cotton," and Southerners were "native to the soil." The statistics of the 1860 census made the same point, though a bit more pedantically. In approximate figures the South had only 15 percent of the nation's industrial establishments and produced a little more than 7.5 percent of the nation's industrial gross national product. A closer look at census statistics reveals that Southern manufacturing had grown rapidly during the decade of the 1850s. Virginia, for example, had a significant iron industry. But songs and statistics agree that the Southern economy was predominantly agricultural, preindustrial.

If the South was agricultural, then was it a land of plantations and columned mansions? No, it was not. The vast majority of Southern agriculturalists were not planters. And the vast majority of planters were not large planters. When we speak of large plantations of several hundred acres and more than 50 slaves, we are talking about only several thousand units, ten thousand at the most. If we use slaveholding as an index to planterhood, we find that most (three-fourths) Southerners did not own slaves. Of those who did own slaves, almost three-fourths owned fewer than ten. In terms of numbers, the South was a land of farms, not plantations. This is not to suggest that plantations and planters were unimportant. As we shall see, the plantation had an economic importance which did not relate only to numbers of units. And planters, as a class, possessed political power and social status which far outweighed their numbers. Nevertheless the fact remains that most Southerners earned their daily bread in ways other than planting.

Tradition and myth hold that those antebellum Southerners who were not planters or slaves were "po' white trash." Indeed there was a Southern "mudsill" composed of shiftless folk who, if reincarnated, would feel quite at home on Tobacco Road. Yet a close look at the Southern economy makes it very difficult to distinguish among the poor, the white, and the trash. Hill folk of the Southern Appalachians, for example, may have been poor in terms of money. Yet they were also proud and independent people, no more "trash" than the adventurous pioneers from whom they descended. Historian Frank L. Owsley once pointed out the error of making economic judgments based on appearances. If we take the accounts of travelers and visitors to the antebellum South at face value, we may make serious mistakes. For example, a traveler in the Old South may have recorded what he thought was an encounter with "trashy whites." The traveler saw a cabin in a small clearing off the main road. On the porch was a lean man who apparently had nothing better to do than spit tobacco juice. The man's wife was hoeing a small but neat garden, while four or five children frolicked nearby. The traveler concluded that this family had no visible means of support and was destitute. There is ample temptation for the historian to agree with his source. Yet in the woods beyond the clearing may have been 200 hogs and on the back wall of the cabin may have been dozens of well-maintained traps. The "destitute" family made their living tending livestock and trapping and not a bad living it was. This incident is, of course, hypothetical; but it does illustrate that some of the South's "poor whites" may have had "invisible" means of support and economic significance. Tax records and census returns (when available) tend to support Owsley's contention. The planter–po' white trash dichotomy may survive in the popular imagination; it does not, however, bear up under investigation.

Somewhere between the plantation and mountain cabin were the "plain folk." These yeoman farmers and herdsmen were perhaps the "forgotten men" of the Old South. Some of them were subsistence farmers who raised or made most of life's necessities and did not participate in the South's commercial economy. Others were herdsmen who made their living from cattle, horses, hogs, and sheep. The majority of the plain folk were quasi-commercial farmers. That is, they produced for most of their own subsistence and the marketplace as well. These middle-class farmers produced livestock, grains, and garden produce for sale both locally and regionally. They did not generate a lot of economic activity as a group; but the farmer class was "comfortable"—their needs were simple and usually filled.

Some historians have suggested that these non-planter, "plain folk" farmers were the backbone of the Old South. The planters, they argue were window dressing which too often had obscured the "real" South of the plain folk. To the extent that such an argument rebuts the "moonlight and magnolia" and the planter/po' white trash mythology, it has validity. The issue is that of emphasis. Economically or otherwise we cannot ignore the planters and their influence any more than we can discuss oil companies without mentioning John D. Rockefeller.

On plantations Southerners produced their chief "exports"—cotton, rice, tobacco, and sugar. If we look at the South as an economic "nation," we see factories and farms serving largely local or regional markets (with the exception of livestock production). Plantations were the sources of the South's cash crops sold in the North or in Europe. These raw staples were the chief output of the South as an economic unit. And cotton was chief among them. By 1860 the South produced more than five million bales per year, which represented a majority of the world's supply (for example, after the mid 1840s four-fifths of Great Britain's raw cotton came from the South).

Europe and the North depended upon Southern cotton and other staples. The South depended upon Europe and the North for manufactured items and credit. It proved a bad bargain for the South. Southerners assumed a "colonial" economic status vis-à-vis the North and Europe; they resented this circumstance, but could or would not alter it.

Influential Southerners continually called upon their fellows to diversify the Southern economy and make the South self-sufficient. J. D. B. DeBow in his *DeBow's Review* along with numerous newspaper editors urged the construction of railroads and the establishment of industries in the section. Southerners held commercial conventions and echoed the theme. Yet despite the impressive industrial growth rate in the 1850s, the South lagged pitifully behind the rest of the United States in industrial development. Perhaps the major barrier was a lack of investment capital. Plantations did not produce fluid capital. The South did not have much specie, and those who had investment capital more often than not "plowed" it into more land and slaves to expand the plantation economy. The result was a vicious circle which made cotton "King" in the South, but forced Southerners to import the "King's" throne and sceptre.

This gloomy summary of the colonial state of the Southern economy is of course within a capitalist frame of reference. But did the South in fact have a capitalist economy? Historians disagree. A few decades ago as we have seen, the "agrarians" argued that the economy of the Old South was more communal and feudal than capitalistic. Other scholars later responded that the South was indeed capitalistic or at least a capitalistic mutation. After all, they contended, Southerners invested capital, produced a cash crop, and often depended upon credit in the money market to finance their ventures. In economic terms slavery was nothing more nor less than a peculiarly brutal and blatant form of labor exploitation. Thus the argument concluded, Southern planters were "cotton capitalists."

In recent years some historians have moved to reconsider the issue. They argue that the plantation economy was neither communal nor capitalistic. Rather it was something unique unto itself, some middle ground between the medieval manor and industrial capitalism. Southerners, the argument goes, used some of the devices of capitalism without accepting the culture of capitalism. As a society they chose to expand the plantation system, rather than diversify and specialize their economy in the manner of capitalist societies. The planters' sense of paternalism and aristocratic position rendered them prebourgeois as well as preindustrial and constrained them from acting and thinking in ways we associate with capitalists. Hence the plantation South was at most superficially capitalistic, post feudal, but prebourgeois.

Slavery

In 1860 just under four million black slaves lived in the United States. The conditions of life for these people were so varied that they defy generalization. Slaves worked as unskilled, agricultural, gang labor. They were domestic servants, cooks, maids, butlers, and coachmen. They did skilled, semi-skilled, and unskilled industrial labor. They did general farm labor. They did construction work, maintenance work, and road work. In short, slaves did almost every kind of work there was to do.

Slaves did this work on plantations and farms. They lived in cities and towns. They lived in subtropical Florida and temperate Delaware. Slaves lived in snug houses and in squalid hovels. They lived under the eyes of their masters; they made their own living arrangements and seldom saw their master after the workday ended. Slaves worked under the direction of a white overseer or black "driver." They worked side by side with their master. They served whites who rented them. Some masters indulged their slaves; others brutalized and degraded them. The slave experience, then, existed in about four million varieties.

In the midst of this diversity, however, there were some constants. Slavery, at its roots, involved a fundamental psychological relationship of mastery and dependence. This relation might exist between slave and master, slave and overseer, or slave and driver. It might be grounded in greed, fear, hate, love, or some combination of these drives. Beyond all the variables pointed out above, the slave experience involved some basic human relationship between master and slave.

This relationship of mastery and dependence, of course, had its effect upon the slave. The time has long passed when apologists for slavery could portray the "peculiar institution" as just healthy, carefree, outdoor work performed to the tune of countless banjos and generously rewarded with watermelons. Historian Stanley M. Elkins has contended that the slave experience produced slavish personalities among its victims. In brief Elkins' thesis suggests that slavery in the United States involved wrenching Africans from their homeland and placing them in an unfamiliar, authoritarian environment. The slave's new circumstances demanded that he acquiesce or die. And acquiescence in turn required him to accept a presumption of inferiority and to act out subservience. The result was a child-man who looked upon his master as a father figure, and who for the sake of security supported the system which enslaved him. This psychological response to slavery, Elkins concludes, robbed the slave of his personality and created the stereotypical "Sambo," "Uncle Tom" personalities among black people.

The Elkins thesis is sweeping and damning. It furnishes perhaps the greatest indictment of slavery; but it also tells black Americans that their heritage is that of Sambos and "bootlickers." In response to the Elkins thesis, recent scholarship on Southern slavery has focused upon the degree of resistance offered by slaves to the system and upon the degree of underground black culture created by slaves. Researchers have found ample evidence of both active resistance (revolts, escapes, individual acts of violence) and passive resistance (malingering, destruction of property) to slavery. Songs and folk tales are two examples of a self-conscious black culture which the slave experience could not and did not destroy.

Taking into account all the variables possible in the mastery-dependence relationship of slavery, it seems that slaves responded to their experience in one of three ways. Some acquiesced and became child-people and Sambos. Others resisted their bonds in every way they could at every possible opportunity. Still others, perhaps a majority, played at their prescribed role, retained their basic humanity, and "used" their role to their own advantage. This response is best expressed in the title of a collection of slave narratives edited by Gilbert Osofsky, *Puttin' On Ole Massa.* One of the anecdotes cited by Osofsky in his introduction provides a good example. Pompey's master was preparing to fight a duel and apparently needed some morale building.

> Pompey, how do I look?
> O, massa, mighty.
> What do you mean "mighty," Pompey?
> Why, massa, you look noble.
> What do you mean by "noble"?
> Why, sar, you just look like one *lion.*
> Why, Pompey, where have you ever seen a lion?
> I sees one down yonder in the field the other day, massa.
> Pompey, you foolish fellow, that was a *jackass.*
> Was it, massa? Well you look just like him.

Some slaves probably played Sambo, rebel, and Pompey at various times in their lives. It is clear that the slave experience was a good deal more than physical and that slavery's most profound effect was upon the minds and spirits of its victims.

It is also clear that slavery affected not only slaves, but masters as well. The "peculiar institution" inspired in the master class high-minded paternalism. It also encouraged sadism. Some historians have suggested that slavery created among Southern whites a penchant for command, an authoritarian attitude, and an inclination toward violence. The position of master over other human beings no doubt did expose the best and worst among human responses. However kindly a master might intend to be toward his bondsmen, the potential for viciousness and cruelty always remained.

Slavery affected not only white masters. Researchers may argue about which came first, racism or slavery. The fact remains that slaves were black people, and white people were not slaves in the Old South. And as early as the mid-seventeenth century many whites had come to believe that black and slave were synonymous terms. Southerners, of course, were not alone in their racism; the presumption of black inferiority and racist actions were national phenomena. Yet because of the tendency for slavery to become more and more a Southern institution in the nineteenth century and because of the numbers and proximity of blacks in the South, white Southerners more readily translated racist assumptions into racist actions. Racism could be largely an abstraction in Minnesota; it was not so in South Carolina.

Slavery not only served as cause and effect for white racism in the South. It also produced a kind of ideological schizophrenia among the master class. As Americans, Southern whites professed freedom and liberty. Yet they practiced slavery. The resultant mental contortions and guilt were less than healthy.

Even more disturbing was the outright fear which came from holding four million people in bondage. Revolts and rumors of revolts fed this fear. Will we awake one night looking at the wrong end of a broadax? The most liberal Southerner on the question of emancipation paused when he reflected upon the consequences of freeing a captive population. Fear was certainly one reason that nonslaveholders supported an institution in which they had no apparent stake.

Slavery, then, was much more than a crude economic system of labor exploitation. Just as free labor capitalism influenced the Northern mind, slavery affected the minds and viscera of slaves and masters and nonmasters in the South.

Aristocracy

The lords of the lash are not only absolute masters of the blacks . . . , but they are also the oracles and arbiters of all non-slaveholding whites, whose freedom is purely nominal, and whose unparalleled illiteracy and degradation is purposely and fiendishly perpetuated.

The preceding invective came from the pen of Hinton Rowan Helper, a North Carolinian. Helper was the son of an illiterate farmer who, among other things, wrote into his book *The Impending Crisis of the South: How to Meet It* (1858) a bitter class analysis of Southern society. Helper opposed slavery in his book, not so much out of a sense of justice toward black men, but more in a class-conscious concern for nonslaveholding white men. Slavery, argued Helper, produced and perpetuated the small, aristocratic planter class. The vast majority of white Southerners could not afford the capital outlay involved in purchasing land and slaves in quantity. Thus the "peculiar institution" kept a few rich men rich and many poor men poor. Abolish slavery, he concluded, and in time the South would achieve social and economic democracy.

Helper may have oversimplified a bit, and some of his analysis suffered from rhetorical "overkill." Yet the North Carolinian had a point. There was a planter aristocracy in the Old South which held social, economic, and political power way out of proportion to their numbers. And this planter power was indeed class power. The planter class functioned as an aristocracy in spite of the fact that many among them were more nouveau riche than aristocrats, and in spite of the fact that the aristocrats themselves did not always hold political office.

The cotton boom of the 1820s, 30s, and 40s "made" large numbers of planters. Until the 1850s there was a high degree of social mobility among the planter class. "Dirt farmers made good" do not fit any conventional definition of aristocrats. Newly rich planters, however, did in fact act like aristocrats. They did so in part because of the nature of the plantation system. The plantation was almost by definition an isolated empire; it required extensive management and paternalistic concern from the planter to degrees unknown on farms or in factories. With the need to operate and care for his dominion, in the manner of an aristocrat the planter drew also upon the *ideal* of landed gentry. Planters, often with the zeal of the convert, believed themselves to be the most recent link in a chain which began with the feudal lord, passed to the English squire, thence to the Colonial Virginia tobacco planter, and finally to them. No matter if the planters believed a myth. Planters, in general, believed and tried to act up to their belief.

The planters, as genuine or would-be aristocrats, exercised political power and influence in the Old South. They did so both directly and indirectly. W. J. Cash has observed that, "of the eight governors of Virginia from 1841 to 1861, only one was born a gentleman. . . ." Yet however democratic political machinery became in the South, the class interests of the planters prevailed. The seven non-gentle-born Virginia governors between 1841 and 1861 may not have been aristocrats; they did, however, serve the planters' interests in the state.

If, in general terms, the planters were an aristocratic class as Helper contended, why did the more numerous non-planters not challenge them? Why did the "plain folk" not rise up in their best class interests, abolish slavery, and destroy the economic base of planter power? These are logical questions which require at least tentative answers if we are to understand Southern society.

Several circumstances tied the plain folk to the planters in apparent denial of their class interests. Indeed there was an economic tie. Plantations were never wholly self-sufficient economic units, however much the planters tried to make them so. Nor could the planters import all their needs from Europe or the North. Thus planters and farmers exchanged such things as grain and livestock for mutual advantage. The farmers made profits and the planters could concentrate more on the production of their staple crops.

There were also ties of kinship, neighborliness, and paternalism between planters and plain folk. It was difficult for the small farmer to see his nearby planter neighbor as his class enemy, if the planter attended the same church, patted the farmer's children on their heads, and was the farmer's second cousin.

Ambition, too, made the plain folk reluctant to challenge the plantation aristocracy. The farmer may have been a proto-planter. The plantation ideal not only influenced the planter; it served as a goal for the non-planter as well.

Finally, race united Southern whites. Slavery might pose a barrier to the plain folk's class interest as Helper said; but slavery also subordinated four million potential economic competitors. Moreover the slave system effectively restrained four million potential physical enemies. The fear of what one scholar has termed "racial adjustment" may also have been sufficient cause of the support offered by plain folk to the planter aristocracy.

The Southern Mind

"Minds" are difficult. Most scholars have long agreed that a distinctive mind existed in the Old South—that antebellum Southerners were somehow different. Unfortunately scholars have never agreed about the traits and characteristics which composed this Southern mind. In truth, among the South's 11 million people in 1860, there were 11 million variations of the Southern mind. Nevertheless, if we are willing to generalize, we can identify some distinctive elements shared in some degree by 11 million minds. If we catalog the characteristics most mentioned by scholars, we can suggest that Southerners had individual, personal, romantic, proud, violent, and provincial mental traits.

1. Individualism

Because the Old South was predominantly rural—in many areas little removed from the frontier—Southerners tended to live rather isolated lives. Many factors within this isolation tended to emphasize the assertion of self. Planters perceived themselves as masters of their plantation kingdoms. Farmers looked with pride upon fields which had been wilderness. Neither farmer nor planter worked for anyone but himself. It was small wonder that Southerners had little consciousness of a corporate identity, beyond their immediate family or community.

2. Personalism

One Southern historian, David M. Potter, has suggested that a set of personal relationships with men and land was the diagnostic feature of Southern life. Potter's idea of a persistent "folk culture" hinges upon a high degree of personal, as opposed to institutional, relationships among Southerners. Even in cases in which the relationship was degrading, Southerners tended to emphasize the personal aspects and thereby make the relationship more meaningful. Perhaps the Southern attitude toward the law was a good example. In the halls of Congress and in the press Southerners often lapsed into legalism, citing the law as an absolute in whatever argument they were advancing. Yet on a plantation the law was often whatever the master said it was. Duels and gouging matches often substituted for trials and suits. And a ready defense for anyone accused of murder was that the victim "needed killing." The law was in the South more a personal affair than an institutional abstraction. Personalism also extended to paternalism and accounted for instances of slaves' loyalty to masters. In general the South was a society of men, not institutions.

3. Romanticism

As we have seen, Americans in the mid-nineteenth century had a romantic world-view. Southern romanticism was a distinct mutation of the prevailing national mood. In general Southerners tended to idealize themselves and to think themselves into romantic molds. Elsewhere in the nation, romanticism might help trigger a reform impulse, but not in the South. Others might see distant romantic ideals and strive for them; Southerners generally found romantic ideals in the status quo and proclaimed them. Southerners as a group read themselves into Sir Walter Scott's novels and identified with ideals of the past. Virginians, for example, held jousting tournaments. And Southerners created that nineteenth-century apotheosis of courtly love, the Southern belle. The ideal of the belle, like the ideal of the planter, was more vision than reality. Indeed the Southern lady often found the pedestal on which society expected her to stand more of a cage than a place of honor. Nevertheless the Southern belle was the ultimate expression of Southern romanticism. And however false the Southerner's chivalrous self-concept may or may not have been, he believed and acted upon that romantic image more often than upon the harsher reality.

4. Pride

Our hypothetical Southern mind expressed pride more than it explained it. In a healthy context the Southerner was proud of his identity as an individual and of his way of life. Occasionally however Southerners tended to "protest too much." Pride then took on a defensive overtone and perhaps bespoke guilt. Much of the Southern reaction to the sectional crisis reflected this unhealthy sort of pride. Politicians demanded that slavery extend to areas unsuited for the conventional employment of slave labor to reassert the right of the slave system. To deny the extension of slavery and the righteousness of slavery was to strike a sensitive spot in Southern pride. Southern slaveholders said freedom, but practiced its opposite. Criticism of this circumstance, both rational and irrational, evoked an aggressive defense. And often the degree of Southern over-reaction to threats real and imagined revealed more about the Southern mind than about the issue at hand.

5. Violence

Naturally, Southerners were not the only violence-prone Americans. Yet the practice of dueling persisted in the South after it had been outlawed elsewhere. The Southerner's pride and individualism tended to lead him to violent acts in defense of dignity and honor. The maintenance of the slave system depended upon physical coercion and punishment. The proximity to frontier conditions in the South contributed to the number of fights and brawls. It is easy to overstate the Southern penchant for violence; comparative statistics, if they were available, might reveal that Americans as a group were violent people in the nineteenth century. Still, it was a Southerner, Preston Brooks, who beat Charles Sumner senseless on the floor of the Senate over a slur Sumner made about a relative of Brooks. In a sense Brooks committed a classic, symbolic act of Southern pride and violence.

6. Provincialism

State's rights was more than a political doctrine in the Old South. The concept expressed also a long-held pattern of ascending loyalties which radiated outward from self, to community, to region, and to state. When loyalty had filtered through that many steps, there was often not much enthusiasm left to share with the nation. The Southerner, in rural isolation, naturally developed a provincial outlook. And, as we shall see, when "outsiders" attacked his life style he responded by narrowing his horizons still further.

If the South's 11 million minds did share some or all of these characteristics, and if the corporate Southern mind was distinct from the "mind" of the rest of the nation, we must make at least two observations about that mind. First the traits and characteristics listed and defined above have healthy and unhealthy aspects associated with them. An individualistic frame of mind may yield an egomaniac or an admirably independent person. The point is that the Southern mind was not sick because some Southerners seem to have been, nor noble because other Southerners seem to have been.

The second observation about the Southern mind is that during the mid-nineteenth century it was becoming dangerously closed. Historian Clement Eaton has documented this tendency in the Old South to permit little deviation from an accepted "truth." That "truth" was that the South was "the best of all possible worlds" and that slavery was a "positive good." Eaton has shown that Southern institutions, the church, schools, the press, and politics actively excluded otherwise-mindedness. The result of this growing adherence to the Southern "line" was the creation of a kind of "Cotton Curtain." Southerners were quite willing to believe the worst about the North (and vice versa), because they rarely heard or read anything else. In this kind of atmosphere, full of defenses for real and imagined threats, Southerners began to question the value of continued union with the Yankees.

Southern Nationalism

Sometime between 1830 and 1860 Southern sectionalism became Southern nationalism. As sectionalists, Southerners saw themselves as part of a larger union and asserted their interests within that union. As nationalists, Southerners perceived themselves to be more Southern than American and viewed the union as an unfortunate circumstance.

One man more than any other was crucial to the Southern change of heart. That man was John C. Calhoun. Born in upcountry South Carolina, Calhoun first won political office as a representative of the backwoods farmers against the entrenched power of low country planters in the South Carolina legislature. In 1811 Calhoun went to the United States Congress and soon joined with other Southerners and Westerners in enmity towards England. The "War Hawks," as the group was called, encouraged and supported the Madison administration in the War of 1812. When that war ended, Calhoun had acquired such a reputation that President James Monroe named him Secretary of War. Calhoun the superpatriot had voted for the National Bank and the tariff in Congress, and as Secretary of War he pursued a broad nationalist policy. In the election of 1824 and again in 1828 the South Carolinian won the office of Vice President. He appeared certain to succeed Andrew Jackson to the Presidency in 1832.

Many factors prevented Calhoun from becoming President. Not the least of these was his growing concern for South Carolina and the South during the years 1824–1830. During this period Calhoun became a sectionalist. He became convinced that the South's interests were distinct from those of the rest of the nation. And he believed that the South's interests were being ignored. It was largely for these reasons that he formulated the Doctrine of Nullification. According to this theory any state could nullify or void a law or policy which threatened its safety or basic well-being. Calhoun led South Carolina's struggle to nullify the tariffs of 1828 and 1830, because he hoped that nullification would preserve the Union and the South by providing a middle ground between submission and revolution. During the Nullification Crisis of 1832, Calhoun resigned the vice-presidency. He returned to Washington as Senator from South Carolina. Within a few months Calhoun had made the transition from national to state office; the change in his mind was already complete.

For the rest of his life Calhoun served as a sectional spokesman, mostly in the Senate. The South did not often rally to the Carolinian; he never united Southerners in their sectional self-interest. Still, Calhoun tried. He advanced the "gag rule" against the introduction of abolitionist petitions in Congress. He sought to further Southern sectional interests in alliance first with the West and then the Northeast. He switched political parties in hopes of securing a better deal for himself and the South. He tried to annex Texas and supported the Mexican War. Whenever the South had a stake in any national issue, Calhoun spoke for her.

Calhoun thought for the South also. As his section became a minority in Congress, Calhoun became a champion of minority rights. He never abandoned the principle of nullification. There must be some way, he argued, in which a minority interest can protect itself against a majority. He spun theories in his head and played politics in the Senate—all for the salvation of the South as he perceived her.

By 1850 Calhoun was old and sick. But he was still in the Senate when the issue of what to do about the land won in the Mexican War had come to a head. Calhoun's final speech in the Senate was a sectional ultimation. The Carolinian was too weak to deliver the speech himself; he merely nodded as a clerk read it for him. Calhoun pled for union and the South's place in that union. Days later he died; his last words were, "The South, the poor South."

Those who followed Calhoun revered him and honored his memory. They appropriated his sectional logic and turned it to the uses of Southern nationalism. The Southern leadership in the 1850s was a new generation. They had not known the nationalism of 1812; they had taken Calhoun's threats of nullification and secession seriously. Of course more was involved than misusing Calhoun. Even before the South Carolinian died Southern leaders were chafing at his attachment to the Union.

Calhoun led the South from nationalism to sectionalism. He pursued the Southern good within the context of Union. When he died, he left a host of disciples whose sectional loyalty had imperceptibly become Southern nationalism. Perhaps because they did not recognize the dividing line, they crossed it.

The obvious question is, why? Perhaps the answer is incorporated in this chapter and the one preceding it. For those two chapters seem to have described two nations instead of the component parts of one. Perhaps Southerners became Southern nationalists because their interests, ideologies, and life styles were irreconcilably at odds with those of the rest of the United States. It may have been ironic, but no accident, that just over 50 years after Appomattox a Southern president of the re-United States led the nation into a war for the cause of "self-determination of peoples."

. . . as it was in Beaufort, South Carolina.

*. . . as presented in an illustration
for* Uncle Tom's Cabin.

. . . as seen in idylic tones.

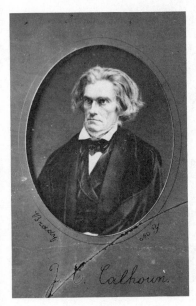

John C. Calhoun.

William H. Seward.

Henry Clay.

Stephen A. Douglas.

Lincoln's Inauguration.

Davis' Inauguration.

THE WAR 4
OF THE
"WORLDS"

By 1850 South and North lived together in a very uneasy union. During the 1850s a series of rude shocks made "nations" out of sections and drove these "nations" to the point of separation. If we oversimplify to the point of absurdity the preceding two chapters, we can see the following dichotomy of "worlds."

North	South
free-market capitalism, work ethic	pre-capitalist agrarianism
expansive nationalism	localism
free labor	slave labor (emphasis)
zeal for perfection	celebration of status quo
industrialism (emphasis)	plantation-slave agriculture
social democracy	social aristocracy

Americans had a war in 1861, not because different "worlds" and ideologies existed in the North and South. War came because these world views came into conflict. Northerners and Southerners expressed their ideologies in political terms and acted them out in the political arena. But politics failed to accommodate the conflicting ideologies, and thus the recourse to force.

Why? Were separation and war inevitable, "irrepressible" as William H. Seward phrased it? Surely the overwhelming majority of Americans, North and South, did not desire four years of bloodletting which produced more than 600,000 graves. If no one, or very few people at most, wanted war, then why could no one stop it? Were politicians blind or simply inept? Was the political structure of the United States in the 1850s unable to accommodate a conflict of interests and ideologies as deep as that of the North and South?

Hindsight is a very mixed blessing for historians. We now know the awesome tragedy that the Civil War became. The participants in this history did not know that sectional impasse would lead to secession, that secession would lead to war, or that the war would be long and bloody. Americans in the 1850s were trying, as most people of any age try, to muddle through one day at a time. They made decisions and took action in accord with their interests and their ideals as they perceived them.

Those political decisions and actions were conditioned by ideologies. They led to tragedy in part because of the issues involved, in part because of the men involved, and in part because of the political structure and institutions involved. To separate these parts—to say that the war came only because of chance, or of bungling men, or of flawed political structures —would be ahistorical. In the real political world of the 1850s men, issues, and structures were bound up in each other. Historical hindsight can help us understand the 1850s only if we apply it to what we perceive to be past reality. And that reality was composed of a deep dichotomy of ideologies and a political amalgam of issues, men, and institutions.

The Chain of Events

The Union was unstable in 1850. Let us now accept the diverse "nationhood" of South and North and outline the events which led to the final crisis. Ironically the decade began with a compromise.

The Compromise of 1850

It all began with David Wilmot. A Pennsylvania Democrat, Wilmot offered a proviso as an amendment to a wartime appropriation bill. The Wilmot Proviso made the appropriation conditional on the exclusion of slavery from any territory acquired as a result of the war with Mexico.

Wilmot's Proviso opened the Pandora's Box of the status of slavery in the territories.

The controversy sputtered throughout the war and came to a head in 1850. In general terms the South, led by John C. Calhoun, insisted that the Constitution guaranteed the sanctity of slave property in the territories. The North argued that Congress had constitutional authority to organize territories and therefore could prohibit slavery as the Confederation Congress had done in the Northwest Ordinances. A third viewpoint was developing as a possible compromise. Squatter or Popular Sovereignty was a doctrine which advocated a hands-off attitude on the part of Congress. Let the people who settle a territory decide and write into their state constitution a policy on slavery urged Lewis Cass of Michigan and Stephen A. Douglas of Illinois.

From January through September of 1850 Congress wrestled with the sectional issue. Indeed the Union seemed to many more likely to break apart in 1850 than it did ten years later. What emerged as the Compromise of 1850 was an omnibus (for all) package of five separate acts. Very few members of Congress voted in favor of all five acts. Yet the understanding proposed by Henry Clay and pursued most vigorously by Douglas was that the package as a whole constituted the compromise. The substance of each of the five acts was:

1. California was admitted to the Union as a free state.
2. Congress organized and defined the New Mexico territory leaving slavery to the settlers. In the same act Congress defined the boundary of Texas and agreed to pay $10 million to Texas (thereby in effect assuming Texas' debts).
3. Congress organized Utah as a territory leaving slavery to the settlers.
4. Congress passed a stern Fugitive Slave Act which provided Federal officials to aid in the recapture of runaway slaves. The Act compelled all citizens to aid in the recapture and provided fines and imprisonment for those who did not.
5. Congress abolished the slave trade (not slavery itself) in the District of Columbia.

The Compromise of 1850 thus incorporated the untried doctrine of popular sovereignty. The package offered concessions to both North and South and hope to all. Many well-meaning Americans believed that the Compromise was a "final" solution.

Reaction to the Compromise

In one sense only was the Compromise of 1850 a final solution; it represented, symbolically at least, the last gasp of virtually a generation of American statesmen. John C. Calhoun died in March of 1850. Henry Clay died in June, 1852. John Quincy Adams died in 1848. Thomas Hart Benton lost first his Senate seat then a House seat in the 1850s. Daniel Webster died in October 1852. Andrew Jackson died in 1845 and James K. Polk, in 1849. Within a very few years the generation of American leaders who knew and expressed the nationalism of the eighteen-teens had disappeared. The new generation of political leaders had not known a national period; they rose to prominence amid partisan and sectional strife. Thus men like William H. Seward, Salmon Chase, Jefferson Davis, and R. M. T. Hunter were conditioned to internal conflict. Potential compromisers like Cass and Douglas lacked not only the stature of Clay, but also the trust and good will of their partisan-minded colleagues.

Although Southern radicals attempted to undo the Compromise of 1850 before it passed Congress, most Southerners seemed willing to give the settlement a trial. The Georgia Platform, for example, adopted by a state convention, accepted the Compromise but warned that Georgians would not abide legislative encroachments upon slavery.

Georgians and others from slaveholding states soon found fault with the enforcement of the Fugitive Slave Act. Some in the North acted out their hatred of slavery. Vermont in essence nullified the Fugitive Slave Act by passing "personal liberty" laws. These laws granted state citizenship and constitutional protection to all who resided in the state. Thus a slaveholder in pursuit of his escaped bondsman faced a legal roadblock in potentially unfriendly state courts. In addition, a few well-publicized rescues of fugitives by sympathetic Northern people and local officials made Southerners believe that the free states had broken faith and destroyed the Compromise.

In the North the Compromise of 1850 became a divisive issue, especially within the Whig Party. Whigs in New York, for example, split over the Compromise and rallied to the leadership of Seward who opposed the Compromise and President Millard Fillmore who supported it. Indeed the Compromise of 1850 was an important issue in the ultimate disappearance of the Whigs as a national party. Could moral men compromise with slaveholders?

Uncle Tom's Cabin

Harriet Beecher Stowe's novel brought home to the literally millions of Americans who read it or saw it acted on the stage the potential horrors of slavery.

Uncle Tom's Cabin was an indictment of slavery and all who allowed the system to exist. The author insisted that God Himself moved her pen and inspired her imagination. The characters in the novel are not the cliches they became in stage adaptations; they are powerful people. None is more powerful than Uncle Tom who lives the religion which whites in the book only profess. The novel portrays divergent "worlds"—New England where men must do for themselves and Louisiana where men have things done for them. Yet Northerners and Southerners share the blame for slavery in the novel, and characters from both sections participate in the institution's cruelty. *Uncle Tom's Cabin* dealt with slavery in all its subtleties; yet it was not a subtle book. It made slavery and the plight of slaves concrete, instead of abstract. And it moved Americans (in the North) to accept a share of the nation's corporate guilt over slavery and do something about it. In just over a year the book sold approximately 2,500,000 copies throughout the world. And Abraham Lincoln when he met Mrs. Stowe in later years greeted her, "So this is the little lady who made this big war."

The Election of 1852

The Democrats nominated Franklin Pierce of New Hampshire as a compromise "Northern man with Southern sympathies." The Whigs chose Winfield Scott, who ran as a military hero. Northern and Southern Whigs split over slavery, and the Southerners felt ill at ease in their party. Although the popular vote was fairly close, Pierce won a landslide victory in the electoral college (254 to 42). The election offered further evidence of the Whig demise, and the party never again contested a presidential election. As President, Pierce more often than not attempted to reconcile the increasingly hostile ideologies of North and South by appeasing the South.

The Kansas-Nebraska Act (1854)

Popular Sovereignty as incorporated in the Compromise of 1850 applied only to those territories (Utah and New Mexico) in which the introduction of plantation-style slavery appeared a remote possibility. In 1854 Douglas presented the Senate with an opportunity to test the doctrine in Kansas where the introduction of slavery was a very real probability. Douglas, the "Little Giant" from Illinois, believed that he had found in Popular Sovereignty the means to avoid sectional strife and to make himself President of the United States. In addition, the organization of Nebraska added weight to the Illinois senator's advocacy of a central route (through Chicago) for a transcontinental railroad. Letting the people decide about slavery seemed to enforce democratic idealism and western expansion. Douglas' bill inspired three months' debate in Congress and considerable suspicion in all sections of the country before it became law as the Kansas-Nebraska Act.

The final version of the Kansas-Nebraska Act repealed the Missouri Compromise of 1820, thus undoing the sectional compromise of an earlier generation. Actually the act upset much more than a 34-year-old settlement.

In Ripon, Wisconsin, in February, 1854, a number of politically homeless Northern Whigs, Democrats, and Free Soilers met and organized the Republican Party. The party formed in opposition to the Kansas-Nebraska Act was a sectional expression. It appealed to former Democrats who were tired of trying to compromise with Southerners. It attracted old Whigs, especially after the Know-Nothing enthusiasm waned in the late 50s. The Republican platform proclaimed advocacy of "Free Soil, Free Labor and Free Men." It was anti-slavery, but more. The Republicans appropriated the nation's faith in laissez faire, hard work, and the American dream. Their platform appealed to America's reforming idealism and sense of mission. In short the Republicans were canny politicians and devoted idealogues at the same time; they were the practical, political expression of the Northern world view.

Many Southerners liked the Kansas-Nebraska Act little better than did the Republicans. Some politicians and newspaper editors suspected Douglas of being in league with abolitionists and of plotting to make Kansas free soil. Ironically, Popular Sovereignty and its political expression the Kansas-Nebraska Act had the reverse effect of that Douglas intended. The act and its implementation in Kansas heightened sectional feelings. And North and South eventually agreed that Stephen A. Douglas should never become President.

Ostend Manifesto (1854)

Northerners who looked upon the Kansas-Nebraska Act as a "slaveholders' plot" found other more dramatic evidence in the expansion schemes of some Southern adventurers and diplomats. In 1851 General Narcisco Lopez recruited a band of Southerners to carry out a revolt against the Spanish in Cuba. The revolt failed and the Spanish executed Lopez; but many Americans recoiled at the possibility of free-lance conquest of additional slaveholding territory. They recoiled some more in 1855 and again in 1857 when William Walker and a party of Southern adventurers attempted (unsuccessfully) to conquer Nicaragua. These unofficial attempts at conquest were embarrassing; embarrassing too, however, was the official pronouncement of the minister to Spain, Pierre Soulé.

In the midst of a dispute with Spain over the seizure of an American ship in Havana Harbor, Soulé sent a dispatch from Ostend, Belgium, to Secretary of State William Marcy. The Ostend Manifesto asserted that Cuba was essential for the security of slavery in the United States, and therefore the country ought to try to buy the island from Spain. If the Spanish would not sell, Soulé continued, the United States should use military force and take Cuba.

Marcy reprimanded Soulé for his rashness, and Soulé resigned his post. However in March, 1855, American newspapers secured and published the Ostend Manifesto. In the North many believed that the "plot" to expand the "slaveocracy" had made the transit from private adventure to public policy. The Northern and Southern "worlds" not only conflicted with each other, they actively competed for room to expand.

"Bleeding Kansas"

Kansas was the test case of Popular Sovereignty in action. Pro-slave and free-soil activists throughout the United States focused energy and attention upon the settlement of Kansas. Many settlers moved to Kansas for the same reasons settlers had moved to other western territories—to make a new start, to farm good land. Others went to Kansas to prove something about slavery and the distribution of sectional power. Even before the Kansas-Nebraska Act became law, the Massachusetts Emigrant Aid Society formed to promote the settlement of Kansas by free soilers. In Missouri similar groups formed to promote proslavery settlement. The atmosphere was not conducive to the kind of simple frontier democracy in which Kansans could determine rationally the destiny of slavery in their community.

The issue was expansion—expansion of life-styles which had assumed the right-wrong fervor of ideologies. Perhaps North and South could co-exist uneasily within long established boundaries; but both sections perceived the need to grow, not just for the sake of free labor capitalism or the slave-plantation system, but as a matter of moral right. Soon they proved that North and South could not co-exist peaceably in Kansas.

Along with the bona fide settlers came ideologues on both sides of the issue. And on election days gangs of "border ruffians" from Missouri came to Kansas to vote for slavery and intimidate the free soilers. By the end of 1855 Kansas had two territorial legislatures (one pro-slave and one anti-slave) and two territorial delegates to Congress. A succession of appointed governors were unable to keep peace or ensure fair elections.

In 1856 civil war began in earnest. Border ruffians sacked Lawrence, a free-state stronghold, in May. John Brown, a free-soil zealot from Ohio, avenged the sack of Lawrence by executing five proslavery settlers near Pottawatomie Creek. Throughout the summer settlers and intruders sniped and burned in eastern Kansas. Finally Federal troops succeeded in bringing a temporary calm in the fall of 1856.

Outside Kansas, Americans reacted in partisan alarm to the violence.

Perhaps the most alarmed American was Stephen A. Douglas whose cherished compromise had backfired so disastrously. In Congress Douglas pressed for Kansas statehood, no doubt hoping that adoption of a state constitution would settle the fate of slavery in Kansas and bring peace. In the course of the debate on Kansas, Massachusetts Republican Charles Sumner delivered a bitter polemic, "The Crime Against Kansas." In the course of the speech Sumner directed special invective against the character of South Carolina Senator Andrew Butler who was not present. Next day Representative Preston Brooks, a nephew of Butler, avenged his kinsman by beating Sumner senseless with a cane on the floor of the Senate. At this point the violence had come full circle, from Congress, to Kansas and back to Congress.

The Election of 1856

Congress adjourned in 1856 without settling anything about the immediate future of Kansas. The question thus became a campaign issue in the presidential election. The Republicans nominated John C. Frémont and flayed the Democrats for "Bleeding Kansas" during the campaign. Democratic nominee James Buchanan of Pennsylvania stood by the Kansas-Nebraska Act and tried to strike a national pose. The Know-Nothing Party, an amalgam of nativist societies and moderate Whigs, nominated former Whig President Millard Fillmore and campaigned for nativism and sectional moderation. Buchanan won. But the Republicans garnered more than a million votes to finish a strong second. Fillmore and the Know-Nothings made a poor electoral showing and discredited nativism and Whig moderation.

The new President tried to keep sectional passions at bay. Like Pierce, however, Buchanan left himself open to charges of being a "dough-face," a Northern man with Southern sympathies.

Dred Scott's Case (1857)

Dred Scott was the body-servant of John Emerson, an Army doctor. In the course of his service Emerson took Scott into Illinois and Wisconsin, a free state and a free territory. When Emerson died Scott sued the doctor's estate for his freedom on the grounds that his sojourns onto free soil made him a free man. *Dred Scott v. Sanford* took 11 years to reach the Supreme Court for a final decision. The Court, presided over by Chief Justice Roger B. Taney, ruled that because Scott was a slave, he was not a citizen and therefore could not sue in state or Federal courts. The court went further and ruled that local law (state or territorial) could not deprive a slaveholder of his "property" or alter the status of enslaved persons. The Court went on to declare the Missouri Compromise unconstitutional because it denied a man's right to hold slave property in special and arbitrary cases.

Members of the Taney Court reached this decision in various ways and split six to three on the major issues. Nevertheless, by implication, the decision rendered the doctrine of Popular Sovereignty meaningless. If the people of a territory could not interfere with slave property, then in no way could people make their territory free soil. Abraham Lincoln made this very point in one of his debates with Stephen A. Douglas during the senatorial camapign of 1858 in Illinois. Douglas responded that local laws and ordinances (a slave code) were a sine quo non of slavery. Thus settlers could effectively prohibit slavery in a territory by failing to pass and enforce a slave code (Douglas' Freeport Doctrine). Indeed, Douglas had a point. But in the face of "Bleeding Kansas" and the Dred Scott Decision, Douglas and Popular Sovereignty were bankrupt.

Kansas Again

In 1857 a proslavery convention meeting at Lecompton drew up a proposed constitution for Kansas. Free staters had boycotted the election of delegates to the convention, and the free-state legislature meeting of Topeka denounced the Lecompton Constitution. President Buchanan's appointee as territorial governor, Robert J. Walker of Mississippi, became convinced that the majority of Kansas opposed the work of the Lecompton Convention. And indeed when Kansans finally voted in a fair election, in January, 1858, they confirmed Walker's opinion by soundly defeating the Lecompton Constitution.

The President, however, desired nothing so much as to be rid of the Kansas issue. At the urging of the Southern members of his Cabinet, Buchanan submitted the Lecompton Constitution to Congress and recommended admission of Kansas as a slave state. Walker then resigned claiming that Buchanan had betrayed him. The Administration-backed English Bill provided for another vote by Kansans, but stated that should the Lecompton Constitution again fail at the polls, Kansas would have to wait for admission until its population reached the level required for a Congressional representative (around 90,000). In August, 1858, Kansans did again reject the Lecompton Constitution, and Kansas remained a territory until 1861.

Naturally the man most disgusted by Buchanan's highhandedness on the Kansas question was Stephen A. Douglas. Following a stormy personal confrontation with the President, Douglas formally broke with the Administration. Kansas, therefore, had not only provided fuel for sectional partisans (especially the Republican Party); it also rent the Democratic Party. And in the late Fifties the Democratic Party was the only viable political organization even trying to maintain a national stance. Significantly the Democrats lost heavily in the Congressional elections of 1858, and the Administration lost effective control of the House of Representatives.

Harpers Ferry, 1859

We have not dealt with people, as individuals, for some pages. We have spoken of ideologies, and we have recited the issues and events by which those ideologies were translated into political activity. This "big picture" is important. But what about people; how did all this affect individuals?

John Brown was certainly not the epitome of the Northern "world," yet he incorporated much of the American world view. He was born a New England Calvinist. God, for John Brown, was a God of justice and omnipotence. John Brown often feared that he fell short of that justice, but he did his best. He was an intense apostle; he worked hard and drove others to do likewise. He was a stern father and husband. And John Brown and his God agreed in their righteous hatred of slavery. Slavery was a stain on the social fabric, and slaveholders were guilty.

For all his hard work and faith in his dreams and ideals, Brown consistently failed in business and social relations. "Success" came first when Brown was in his fifties in Kansas. His "massacre" on Pottawatomie Creek in 1856 brought him measures of fame and notoriety, and his adventures convinced him that God might yet make John Brown His instrument. Brown returned to the East and mapped his Holy War on slavery and slaveholders. He planned to foment a slave revolt in Virginia, maintain a stronghold in the Appalachians, and export insurrection throughout the South. Brown secured money from influential abolitionists and attacked Harpers Ferry, Virginia, on October 16, 1859.

Because he believed himself called by God to do this work, Brown did not plan very carefully. He was convinced that God would use him to God's purpose whether the Harpers Ferry scheme succeeded or not. Doubtless Brown's backers and followers in the raid would have preferred him to pay more attention to mundane matters like success.

The raid did take Harpers Ferry by surprise and enjoyed some initial success. However, slaves from the surrounding area did not flock to Brown's banner. The old man and his less than two dozen raiders were no match for the aroused citizenry and the United States Marines (led incidentally by Colonel Robert E. Lee). The soldiers took Brown and what was left of his band prisoners on October 18.

The state of Virginia indicted Brown for treason and for inciting servile insurrection and tried him at Charles Town. Brown was a failure at raiding, but to him that was no matter. He had struck God's blow for freedom, and that was sufficient. Brown acted out his martyrdom and went unflinchingly to the gallows in early December.

John Brown the zealot was one of a kind. Many Southerners believed that he was typical of Yankees in general and abolitionists in particular. He was not. Yet Brown partook of the American tradition. He struck a blow for his convictions and pursued his and his nation's righteousness to the ultimate degree. He translated the ideology of the American "world" into moral right, and then his soul marched on to become a part of that ideology.

Edmund Ruffin watched John Brown die. Ruffin was a Virginian, a planter, and a Southern zealot. In his youth Ruffin had aspired to political leadership, and failed. He lacked the hail-fellow-well-met manner necessary to succeed at politics. Ruffin turned then to the science of agriculture and won recognition as an intellectual. He published a journal, *The Farmer's Register,* and through it and his scientific discoveries almost single-handedly brought about an agricultural renaissance in the previously worn-out soil of the seaboard South.

During the 1840s and 50s Ruffin became a professional revolutionary. He was convinced that the North and South were incompatible and that the sooner the South realized this the better. Ruffin traveled throughout the South preaching secession and a Southern republic as the only salvation for the Southern soul.

In the fall of 1859 Ruffin was over 60 years old; he despaired of his mission as prophet of Southernism. He had watched Northern aggression grow and warned his fellow Southerners. Yet even though he and other fire-eaters had won converts, secession seemed still remote. The day before he heard of John Brown's raid, he wrote in his diary, "I have lived long enough. . . ."

When Ruffin heard the news from Harpers Ferry his mood brightened. Perhaps this would be the beginning of his revolution. Accordingly, despite his years and cold weather, he went in late November to what he termed the "seat of war." At Harpers Ferry Ruffin wormed his way into a military company, a detachment of cadets from the Virginia Military Institute. Thus the old man in a borrowed military overcoat marched with boys still in their teens to the place of execution. He watched John Brown hang and liked what he saw. He carefully recorded the time and degree of the convulsive movements of Brown's arms and legs in his diary and grudgingly admitted that Brown had displayed "animal courage."

Later Ruffin collected some of the pikes with which Brown had armed his followers and sent them to Southern governors with appropriate labels and propaganda. Still later, he went to Charleston in the midst of the Sumter crisis. There he slept in his clothes on the night of April 11-12, so that he would be ready to fire the first gun on the Fort (after Captain James's signal shot).

Ruffin was not exactly the typical Southerner. He was an extreme expression of the ultimate Southern ideology, just as Brown was for the Northern world-view. Ruffin believed that the South was the "best of all possible worlds," and he devoted his life to the preservation of the Southern "world."

The events at Harpers Ferry in the fall of 1859 were tragic. They were tragic for Edmund Ruffin, because they marked the beginning of the end for his "world." Certainly they were tragic for John Brown, even though they made of him a martyr. Yet the deepest tragedy was reserved for a third man present at Harpers Ferry—Robert E. Lee.

Lee, like Ruffin, was a Virginian; like Brown, Lee detested slavery. Lee was a man of two worlds, Northern and Southern. Ultimately he decided that he was more a Virginian than an American, and he probably was. He became in time for Southerners the personification of all things Southern. But in 1859 Lee was a soldier. He had fought for the Union, and he had lived a large portion of his life outside the South. When Lee made his decision in 1861 he agonized over his choice. Offered command of the armies of the United States, Lee chose to go home to Virginia. Ruffin and Brown were symbols, no, caricatures, of their respective ideologies. Lee was something else. Lee's agony and his decision to fight for his homeland reveal not so much about the nature of the contending "worlds." Rather Lee demonstrated the strength and depth of ideology in mid-nineteenth-century America.

The Making of the President, 1860

In 1860 the United States had suffered severe shocks to its political equilibrium. In the midst of instability, men and ideologies faced a presidential election.

The Conventions

On April 23, 1860, a divided Democratic Party convened at Charleston, South Carolina. Stephen A. Douglas hoped to salvage the nation, the party, and himself. He failed. Southerners demanded from the convention positive protection for slavery, and by implication the Southern "world," in the territories. The Douglas people chose not to allow the Democratic Party to become a tool of Southernism, and they had the votes to prevent it. Then in the midst of a platform fight, William Lowndes Yancey led a walkout of eight Southern state delegations. On May 3 the Convention adjourned after 57 ballots without nominating a candidate. In June the

Northern Democrats again convened, this time in Baltimore, and nominated Douglas and Herschel V. Johnson of Georgia. A Southern rump convention in Richmond chose John C. Breckinridge of Kentucky for President and Joseph Lane of Oregon for Vice-President. Before the campaign even opened, the last national political party in the country had come apart. ᵥ

One would-be national party did try to stand for moderation in 1860. In May a group composed essentially of ex-Whigs met in Baltimore, called themselves the Constitutional Union Party, and nominated John Bell of Tennessee for President and Edward Everett of Massachusetts for Vice-President.

The Republicans met in Chicago on May 16 (after the Democrats' debacle at Charleston), and smelled victory. William H. Seward led presidential nominees for two ballots. Seward had been in public life long enough and conspicuously enough to earn the nomination. But these very factors had made enemies for Seward. On the third ballot, therefore, the Republicans went to Abraham Lincoln whose public life to that time had been short, soundly Whig-Republican, and relatively "safe." The Illinois lawyer had served in the state legislature, spent an unproductive term in the House, and attracted attention and sympathy during his unsuccessful campaign for the Senate against Douglas. Lincoln's debates with Douglas sparked national interest, and even though Lincoln lost the election he gained a place in the popular mind as the "folksy," capable foe of the discredited "Little Giant." To balance the ticket the Republicans chose Hannibal Hamlin of Maine as Lincoln's running mate.

The Platforms

Douglas and the Northern Democrats reendorsed Popular Sovereignty and pledged to support the Supreme Court. In addition Douglas wooed Southern support by promising to acquire Cuba.

Breckinridge also incorporated designs on Cuba into his platform and restated the Southern position on slavery in the territories. Bell and the Constitutional Unionists stood for the Constitution and the Union, whatever they were. The Republicans opposed the expansion of slavery, as expected, and they offered other sectional planks to expand their popular base in the North. Lincoln espoused a higher tariff, internal improvements, government subsidies to railroads, and a homestead law (offering public land free to bona fide settlers). Diverse as the platforms were, only the Republican statement had much significance or impact on the election.

Symbol supplanted platform in 1860. Lincoln and Breckinridge led ideologically sectional tickets; they prompted a sectional response. The Republicans were artful in choosing Lincoln over Seward and broadening their antislavery base in their platform. But the Republicans would have had to commit incredible blunders to lose in 1860. Lincoln could beat Breckinridge because the source of his sectional support controlled more than twice the electoral votes. And the two blatantly sectional candidates faced one discredited moderate (Douglas) and one uncredited moderate (Bell). From hindsight, at least, it appears that the Republican Party could have run almost anyone in 1860 and won.

The Results

Candidate	Popular Vote	Electoral Vote
Lincoln	1,866,352	180 (18 free states)
Douglas	1,375,157	12 (Missouri and three New Jersey votes)
Breckinridge	847,953	72 (11 slave states)
Bell	589,581	39 (Virginia, Tennessee, and Kentucky)

To whatever degree that votes reflect temperament, the election of 1860 demonstrated the depth of division in the country. If Lincoln and Breckinridge represented opposite poles, then 2,714,305 Americans voted their polarization. If Douglas and Bell stood for moderation and some kind of compromise, then 1,964,738 voted their fear of sectional confrontation. If we look at the election in terms of mood, "showdowners" clobbered "compromisers." The sectional candidates garnered 58 percent of the total vote, and in most traditional political analyses 55 percent is sufficient to define a landslide.

Secession

On December 20, 1860, South Carolina threw down the gauntlet. Elected representatives of the people met in convention and voted to secede from the Union. South Carolinians believed that secession was legally undoing what the state had done in 1788 when a convention had ratified the Constitution. Secessionist radicals spoke and thought in Lockean terms and compared their revolution to the one their forefathers had begun 84 years earlier. Beneath legalism and theory was fear. South Carolinians were convinced that Lincoln and the Republicans were about to overturn their "world" and impose an alien "world view" upon them. Their response was aggressive defense.

South Carolina's action obviously challenged the government of the United States. South Carolina also challenged her sister states in the South. Southern radicals had been talking and thinking for a long time about secession and a Southern nation. Many believed that the Southern states should concert action and break away from the Union in a block. Timing was crucial to such a scheme, however. The states of the Deep South (at least) would have to reach the same level of malaise at the same time and would have to agree in advance upon the form and stance their concert would take. Ultimately the South Carolinians determined that concerted secession was over-complicated and too likely to miscarry. Thus what South Carolina did was to present the South with a fait accompli. In the aftermath of secession, the South Carolina convention dispatched agents to other slave states in search of allies. South Carolina was telling her sister states to "put up or shut up."

In the Deep South response to South Carolina's secession came swiftly. By February 1, 1861, six states had followed South Carolina out of the Union (Mississippi, January 9; Florida, January 10; Alabama, January 11; Georgia, January 19; Louisiana, January 26; and Texas, February 1). In each of these states a special secession convention met, deliberated, and decided. The people of the seceded states spoke only through their elected representatives. A majority of voters chose secession in their selection of convention delegates. Yet the secessionist leaders were correct in believing that they had a good deal less than a unanimous mandate.

At Montgomery, Alabama, delegates from the seven seceded states met on February 4, 1861, to form a new union. The Montgomery Convention expressed a certain amount of bravado; for the most part, though, it was a conservative body. Perhaps the secession euphoria had worn thin. Probably the delegates realized that to succeed, their revolution needed all the good will it could muster, in the North, in Europe, and also back home in the South. In five days the Convention adopted a provisional Constitution of the Confederate States of America, elected a provisional President and Vice President, and resolved itself into the Provisional Congress. At every turn the convention tended toward moderation and unanimity, to present a solid front to the world and to themselves.

The Confederate Constitution was strikingly like that of the United States. Ironically the preamble proclaimed a "permanent" union, implying that the "sovereign" states could not secede from the Confederacy. The Constitution sanctioned slavery but forbade the foreign slave trade (something for which Southern senators and congressmen had crusaded in the old Union in 1859). The President was to serve six years and be ineligible for reelection. The Post Office Department was to be self-sustaining. The President could veto portions of bills and thus avoid "riders." Other than these changes (some were improvements), the Confederate Constitution resembled in form and content that of the "Old Union." The delegates of Montgomery no doubt believed that the "old" Constitution would serve well enough now that there were no Yankees around to pervert it.

Moderation ruled in the choice of executives, too. The convention looked past those men who had stood in the forefront of the secession movement and chose (unanimously) Jefferson Davis who had wept when he left the United States Senate. Davis had tried to take up Calhoun's mantle as Southern spokesman in Congress. A Democrat, he had guarded Southern interests and threatened secession, but he himself had no direct part in disunion. Davis looked like a President; he was tall and almost handsome. He had a "correct" record as a Senator, and, significantly, he had military experience, actively in the Mexican War and administratively as Pierce's Secretary of War.

The Convention "covered its bet" in the choice of Alexander H. Stephens for Vice-President. Stephens, a Georgian, never chose secession; he simply followed Georgia out of the Union. He was a short, wizened Whig with legal, instead of military, experience. Stephens and Davis were "safe." Together they appealed to many members of the Southern body politic. In the Confederacy, however, they did not long remain together, politically or even physically.

The Confederate provisional executives were inaugurated on February 18. They, the Cabinet, and Congress then began talking about peace with the United States and preparing for war.

Quid Nunc

Classically educated newspaper editors on both sides of Mason and Dixon's line used the phrase *quid nunc*—what now?—a great deal during the winter and spring of 1861. South Carolina and her sister states had taken the initiative and pressed it when they founded the Confederacy. The next move belonged to those in the still United States—President Buchanan, Congress, and the states.

The President took a firm stand for equivocation. He said in essence, you Southern states cannot secede, but I cannot stop you. As the crisis deepened, Buchanan's vacillation became more sophisticated. Early in the Fort Sumter crisis in January, the President sent an unarmed ship, "The Star of the West," to Sumter to resupply the fort. However, when South Carolina guns fired upon "The Star of the West," her captain aborted his mission. Buchanan did make the proper gestures (he also ordered the collection of federal taxes, if possible). But he shrank from confrontation and counted the days until March 4 when he would no longer be President.

In Congress Kentuckian John J. Crittenden, who occupied Henry Clay's old seat in the Senate, proposed a sectional compromise. Crittenden proposed a revival, extension, and sanctification of the Missouri Compromise line (36° 30′) by unamendable amendment to the Constitution. The line was to divide slave territory from free soil and settle once and for all the question of slavery. Alas Crittenden proved more capable of filling Clay's seat than his shoes. Given the situation, he could do little else. Lincoln and the Republicans found Crittenden's compromise unacceptable and said so. Having won a mandate to "Americanize" the nation from the voters, the incoming Administration was not about to shrink from the task or compromise its principles.

The Virginia General Assembly and ex-President John Tyler called and led respectively a Peace Convention in Washington. The convention of state delegates met in Washington on the same day (February 4) that the Confederate convention met at Montgomery. Moderate men were present, and they wanted to find a compromise. But the "Old Gentleman's Convention," as it has been termed, could neither arrest the progress of events in Montgomery, nor find a common ground with the incoming Republican administration. Peace and its practitioners just seemed passé in 1861.

The American people seemed to take the secession crisis either too seriously (as participants), or not seriously enough. Many Northerners were convinced that secession was just another Southern bluff. Indeed many Southerners held the same view. Secession was merely a replay of nullification—a little more bluster and then some kind of settlement. Others were quite content to let the Southern states secede and say good riddance. Moderation just never mobilized.

In the unseceded states of the upper and border South, however, people could not ignore the crisis. Most of these states had potential secession conventions in session. But these conventions had large conservative majorities. In Kentucky, Arkansas, Virginia, Missouri, North Carolina, and Tennessee, while the radicals ranted, the conservatives held on and said, "*quid nunc.*"

Enter Lincoln

Abraham Lincoln maintained an almost unbroken silence from his election until his inauguration. He "leaked" his disfavor with the Crittenden Compromise; otherwise however Lincoln was content to watch Buchanan squirm. Lincoln's silence convinced many people that he shared the general frustration and indecision about the secession crisis. In fact many Republicans did not expect Lincoln to count for much in the new administration. While Seward might not be an attractive candidate, he could be a "prime minister" in the new government; Lincoln would be a "front man" while Seward ran the country. Not the least of those who held this view was William H. Seward.

Lincoln came to Washington in full knowledge of what others were saying and thinking about him. He came to Washington, into the midst of confusion, with three firm convictions: (1) He would be his own President. (2) He would preserve the Union. (3) He would not compromise on slavery extension. He said these things in his inaugural address, but somehow few people heard or believed him. Most heard Lincoln say conciliatory things to the South and missed the firmness with which he pledged to end the expansion of slavery and save the Union.

As the crisis developed, Lincoln seemingly devoted most of his energies to dispensing the "loaves and fishes" of patronage to voracious Republican placemen. The issue of federal installations on Confederate soil grew and sharpened. Attention focused upon Sumter and Fort Pickens, off Pensacola, Florida. Lincoln waited. He talked to border-state men and hoped that Southern unionists would assert themselves. Lincoln realized that the confrontation would have to come. When it did, however, he wanted as much of the upper South as possible on the side of Union.

The President did not share his thinking with his Cabinet. That body was a political construction in which the two strongest men, Secretary of State Seward and Secretary of the Treasury Salmon Chase, despised each other and patronized the President. Thus Seward, the would-be "prime minister," decided on April 1 that his time had come.

Seward sent a memorandum entitled "Some Thoughts for the President's Consideration" to Lincoln. In it Seward asserted that the Administration had no policy, and that it was high time to adopt one. Then Seward proposed to provoke war with at least Spain and France (perhaps England and Russia, too) for the purpose of rallying all Americans to the Union cause. Finally, Seward himself offered to oversee the war and the rallying. In a display of incredible self-control Lincoln responded. He wrote to Seward that the Administration did indeed have a policy and he the President would carry out that policy.

Lincoln had asserted his authority as President. A few days later he asserted the authority of the Union and the righteousness of the Administration's ideology by sending the *Harriet Lane* to Charleston Harbor. Later still Lincoln confirmed his stand by calling for 75,000 volunteers to "put down combinations in rebellion." The war of "worlds" had begun.

ARMED 5
MOBS

Fort Sumter, or more precisely Abraham Lincoln's subsequent call for volunteers, settled two questions. There would be a war over secession, and more states would secede. Since we need to know precisely who the contestants were before we can discuss the war, let us first deal with the border-state crisis.

Secession: Round Two

In 1861 the Border States agonized over secession—Maryland, Delaware, Missouri, North Carolina, Kentucky, Virginia, Tennessee and Arkansas. Each of these states had ties with the deep South and its "Cause." Each of these states also shared common cause with the Union. Ultimately the Border split, four Confederates and five (including West Virginia) Union.

The original Unionist quartet—Missouri, Maryland, Delaware, and Kentucky—had blocs of devoted Confederate sympathizers living within them. In fact two of the four (Kentucky and Missouri) had stars in the Rebel flag. The Confederate foursome—Virginia, Arkansas, North Carolina, and Tennessee—all had massive troubles with "tories." East Tennessee and Western North Carolina were often no man's lands in which anyone in uniform was evaded or shot. And Virginia's western counties seceded from the state during the war to become West Virginia. The Border States supplied many soldiers to both sides. Perhaps the most significant factor about the border anguish was the most obvious (and thus the easiest to to overlook). None of these states, however divided their mind, could remain neutral during the conflict. Only Kentucky attempted neutrality, and the posture vanished as soon as the first soldier set foot on Kentucky soil. The impossibility of neutrality bore ample witness to the strengths of the opposing ideologies and to the contagion of war.

Let us now look briefly at what happened to the Border in the aftermath of Sumter and Lincoln's call for volunteers:

Maryland   Governor Thomas H. Hicks helped hold his state in the Union by refusing to call the legislative special session necessary for secession or a secession convention. While most Marylanders applauded Hicks, on April 19 a Baltimore mob hurled stones and epithets at federal troops marching through the city. Lincoln used troops and Hicks effectively to keep secession sentiment from growing.

Virginia   The secession convention held out for moderation until the news from Fort Sumter and Washington reached Richmond. Amid visible Southern enthusiasm and none too subtle radical pressure, the convention voted 88–55 on April 17 to secede. Dissenting delegates from western counties met following the vote to help create West Virginia.

North Carolina   On January 28 North Carolinians voted by a narrow margin not to call a secession convention. The Sumter Crisis induced Governor John W. Ellis to call a special legislative session, which in turn called a secession convention, which in turn seceded on May 21.

Tennessee   In response to Sumter and to the arguments of Governor Isham Harris, the legislature in secret session allied with the Confederacy on May 1 and adopted a Declaration of Independence on May 6. Earlier, Tennesseans had voted against calling a secession convention. In June, the people ratified the May 6 Declaration. Significantly, East Tennesseans rejected secession by more than a 2 to 1 majority.

Kentucky Pro-secessionist Governor Boriah Magoffin proclaimed neutrality in the wake of Lincoln's call to arms and forbade Kentuckians from any part in the ensuing conflict. When Confederate General Leonidas Polk violated the state's neutrality, Union troops followed, and Magoffin's posture collapsed. The regular legislature affirmed its loyalty to the Union, even though many Kentuckians were active in the Confederate cause. For his part Lincoln let Kentucky alone, guessing correctly that the Confederacy would drive the state back into the Union fold while attempting the opposite. The contrast between this "kid gloves" approach in Kentucky and his hard line dealings with Maryland and the success of both methods bore witness to the President's genius as a political leader.

Missouri A state civil war decided Missouri's fate. United States General Nathaniel Lyon and a hard core of Unionism in Saint Louis held the state in the Union. Like Kentucky, Missouri maintained a Confederate government in exile and sent Senators and Congressmen to Richmond.

Arkansas The hitherto conservative secession convention voted the state out of the Union on May 6 by a margin of 69–1. Again, Sumter and the call to arms sparked radical action.

The Confederacy welcomed its newcomers and made efforts to share with second-round seceders the plums of office and privilege. Virginia received the warmest welcome. In May the Provisional Congress voted to make Richmond capital of the new nation. Thus it was from Richmond and Washington, cities only about 100 miles apart, that the rival governments began to consider the ways and means to win the war begun at Fort Sumter.

Strategy

When statesmen called in generals to talk about this war, what did they say? We do not know precisely, but subsequent events indicated that early councils of war in Washington and Richmond produced no startlingly new ideas. Generals, like other men, act upon experience: personal experience and the collective experience which forms the conventional wisdom of their profession.

In 1861 the "sons of Mars" looked primarily to two patristic sources, Baron Antoine Henri Jomini and Karl von Clausewitz. Jomini had something of a Boswell-Johnson relationship with Napoleon and translated much of Napoleon's genius from words and deeds to paper and ink in his

Treatise on Tactics. Clausewitz was a Prussian whose treatise *On War* was a bible for nineteenth-century warriors.

From Jomini and Clausewitz American military men thought they had learned several lessons. Warfare was an extension of politics Clausewitz taught, but once the shooting starts generals must forget political objectives and destroy the opposing army. To do this, said Jomini, a good general applied strength against weakness. The good general must have a large army, and he must move, or maneuver, his army in such a way as to take advantage of mass. The good general must carry the battle to the enemy and maintain an offensive posture as often as possible; the defensive was only valuable to gain time and opportunity to regain the offensive. Naturally the good general took advantage of technology and perfected organization and execution. If we had to sum up the strategic wisdom of Americans in two words, those words would be *maneuver* and *mass;* war was the business of moving friends and smashing foes.

Neither Jomini nor Clausewitz was around to tell Americans how to win the war begun at Fort Sumter. Thus with the ground of abstract military wisdom, the generals in Washington and Richmond began to think strategically about their specific war. First the vital statistics:

	North	*South*
States	22	11
People	20 million	11 million
Railroad Mileage	20,000	10,000
Farms, Cash value	4.8 billion	1.9 billion
Manufactures, Cash value of products	1.5 billion	155 million

Add to these figures the fact that the United States began the war with a small but established navy and the wonder was that the South even bothered to try. Yet the race is not always to the swift. Confederates could and did point out that the American colonies had entered their war for independence against even longer odds, and won.

". . . Put down combinations in rebellion. . . ."

Lincoln's phrase, used in calling for the 75,000 volunteers, set the necessary guidelines for United States strategy. To "put down" anyone, Northern troops would have to be the aggressors; they would have to invade the South and root out the rebels. Thus the fundamental question put to Northern generals was, how? How can the Union best conduct an offensive war?

The ranking general in the United States Army was Winfield Scott. Scott was a relic. He first won fame in the War of 1812; in 1861 he was sick, old, and fat, but he had a plan. Scott's idea was to take full advantage of the census returns and crush the would-be Confederacy with a war of attrition. He proposed to blockade Southern ports and assault Southern soil at myriad points. Scott called his plan "The Anaconda," and like that snake, the Union war effort would exert continuous, increasing, choking pressure. While the army and navy strangled the South and occupied as many Southern troops as possible, Scott proposed to send assault columns into the Southern interior to destroy rebel armies and thus the resistance.

The Anaconda was a good idea. It eventually won the war. But Scott did not stay around long enough to oversee implementation of his plan (he resigned from the service in the fall of 1861). The trouble was that Scott's idea promised victory but cost time, money, and energy. The Union War Office paid lip service to Scott's ideas, but for a time at least placed more emphasis and enthusiasm upon shortcuts to the Anaconda. Richmond was so close; and if the Rebellion lived in Richmond, why not go there and scotch it. The war lasted long enough to catch up with the Anaconda, and Ulysses S. Grant in essence revived Scott's plan in 1864. Until Grant's ascendancy, Union generals seemed unwilling to admit the need for more than one decisive thrust. And until Grant, these thrusts were characterized by their indecisiveness.

". . . all we ask is to be let alone. . . ."

Jefferson Davis, in his "war message" to the Confederate Congress, prescribed the South's strategic pose. Davis knew something about census returns and he also realized that Confederate arms could win the war simply by not losing it. Even if the South had possessed the human and material resources to do it, there was no need to capture Boston. All that was necessary was for the Confederacy to exist, to maintain its independence.

A defensive posture was not merely in keeping with logistical reality for the South. The pose of a pacific nation under assault by an aggressive neighbor offered the Confederacy promise of help from abroad and solidarity at home. Defense, then, was the order of the day.

But there are various kinds of defense. Did Davis and his generals propose to conduct some sort of static, entrenched defense? Events indicate that they did not. Just as Scott proceeded from his awareness of Northern strength and his appreciation of the importance of logistics and offensive action to construct the Anaconda, so did Davis and his generals base their strategic planning upon their present circumstances and conventional military wisdom. The Confederates never named and wrote down a plan; nevertheless they had and used one. In Jomini's writings there is a reference to an "offensive-defense." This paradoxical concept called for an army to stand on the defense, to allow the enemy to advance, and then, when time and circumstances were favorable, to attack the invader and destroy him.

The Confederates had more than an intellectual explanation of the "offensive-defense"; they had an object lesson from that other American revolution. George Washington had lost Boston, Philadelphia, New York, and any other place that the British really wanted. Yet Washington won the war. He won because he kept his army in the field and fought only when he could win. Could the Confederate rebels do the same thing? Davis believed, even in 1865, that they could.

Tactics

Strategy, in general terms involves winning wars and campaigns. Tactics deals with battles. In the minds of American generals "winning a battle" meant various things. Warriors, North and South, appropriated Clausewitz's concept that to win a battle, a commander must destroy the enemy's will to fight by destroying the enemy. Yet most Civil War commanders were satisfied with a great deal less and often fell back upon the eighteenth-century notion, supported to some degree by Jomini's emphasis upon control of decisive terrain, that victory meant driving the enemy from the battlefield.

However they defined it, generals sought victory in mass and maneuver. The most obvious way to win an engagement was to gather a lot of soldiers in one place at one time, line them up, and run over an opposing army (Sketch Map 5.1).

Such "collision" tactics, however, were crude and costly. They depended almost entirely upon mass. As we shall see, even the best commanders used point-blank, frontal assaults, but only when they had reason to believe that such action would succeed. More often they depended upon envelopments or flanking movements. The idea was to hit the enemy in his front and on his flank (side) at the same time (Sketch Map 5.2).

Thousands of men, lined up almost shoulder to shoulder, moved about the battlefield in a series of drills now restricted to parade grounds. The difficulty of controlling and moving these mass formations made flanking movements more successful. Those thousands of men could not face two directions at the same time, and once a formation broke and became individuals, the unfortunate commander could no longer control his troops.

Even better than one flanking movement or envelopment were two of them (Sketch Map 5.3).

A "reserve" force, if the general had one, often proved indispensable during a battle. Reserves, sent into the fray at the decisive moment (to

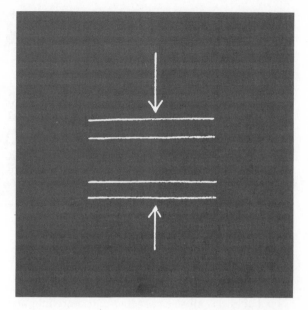

Sketch Map 5.1.

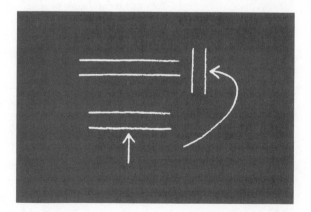

Sketch Map 5.2.

conduct or counter a flanking movement or to bolster used-up troops), often won the day. If nothing else, reserve units could prevent retreats from becoming routs and keep an army alive and together to fight another day.

Infantry was the most important component of any Civil War army.

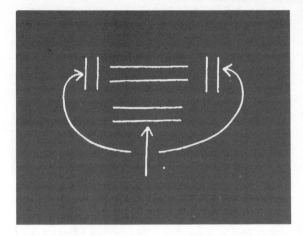

Sketch Map 5.3.

Men on foot with rifles in their hands and a knapsack or blanketroll on their backs did all this charging and marching and flanking. Foot soldiers sometimes fought more or less on their own as sharpshooters. They also served in loose skirmish lines to "feel out" their enemy and find (the hard way) his strengths and weaknesses. For the most part, however, infantry fought in tight formations whose object whether attacking or defending was to deliver massed fire on their foes.

Artillery also dealt in firepower. The guns whether big and fixed or light and highly mobile were supposed to neutralize the enemy's fortifications and guns and to destroy his formations and people. And they did so very efficiently. Recent advances in gun technology (rifled cannon, exploding shells, and such) had greatly increased the accuracy and destructive capacity of Civil War weapons. The resultant firepower gave aid (and comfort) to the defense. Civil War artillery fired solid shot of various sizes, exploding shells, and masses of smaller missiles (grape and canister). The men who served these guns often rode on caissons and laughed at foot-bound infantry. But when a thousand pounds of cannon got stuck in the mud, foot soldiers returned the compliment. And because of their capacity for destruction, the big guns were, more often than not, a first priority target on the battlefield.

Cavalry was the glamor arm of the army. Horsemen performed scouting missions, guarded flanks, and shielded the army's movements. A wise commander used his cavalry in these capacities, but realized that man on a galloping horse was no match for massed infantry. The day of cavalry charges against foot soldiers was over.

It all looks so neat and simple with straight lines of ink on flat paper.

But the war was not fought with ink on paper. We now need to leave the headquarters tent and think about the men represented by those neat lines of ink.

The Soldiers

Soldiers were (and indeed still are) the soul of any nineteenth-century army. As a general rule both North and South organized their soldiers into armies like this:

Unit designation	Number of men (Very Approximate)	Commanded by
Company	100	Captain
Battalion	500	Lieutenant Colonel
Regiment	1,000	Colonel
Brigade	2,000–4,000	Brigadier General
Division	3 or 4 Brigades	Major General
Corps	2 or 3 Divisions	Lieutenant General
Army	2 or more Corps	Full General

Of course this was "paper" organization. As the war wore on brigades sometimes had no more men than a company was supposed to have.

In 1861 soldiers were volunteers. One such volunteer was G. T. Anderson; with the aid of his diary let us walk in his shoes for a while.

Anderson was young; he was one of the plain folk from northern Alabama. On April 29, the same day Jefferson Davis was telling his Congress "all we want is to be left alone," Anderson marched off to war with his company, part of the Fourth Alabama Regiment. No doubt he had already learned, by that time, the bare rudiments of soldiering. He had drilled and drilled and drilled. Anderson had learned to handle his weapon, too.

Although he may have had only his own squirrel gun, in all probability his rifle was a .577 Enfield or something very similar. Loading and firing a Civil War vintage rifle was easy—on the drill field. The process (in laymen's language) went something like this:

1. Stand the rifle up and take out a cartridge from the bullet pouch. The cartridge was composed of cone-shaped bullet and powder wrapped in paper.
2. Break (bite) open the paper and ram the elements of the cartridge into the barrel of the rifle with the ramrod.
3. Cock the piece and place a "cap" (explosive device of fulminate of mercury) over the "nipple" beneath the hammer.
4. Aim, pull the trigger.

The hammer struck the "cap" causing a small explosion which in turn caused a larger explosion in the chamber. The bullet then spiraled out of the barrel. The rifle was effective at 1,000 yards, deadly at 300 yards. If G. T. Anderson mastered the manual of arms, he could fire two or three times per minute.

Anderson did not want to leave home and family; he disliked planters and "aristocrats." But he went "for the defence of my country" just as his Northern counterparts were doing. The Fourth Alabama traveled in box-cars toward Northern Virginia. At Jonesboro, Tennessee, on May 4 Anderson received a bouquet of flowers from a "very nice girl with a soul-stirring inscription on it."

On May 5 while at Lynchburg, Virginia, the regiment elected officers. The Confederacy allowed elections at company level, despite complaints from "old army" men. On May 7, Anderson wrote home "for the seventh or eighth time" and, with his regiment, mustered into the service of the Confederate States. The fact that he was a Confederate soldier, instead of an Alabama soldier, made little impression upon Anderson. He was too homesick to care about such technicalities.

Anderson still had no letter from home on May 10: "Why on earth can't a fellow hear from home? They seem to have forgotten that we are in the world. I have a notion not to write anymore until I receive a letter from home." The company boarded a train that day for Harpers Ferry. The weather was rainy and cold, the cars crowded, and the food "a dog would refuse." Anderson was miserable, but still willing, even anxious to fight and have done with soldiering. Finally on May 18, after his arrival at Harpers Ferry, Anderson received a letter from his parents. All was well; the young warrior cried over the letter.

The Fourth Alabama and other regiments from all over the South settled down to camp life at Harpers Ferry very quickly. On May 19 the assembled troops held a dress parade. The commander at Harpers Ferry, Colonel Thomas J. Jackson, until lately a professor at Virginia Military Institute, inspected his charges. Anderson thought that Colonel Jackson was "a large, fat, old fellow; looks very much like an old Virginia farmer." The "fat, old fellow" must not have liked what he saw, because the Fourth Alabama had another dress parade that evening. Anderson did not mind the drilling so much as the fact that it, along with considerable card playing, took place on Sunday.

Men of the Fourth Alabama could only guess at what was going on some miles down the Potomac from Harpers Ferry at Washington. In fact much the same thing was happening at Washington as was going on at Harpers Ferry. Volunteer regiments were arriving, setting up camp, and drilling for war. And the same kind of activity prevailed in Richmond, formally made the Confederate capital the day after Colonel Jackson held his two dress parades on Sunday. The months May and June were occupied in getting ready for a war which had already begun. Yet while the troops assembled, skirmished here and there on land and water, civilians on both sides of the Potomac grew impatient. Especially in Washington in Congress did the restlessness surface. G. T. Anderson would not have to endure the boredom of camp life at Harpers Ferry much longer.

Late in May Anderson's brother Stephen became ill, and then Anderson himself contacted some respiratory disease which almost went into pneumonia. As might be expected, medical facilities in camp were crude. Stephen recovered his health in a private home. Anderson, too, probably depended upon civilian help during his recovery.

On June 14 the Confederates at Harpers Ferry broke camp and fell back to Winchester. General Joseph E. Johnston had assumed command in Western Virginia, and he was "shadowboxing" with a Union force under General Robert F. Patterson. To the east General P. G. T. Beauregard, the "hero of Sumter," had assumed command of Confederate forces which barred the invasion of central Virginia at the little rail junction of Manassas. General Irvin McDowell was trying to build an army of invasion in Washington and trying to forestall Congressional demands that he begin his drive the day before yesterday (Sketch Map 5.4).

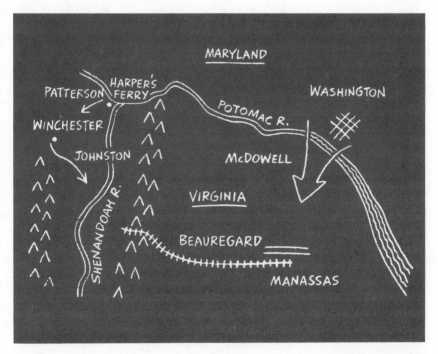

Sketch Map 5.4.

G. W. Anderson heard rumors of peace and hoped. The young Alabaman spoke of his "weary and careworn" body and dreamed of home. On July 4 Anderson heard the sound of Union guns and assumed that the Federals were celebrating Independence Day. He wondered why his own army did not also observe the birth of that other revolution. Actually the guns he heard were not fired in celebration; Patterson's Union army had skirmished with Confederates at Harpers Ferry and begun to advance up the Shenandoah Valley ("up the valley" means that they moved south; the Shenandoah River flows northward). And in Washington, President Lincoln sent a message to a special session of Congress asking for 400,000 troops and $400,000,000 to subdue the South. In Richmond the Public Guard celebrated the Fourth of July by firing salutes to the 11 seceded states. Anderson's peace rumors were only rumors; he would not be going home.

On July 18 the Fourth Alabama received orders to strike its tents, cook food for two days, and get ready to march. Anderson and his comrades left Winchester about 5:00 in the afternoon and marched nearly all night. On the nineteenth, after two hours' sleep, Anderson was on the road again. He learned that Johnston's army was marching to support Beauregard at Manassas. McDowell had begun his drive on Richmond. An hour after dark Anderson reached a place called Piedmont Station (about 20 miles from Winchester) where his unit was to board the train for Manassas. Anderson slept in the rain until midnight and then stumbled aboard the boxcars.

Anderson reached Manassas at 10:00 on the morning of July 20. He was tired and had not eaten in two days. The regiment marched about two miles away from the railroad and made camp in some woods. Anderson got some of the bread and meat issued to his company and did not even notice until the next day that the bread was "full of bugs." He ate and slept for the rest of the day and night. On Sunday the twenty-first, Anderson rose shortly after dawn and waited for orders. "We shall fight, I suppose, before another week."

The woods in which G. T. Anderson spent the night of July 20 belonged to a farmer named Wilbur McLean. Less than a mile away to the north and east ran Bull Run. The creek meandered through rolling country. There were several fords in the vicinity and three bridges, two railroad bridges and one stone bridge over which ran the Warrenton Turnpike. Confederate soldiers were stationed along the south bank of Bull Run for about six miles. Anderson and the Fourth Alabama were part of General Barnard Bee's brigade. This unit along with the others from Johnston's arriving army were available for service wherever needed. Johnston's force brought Confederate strength at Manassas up to about 35,000 men, approximately the size of McDowell's force (Sketch Map 5.5).

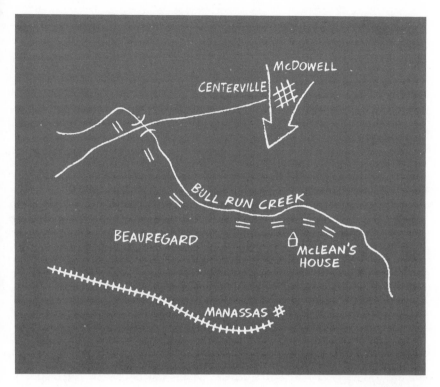

Sketch Map 5.5.

In Wilbur McLean's home were the headquarters of Generals Beauregard and Johnston. There at about the time that Anderson was waking up, the two generals were issuing orders to attack. Anderson would not have to wait a week for his fight.

Irvin McDowell and his brand-new army was at Centreville and still coming. Beauregard decided to strike first. Johnston outranked Beauregard, but Johnston, since he had just arrived on the terrain, yielded command of the impending battle. Johnston was thinking of Patterson's Union army in the Shenandoah Valley and hoping that it had not followed him to Manassas. He agreed that the assembled Southerners must fight immediately.

Beauregard's attack order assumed that McDowell's army would be in or around Centreville. The Confederate general proposed to cross Bull Run and attack McDowell from the right, left, and center. The idea was simple enough, but the order itself was not. One brigade, for example, was directed to "march via McLean's Ford to place itself in position of attack upon the enemy on or about the Union Mills or Centreville road.

It will be held in readiness either to support the attack upon Centreville or to move in the direction of Fairfax Station, according to the circumstances, with its right flank toward the left of Ewell's command, more or less distant, according to the nature of the country and the attack." Napoleon's veteran marshals may have had difficulty following such directions. American amateurs could not be expected to understand. As it happened, though, the generals and their orders had little effect upon what happened in the battle.

Couriers had hardly galloped away from Beauregard's headquarters to distribute his attack order, when reports began to filter in about firing on the Confederate right near the stone bridge over Bull Run. McDowell was not cooperating with Beauregard's plan; he had his troops driving down the Warrenton Turnpike in an effort to get on the Confederate left flank. First, Beauregard dispatched some troops to meet the threat to the left. And first among troops sent were General Barnard Bee's brigade which included the Fourth Alabama Regiment and G. T. Anderson. Next Beauregard prepared a supplementary order. This time he directed that units on the Confederate right get ready to conduct a "demonstration" (show themselves) on McDowell's flank. This action, thought Beauregard, would cause McDowell to turn his army to the left and then he would be in position for the Confederates to execute the original attack order.

Again couriers dashed away with orders. Some of these couriers found the addressees of Beauregard's orders. Others did not. Some commanders received both sets of orders, others one, and still others none. It mattered little, because McDowell was pressing his army on the Confederate left. Finally around noon Beauregard decided to stop writing orders and see what was going on. He and Johnston rode off toward the sound of battle, and as they rode the generals issued verbally the only orders which had any real effect upon the day's action: "Go to the sound of the firing!"

Beauregard and Johnston found that the battle raged over the plateau in front of Henry House Hill. McDowell's troops were swarming across Bull Run and up the first slope against a thin, but firm, line of Confederates. On the very top of the hill was the home of Judith Henry. The old woman was bedridden, and she had refused to evacuate her home when told that a battle might be fought in her front yard. Standing against the blue-coated Federals was the brigade of Virginians commanded by G. T. Anderson's old Colonel, Thomas J. Jackson. Anderson's newest commander Barnard Bee had shouted to his brigade, "There stands Jackson like a stone wall. Rally behind the Virginians!"

Rifles and artillery cracked and boomed. The plateau in front of the Henry House Hill changed possession three or four times in charges and countercharges. Then the battle swept southwestward, as Beauregard and McDowell threw fresh brigades at each other's flank. Johnston, at

Beauregard's request, returned to the headquarters instructing those whom he met on the way to "Go to the sound of the firing!" Beauregard was running out of troops, and the Southern battle line was bending (Sketch Map 5.6).

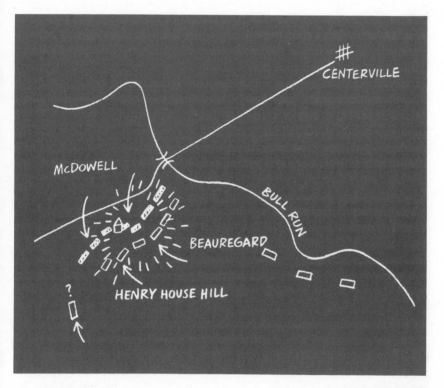

Sketch Map 5.6.

Confederate cavalry commanded by J. E. B. Stuart was "covering" the flank. But cavalry alone was no match for massed rifles and mobile artillery. The Federals swept so far from Bull Run that the civilians (some of them Congressmen) who had driven out from Washington to see the rebellion crushed had to find new vantage points in order to view the action. Beauregard, his army, and his nation were in a desperate situation. The road to Richmond was all but wide open.

Then, about 3:30 Beauregard's bad fortune seemed about to get infinitely worse. A column of dust rose from the South. It must be Union-General Patterson coming from the Shenandoah Valley in pursuit of Johnston. The dust came closer and materialized into troops. Whose troops?

Their flag hung limply in the hot afternoon; it was red, white, and blue, but Beauregard could not determine if it were the Stars and Stripes or the Stars and Bars. It must be lead elements from Patterson's force. Beauregard would have to act swiftly to avoid losing his entire army along with Richmond.

The Southern commander summoned a courier and hastily scribbled a note to Johnston. He asked Johnston to prepare intermediate defenses through which the army could retreat. The courier stood ready to spur his horse. Then Beauregard hesitated. He stayed the rider and again focused his field glasses upon the advancing column and its flag. A weak puff of wind rippled the banner—Stars and Bars. Jubal Early (ironically a bitter foe of secession in the Virginia Convention) was chewing his tobacco furiously and urging his brigade forward. Early's brigade would be the last one on the Confederate left, and soon it would be on the Union right flank.

Beauregard had not been the only one watching Early's dust. Soldiers on both sides had grasped its significance and had paused. Most of those on Henry Hill had been marching and fighting all day. They were scared, drenched with sweat, and bone tired. When Early's brigade came up, the Southerners spontaneously began to move forward. As they did a cry went up, shrill and long, a foxhunter's cry, which thereafter was the "Rebel Yell." Beauregard did not order the advance or the yell, it just happened. And when it happened, McDowell's young soldiers showed their inexperience.

In groups of twos and threes Federals left their places in formations. Sergeants and officers shouted to them while more men began to turn away from the battle. The few veterans in the ranks knew they could not stop an infantry charge all by themselves, so even seasoned soldiers joined the retreat. The Confederates came on, and retreat became rout. Farm boys and shopkeepers had had enough fighting; it was time to stop, to be safe for a while. McDowell's army became a mob. Rout became panic.

In pursuit Beauregard's army became a mob also. Organization all but disappeared on both sides. The civilian spectators joined the race back to Washington. In the confusion Michigan Congressman Alfred Ely ran into a squad of Rebels and became a prisoner. Before the pursuit had gone very far, Southerners in disordered bunches gave up the chase and returned to the battlefield to celebrate. Those few units which pressed on found just enough Federals able to conduct an effective rear-guard action. And so in the midsummer darkness the battle wound down.

Jefferson Davis came up from Richmond in the aftermath of the battle. He and his two generals conferred and decided to consolidate the victory and not to push their ragged columns to Washington. Later these men would regret the restraint and blame each other for it.

Abraham Lincoln saw all too clearly the results of the battle in the faces of those who streamed into his capital. Lincoln was afraid for a while and then determined that he would never again allow Washington to become vulnerable.

The battle at Manassas (Southerners often named battles and armies for land features) or Bull Run (Northerners often named battles and armies for water features) transformed an expedition against rebels into a war. In the United States shock, pique, and determination were the dominant moods. The nation began to prepare for war in earnest. In the Confederate States victory brought relief and exaltation. The new nation was secure for a time, maybe forever.

We shall not always need to pay so close attention to one battle. Bull Run or First Manassas, however, invites our scrutiny. On that ground south of Bull Run the generals and the soldiers showed the stuff from which they were made (some quite literally).

The generals were flawless—in principle, on paper. McDowell was right in trying to flank the Southerners, and, indeed, he came as close as humanly possible to winning the day and perhaps the war. He erred when he allowed Beauregard and Johnston to join and when he did not use Patterson's army to regain the numerical advantage. Beauregard was brilliant so long as he was planning the linkup with Johnston and his aborted attack. Yet at every decisive moment, the men under Beauregard did their decisive things without the commanding general's direction or often his knowledge. And both generals wasted too many men by not getting them into the conflict; whole brigades never fired a shot on July 21 (one Southern unit reportedly crossed Bull Run six times on the day of the battle without even seeing its enemy). However well McDowell and Beauregard planned and thought, the battle was always in the hands of the men with rifles instead of order books in their hands.

Postscript

What did the battle mean to these lesser creatures? For 847 (460 Union, 387 Confederate) the battle meant violent death. Wounds struck down 2,706 more.

Judith Henry, whose house was fought over at the height of the conflict, died in her bed. Her body was riddled with grapeshot and shell fragments.

Wilbur McLean, who owned the farm on which G. T. Anderson and the Fourth Alabama camped on the night before the battle, learned to despise the war and began to consider moving to a safer locale.

Thomas J. Jackson, the "fat, old fellow" who looked like an "old

Virginia farmer" was wounded. But he was also a hero, and he had a new name, "Stonewall."

Barnard Bee, commander of the brigade which included the Fourth Alabama, gave Jackson his sobriquet. A very short while after he did so, Bee was killed.

G. T. Anderson, the homesick but duty-bound Alabama boy, was in the thick of the fighting in front of Henry House Hill. Anderson and his fellows charged some guns of Rhode Island Artillery in the morning. The gunners loaded grape and blazed away. A marble-sized ball of lead struck Anderson in the cheek. He died instantly.

Ruins of Judith Henry's house.

P.G.T. Beauregard.

Joseph E. Johnston.

"A Yankee Volunteer."

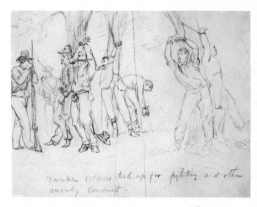

Drunken soldiers undergoing punishment.

"Washing day."

"Dick," the Union company cook.

A cavalryman.

Snowball fight among Confederate troops at Dalton, Georgia in 1864.

"A hard pull."

Sutler's cart.

A QUESTION 6
OF UNION

Abraham Lincoln did not sleep at all on the night of July 21, 1861. Washington was filled with summer rain and frantic people. Most of these people were convinced that the capital was doomed. Civilian observers of the battle at Bull Run clamored into town and spread the word. First, Irvin McDowell sent reassuring telegrams—he would regroup at Centreville, perhaps at Alexandria. Then McDowell wired Winfield Scott that Scott must save Washington. Finally some of McDowell's army arrived. Many of them had walked 45 miles and fought a battle in 36 hours. They were exhausted and not very reassuring as they slept in gutters and doorways, oblivious to the rainwater in which they lay. Scott was less than confident that he could save the city with these men. The President listened all night to sad stories.

Next morning some regiments marched into Washington. Some army remained after all. And the expected Rebel invasion never occurred. The war was still on. It was time to pick up the pieces and begin again.

The nation needed inspiration of the kind that only a Napoleon could supply. Lincoln was no soldier, and he had the wisdom to know it. Winfield Scott was too old to be active, and McDowell was discredited by Bull Run. At this juncture Lincoln called in the only hero he had, George Brinton McClellan, and the press was soon styling him "the young Napoleon." McClellan looked like a soldier and demanded that his troops act like soldiers. He rode about furiously, attending to details, holding reviews. Before long the United States had an army. McClellan was a more honored dinner guest than the President himself. The general even developed the irritating habit of keeping Lincoln waiting, and on one occasion he actually went to sleep and left the President cooling his heels in McClellan's parlor. He liked playing the part of savior and even devoted some time to planning how he was going to do the saving.

Then "young Napoleon" got sick—typhoid fever—and the Union war machine McClellan built had to idle until he recovered. Even when he was well McClellan refused to move until he was ready. And that took some time. Finally the powerful Congressional Committee on the Conduct of the War, a sort of self-styled Star Chamber, summoned McClellan before them. He was polite, but thoroughly mute about his plans to get on with the war. Members of the committee fumed, but did nothing. At last, in January 1862, Lincoln took the initiative and issued General Order No. 1. He ordered a "general forward movement" of all United States forces to begin no later than February 22.

From our vantage point, more than a century removed from the events in Washington during the latter half of 1861 and the early days of 1862, the most intriguing feature of all this was the tenacity with which the Washington government pursued the cause of Union. The events at Manassas provided ample evidence that Southerners were in earnest about separation; why not let them go and have done with it? Of course some Northerners expressed this very sentiment. But the overwhelming majority, both in and out of the government, seemed to have no reservations about the necessity to restore the Union. Why?

The question is easier asked than answered. Part of the answer lay in the dynamic of war itself. Once the nation was geared for war, once men had died in battle, war had a tendency toward self-perpetuation. Never mind what started the conflict—brave men have died; victory is an end in itself. "Are we going to let those sons-of-bitches whip us?" This kind of reaction may explain Washington's perseverance as the war progressed. But in 1861 the war had not yet reached the point at which its very dynamic demanded that it go on to conclusion.

In 1861 the answer was very close to just what Lincoln said it was,

Union. The Union was an important abstraction in the American mind. It was the vehicle in which reformers could do good, the only means of eradicating slavery. It was the best hope of liberal democracy in the world. It was the setting for economic enterprise. It was the sine qua non of the American world-view. If the Union fails, then George III will have the last laugh. No one said these things, at least not in these words; they did not have to. Americans in 1861 acted out their commitment to a perception of reality which seemed to them self-evident.

Southerners, of course, had their own perception of reality, acted out in secession. The battle at Manassas confirmed their dream of a Southern nation. In the aftermath of the battle Confederates spoke of victory in the past tense. Later, when the United States appeared willing to persist in the folly of denying the reality of Southern nationhood, the government at Richmond resumed preparations for war. In the absence of any immediate military threat, the Confederates felt free to proceed with more leisure than they had before McDowell's expedition. And Jefferson Davis had time to consider the more pacific aspects of nationhood. The Southern nation existed. It had undergone initiation rites at Manassas. The time had come for someone other than Southerners to recognize the existence of the Confederacy.

"The American Question"

European nations for a long time had had a habit of intervening in each other's wars. In 1861 the United States and the Confederate States looked upon this tendency with alarm and hope respectively. Basically the United States pursued the diplomatic goal of keeping Europe neutral and out of the American question. The Confederacy wanted, but did not necessarily rely upon, recognition and intervention from one or more European powers.

What were the prospects of intervention? Let us poll the European powers who might have offered or denied aid to the North or South.

Russia— The tsarist autocracy had no stake in preserving a democratic Union. Yet Alexander II was in the middle of plans to emancipate Russian serfs and so was no friend of slavery. Russia tended to favor the North and even accepted the hospitality of Federal ports when the Russian fleet (for reasons related to European politics) took to the high seas in 1863.

Austria— The Confederates believed that they had friends among Austrian aristocrats who saw the South as battling to preserve aristocracy. Yet the Austrian government never wavered in its support of the Union.

Spain— The Confederacy sent an unofficial ambassador to Spain, but that country gave no indication of upsetting the status quo vis-à-vis the United States.

France— Napoleon III was the kind of monarch who just might have taken a chance on the Confederacy. His ministers, however, were more cautious. France needed Southern cotton, but unilateral recognition of the South seemed too high a price. Napoleon III wanted to act in concert with England in the matter, but flirted with the notion of supporting the South and thus extending French influence into the New World as his uncle had done.

England— Lord Palmerston and his government adopted a "wait and see" attitude. England needed Southern cotton, but also depended upon Northern wheat. Some Conservatives were actively in favor of aiding the Confederacy. But workingmen opposed giving anything to slaveholders. Britain was not going to "back the wrong horse." Since her mills had a stockpile of raw cotton, Britain could afford to watch and wait.

Other European nations either had no interest at all in the American conflict or had no navy, and intervention required both motive and method. Britain and France were crucial. Both had strength, and neither would have had too much difficulty rationalizing their support of the Confederacy. Both had economic and political interests in the faraway struggle.

Even before the confrontation at Fort Sumter, in March of 1861 the then Confederate Secretary of State Robert Toombs dispatched a mission to Europe. William Lowndes Yancey, Pierre Rost, and A. Dudley Mann went in search of status for themselves and their nation. These men had what they believed was an important lever—cotton. Europe could have Southern cotton, but the price was recognition and almost certain confrontation with the United States, either at the diplomatic level or in blockaded Southern waters.

In May, 1861, before the Confederates even reached Europe, Queen Victoria extended "belligerent rights" (a halfway status between rebeldom and nationhood) to the South. United States Secretary of State William H. Seward was furious, but the Union had a cooler, shrewder head in London. Ambassador Charles Francis Adams arrived in England on the same day on which the Queen issued her proclamation and went to work with skill and tact to keep Britain out of the war.

Yancey, Rost, and Mann were unofficial ambassadors. They were received in private in Britain and France and treated cordially. But neither nation *did* anything of substance. Accordingly the Confederacy sent two more emissaries to London and Paris.

James M. Mason and John Slidell sailed from Havana on the British ship *Trent* on November 7, 1861. Next day in international waters an

American ship, the *San Jacinto*, overtook the *Trent* and made her "heave to." The American captain Charles Wilkes sent a boarding party, removed Mason and Slidell, and took the Confederates to Boston where they were confined. The British were not happy. While Wilkes received cheers and banquets, England threatened war. Search and seizure on the high seas was a touchy issue in Anglo-American relations. In 1812 the United States had gone to war over just such incidents as the *Trent* affair. Some of the London press screamed for war.

France sent a strong note to Seward. Leading English liberals Edward Cobden and John Bright offered council to Massachusetts Senator Charles Sumner. Adams did what he could to placate Palmerston and Foreign Secretary Lord John Russell. Then on Christmas Day, 1861, Lincoln's Cabinet approved a letter from Seward stating that Wilkes had acted without orders in the matter and that Mason and Slidell would be "cheerfully liberated."

Actually Mason and Slidell were of far greater value to the Confederacy in Boston than they were in Europe. By the time the emissaries reached London, the furor over the *Trent* affair had died down. Mason in England and Slidell in France made little or no headway in accomplishing their objectives. The governments at London and Paris were quite content to wait. If the Confederacy was to have recognition as a nation, it would have to come from the battlefield, not the drawing room or the conference table.

A Question of Arms

February 22 was a big day in 1862. It was, of course, George Washington's birthday. It was also the day on which Lincoln's prescribed "general forward movement" was to commence. And it was the day Jefferson Davis was inaugurated permanent President of the Confederate States.

It rained in Richmond. The weather seemed to underscore the gloom and apprehension which had overtaken the Confederacy. Davis' inaugural address was one of apology and hope, and many Confederate "insiders" could see ample need of both.

All the while the Committee on the Conduct of the War was chaffing at McClellan's inaction in Washington, Union arms had been making unspectacular but significant gains on the perimeters of the Confederacy.

1. Port Royal, South Carolina, November 7, 1861—A combined force of Union army and navy took Port Royal, Hilton Head, and later Beaufort, South Carolina.

2. Mill Springs, Kentucky, January 19–20, 1862—Confederates attacked

and lost the battle and with it a large portion of Kentucky and Middle Tennessee.

3. Roanoke Island, North Carolina, February 8, 1862—Union ships and troops under General Ambrose E. Burnside secured the island and with it most of North Carolina's Outer Banks.

4. Forts Henry and Donelson, Tennessee, February 16, 1862—An amphibious expedition led by General Ulysses S. Grant captured both forts and with them access up the Tennessee and Cumberland Rivers. The Confederate defense was ludicrous; Generals Gideon Pillow and John B. Floyd all but ran from the scene after much less than determined defense. Simon Bolivar Buckner was left to submit to Grant's demand of "unconditional surrender. . . ."

Davis' embarrassment did not end on the battlefield. The Confederate Congress, like its Union counterpart, wanted to know why the war was not yet over and victory secure. Davis and his generals, notably Joe Johnston and P. G. T. Beauregard, had quarreled. Nor was the bitterness confined to the men. Mrs. Johnston reportedly called Mrs. Davis a "squaw."

Davis' Cabinet, too, was unsettled. Secretary of State Toombs joined the army in July, 1861. Virginian R. M. T. Hunter took the post and then left it for the Senate in February, 1862. The all-important position of Secretary of War belonged first to Leroy Pope Walker of Alabama. Walker was overwhelmed by the job and resigned in September, 1861. His replacement was the original Confederate Attorney General Judah P. Benjamin. Benjamin was a clever, capable man, but a poor choice as Secretary of War. More important, the public and press blamed Benjamin for the Confederacy's military reverses.

President Davis, in his inaugural address, admitted that problems existed and promised action. In March he made significant changes in his Cabinet. Benjamin was "out" of the War Office, but named Secretary of State. To the War Department Davis called George Wythe Randolph (Virginian, grandson of Thomas Jefferson) who proved to be capable but a bit too independent to work for Davis. The truth was, Davis preferred to be his own Secretary of War. Thomas H. Watts of Alabama became Davis' third Attorney General (after Benjamin and Thomas Bragg). But speeches and cabinet shuffles would not win the war.

Plans and Hopes

As the campaigning season of 1862 came on, in terms of major armies, the situation looked like this.

—Admiral David Farragut's ships and 12,000 troops threatened New Orleans.

—Union General Samuel R. Curtis had four divisions of troops in northern Arkansas.

—Confederate General Earl Van Dorn and about 14,00 Rebels (including some Indians) threatened Curtis and Missouri.

—Grant was on the Tennessee River heading south with about 35,000 men. An army commanded by Don Carlos Buell was marching to support Grant.

—Confederate General Albert Sydney Johnston was concentrating about 40,000 troops at Corinth, Mississippi.

—Joseph E. Johnston was in position at Manassas with just over 40,000 troops.

—McClellan had built an army of 155,000 with which to take Richmond.

The Confederates hoped that Van Dorn could defeat Curtis and then turn east. Johnston (Albert Sydney) and Van Dorn together might then destroy Grant's invading columns. About McClellan, the Confederates would have to wait and hope.

The "young Napoleon" in March finally revealed his plan to take Richmond. He proposed to transport 100,000 men to the Virginia Peninsula —between the York and James Rivers (Sketch Map 6.1). Once on the peninsula, McClellan could march into Richmond from the east. The distance this way was not all that much shorter than from Washington, but there were advantages in McClellan's route. The troops would not have to storm Johnston's prepared fortifications at Manassas; indeed, if they acted quickly, Johnston would be surprised and isolated. McClellan planned to have McDowell and 45,000 men march out of Washington and "on to Richmond" from the north. Johnston would be trapped between McDowell marching South and McClellan at Johnston's base of supply, Richmond. The Rebels were through.

McClellan's plan had other significant advantages. The terrain between Fort Monroe, where he planned to land his army, and Richmond was flat tidewater country with few hills and rivers to impede the advance. And, most important, the James, York, and Pamunkey Rivers were navigable. The Union Navy could support the invasion, and naval support had already proven decisive in this young war.

War on Water

The Confederate land mass presented Union armies with formidable obstacles; for the navy, though, the Confederacy was a veritable sieve. Broad rivers flowed from the South's heartland and represented highways of invasion and harassment. The Southern coastline was long (3,500 miles). But along that coast were *relatively* few good harbors (Galveston, New

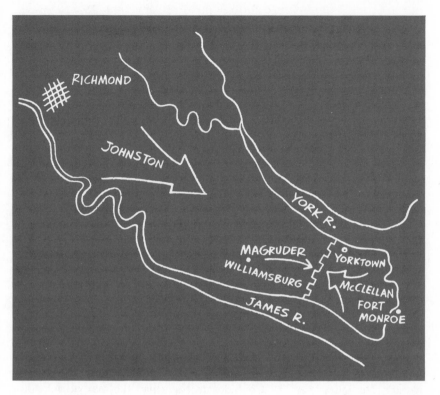

Sketch Map 6.1.

Orleans, Mobile, Pensacola, Savannah, Charleston, Wilmington, New Bern, and Norfolk). Conducting a blockade of the Confederate coast was a formidable, but not impossible, task.

By the spring of 1862 the Union Navy had grown in size and strength. The blockade had become less of the joke it had been in 1861. Combined navy-army task forces had demonstrated their effectiveness at Roanoke Island, Port Royal, and Forts Henry and Donelson.

The guiding hand behind this activity was Secretary of the Navy Gideon Welles. The Secretary was not an "old Navy man." He was not terribly innovative in this thinking. Welles was an efficient administrator though, and he developed a tenacious grasp of essentials. In 1861 those essentials dealt with numbers, technology, and naval strategy. Welles began the war with 42 ships available for service; by 1864 the United States Navy had 671 ships. The old Navy had used wooden ships armed with solid shot. Experience in war proved very quickly that the "old" Navy was too old. Thus the thrust of Welles's expansion was in the direction of iron ships (many armor plated) propelled by steam and a screw propeller (instead of a paddle or side wheel) and armed with exploding shells (capable of piercing anything but armor plate). The Navy not only bore the responsibility for blockading the Southern coast with seagoing vessels. Smaller gunboats and transports plied Southern rivers in direct support of land campaigns.

In late April, 1862, the Union Navy with little or no help from land forces achieved the capture of New Orleans. Admiral David G. Farragut "ran" the Confederate forts protecting the city and found New Orleans all but defenseless. The Confederates had depended upon their forts and river obstacles (such as a "fire raft") to hold New Orleans, and General Mansfield Lovell had only 3,000 troops to face the 12,000 on board Farragut's fleet. Lovell wisely elected to withdraw his force once Farragut had breached his river fortifications, and New Orleans again belonged to the Union, courtesy of the Navy.

McClellan hoped for this same kind of performance from the Navy in his Peninsula Campaign against Richmond. Yet even before McClellan's huge army boarded their transports for Fort Monroe, the Confederates served notice that they could and would challenge the Union Navy for control of Southern waters.

Confederate Secretary of the Navy Stephen R. Mallory had been a United States Senator from Florida and an active chairman of the Senate's Naval Affairs Committee. He was a creative thinker and an energetic worker. He had to be. The Confederate Navy had the task of defending all those miles of coastline and stopping up those river highways into the interior. To do these things Mallory and his men had no ships, virtually nothing from which to make ships, no safe shipyards, and few skilled shipbuilders. Nevertheless the Confederacy built a navy.

Mallory realized that he could never match his enemy ship for ship. He never tried. What he did do was concentrate his resources where they would do the most good. Mallory tried to buy ships abroad, and in some few cases (by hook, crook, and subterfuge) he was successful. He made ships in the South where ships had never been made before. The Confederate Navy was composed primarily of river craft (designed to halt or harass Union gunboats), blockade runners, and "commerce raiders" (pirate ships). The Navy's patriotic pirates made war on Northern shipping, with some success (measured in ships captured and nearly prohibitive insurance rates for Northern shippers). For a time government ships "ran" the blockade along with private enterprisers. Then in early 1864 the Confederate government forbade private "runs"; the Navy held a monopoly on all legal foreign trade—when it could get through.

Mallory's navy pioneered such devices as the submarine (the *H. L. Hunley,* after abortive trials, actually sank a Union ship off Charleston in 1864) and "torpedoes" (mines). But for McClellan's Peninsula Campaign, the most significant of Mallory's innovations was the ironclad ship.

On March 8, 1862, the *Virginia* (rechristened version of the *Merrimack*) steamed into Hampton Roads and with shot bouncing off her iron-plated armor proceeded to sink two Union vessels and threatened to run the Union Navy out of the water. By coincidence the United States, too, had an ironclad, the *Monitor.* Next day the two cumbersome hulks banged away at each other to no avail. The *Virginia,* however, withdrew into the mouth of the Elizabeth River, and when the Federals later captured Norfolk, the *Virginia's* crew had to scuttle her. The Confederate Navy then ordered the crew inland to man river fortifications at a place called Drewry's Bluff, about seven miles downriver from Richmond. Ironically, from there these men were to get another try at stopping the *Monitor.*

Pea Ridge—Elkhorn Tavern

Meanwhile, in another part of the forest, the land campaigns had begun. On March 6–8 Van Dorn attacked Curtis at a place called Pea Ridge or Elkhorn Tavern. The Confederates maneuvered cleverly, got on the Union flank, and drove the Federals up the ridge. Curtis rallied his men near Elkhorn Tavern, however, and the Confederates' Indian allies watched in amazement as the whites charged massed artillery and entrenched infantry. The Rebels could not break through; the Indians decamped; and Missouri remained safely in Union hands. Equally important, Van Dorn's defeat at Pea Ridge prevented him from joining Albert Sydney Johnston for their projected assault on Grant. No matter, a month after Pea Ridge Johnston assaulted anyway.

Shiloh—Pittsburg Landing

Grant's army by April, 1862, had moved up the Tennessee River until it was nearly out of Tennessee. The Union force was camped about Pittsburg Landing on the western bank of the river awaiting reinforcements from Nashville led by General Don Carlos Buell. The Rebels, under Johnston with Beauregard second in command, were concentrating at Corinth, Mississippi, and Grant expected a battle soon.

Johnston was a polished soldier of some reputation. Jefferson Davis admired him and once said, "If Johnston is no general, then I have none." Johnston's Rebels were at Corinth, as Grant believed. But they did not stay there. Johnston decided that his only chance to destroy Grant lay in surprising the Yankees at Pittsburg Landing before Buell arrived. Accordingly, on the third of April, Johnston led his army out of Corinth. He planned to march swiftly, catch his enemies off guard, and drive them into the river. The "forced march," however, turned into a comedy of errors—lost columns, stalled columns, patrols shooting at each other in the woods, and more. This lightening advance traveled 20 miles in three days (remember, G. T. Anderson did 20 miles in a night and a day). Finally on the morning of April 6 Johnston's army was in position. "Tonight," he said, "we'll water our horses in the Tennessee River."

To Johnston's utter amazement, the Federals had not noticed the approach. They were eating breakfast when the Confederates broke out of the woods. Johnston's surprise worked, and the Yankees ran pellmell toward the river as the Rebels came on.

Their initial success was for the Confederates a mixed blessing. Three long columns were supposed to march out of the woods, form battle lines, and sweep forward in unison. This did not happen. The attackers moved forward all right, but in the process they lost their organization. Then, too, what hungry trooper could capture a Yankee frying pan full of breakfast bacon and just leave it to continue the advance? The assault slowed, and the going became more difficult.

Grant had been on one of the river gunboats when attack began. He rushed ashore and found a large portion of his army running to meet him. Quickly he sought to turn the frightened men around and shore up the units who were facing the Confederates. Fast, hard work and the Rebel's lost momentum did the trick. On the last tenable ground, a low range of hills, the Union army at least had a battle line (Sketch Map 6.2).

On the other side of the mass of men killing each other, Johnston was dead. He had ridden forward to keep his drive moving. Union resistance was particularly stern from a little patch of woods known afterwards as the "Hornets' Nest." Johnston was hit in a fleshy part of his thigh; he ignored the wound and continued the work of war, urging his men, placing his artillery batteries. Finally he noticed his blood oozing over the top of his boot and decided to tend his injury. Too late. While Johnston's staff held his head and wrung their hands, the general died from loss of blood.

The battle was now Beauregard's. He pressed the Confederate attack against ever-stiffening resistance. Then as night came on, Beauregard ordered a halt. The men could go no further; they had to rest and regroup. Beauregard planned to renew the attack the next day.

Grant beat him to it. During the night elements of Buell's force arrived. On the morning of April 7, Grant's revived army counterattacked. Another day of fighting and dying and the two armies occupied approximately the same ground that they had when the whole bloody business had begun on the sixth.

Beauregard decided he could accomplish no more in that place and marched his army back to Corinth. Grant let him go.

Shiloh had been the bloodiest battle to that time on the North Ameri-

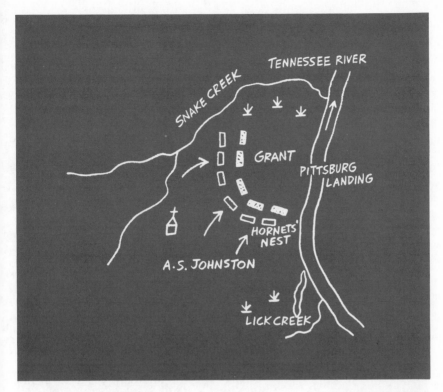

Sketch Map 6.2.

can continent. Twenty thousand men lay among the peach blossoms on the ground. The fight was a draw; but since the Confederates left the field, Federals claimed victory.

Grant was in disgrace because he had been surprised. Rumors made the rounds that the commanding general had been drunk when the battle began. It seemed to fit the pattern of Grant's life. Born in southern Ohio, Grant attended West Point, fought in the Mexican War, and tried his hand at farming and business. In each instance his achievements were mediocre or less. Grant's campaign up the Tennessee River had earned for him some reputation. Shiloh, though hardly Grant's fault alone, burst the bubble, and the War Department shelved him for a time. For most of the remainder of 1862 Union operations in the West were more passive and painfully slow. In strategic terms, the Confederates achieved an accidental advantage from Shiloh. Grant, had he remained in command, would have kept the pressure on in the West.

McClellan's Peninsula Campaign

On the day before Albert Sydney Johnston set out from Corinth (April 4), McClellan declared himself ready to begin his long awaited campaign for Richmond. He had 112,000 troops on the peninsula at Fort Monroe. He was ready to test the Confederates' "Yorktown line" (Sketch Map 6.3).

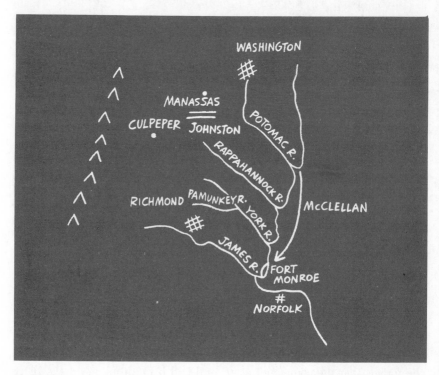

Sketch Map 6.3.

The "Yorktown line" on April 4 was about 12,000 men, incomplete field fortifications, some logs painted black to look like cannon ("Quaker guns"), and John Bankhead Magruder. "Prince John" (for his fastidious dress) did about all he could to make McClellan believe that he had less than his 100,000-man superiority in numbers. And it worked.

Joe Johnston was at first unsure whether McClellan's movement to the peninsula was a diversion. He first abandoned Manassas and an incredible amount of supplies and moved his army to Culpeper. Then on

April 14 he sat down with the President, Davis' military advisor Robert E. Lee, and others to discuss the situation. The meeting lasted 14 hours. Johnston did not want to meet McClellan on the peninsula; Davis would not have a siege at Richmond. Lee and Secretary of War Randolph believed that the peninsula offered as good an opportunity as any to fight McClellan. Finally Davis ended debate; Johnston would fight on the peninsula.

With something less than buoyant optimism Johnston manned Magruder's line with 56,500 men. McClellan with 112,000 was conducting siege operations. On May 4 the Federals made the final grand assault—and found the Yorktown line cleared of Rebels. Johnston had pulled back. Next day the Confederates gave battle at Williamsburg and lost.

Johnston's army resembled McDowell's after Manassas as it stumbled into Richmond after Williamsburg. The Gray situation looked black indeed. New Orleans gone, Shiloh lost, and McClellan's host apparently unstoppable—Richmond was in a state of panic. The Confederate Congress adjourned and went home. Randolph had his department pack its files and move them to the railroad depot. And the President sent his wife Varina to Raleigh, North Carolina. Then on May 15 the *Monitor* and a Yankee fleet steamed toward Drewry's Bluff, the last real obstacle on the James before Richmond. None of these actions were exactly calculated to inspire confidence.

That night Richmond citizens held a mass meeting. Strangely enough their mood was defiant. They could hear guns booming down the James. Yet Virginia Governor John Letcher (whose name hardly fit his bourgeois temperament) shouted that if the gunboats reached Richmond and if they delivered an ultimatum to surrender Richmond or have it shelled, he would reply "Shell, and be damned." As it happened Letcher never had to make such a choice; Drewry's Bluff held. The crew of the *Virginia*, among the defenders there, had the satisfaction of stopping the *Monitor* from the land with torpedoes (mines), ships sunk in the channel, and shore batteries. Perhaps the ultimate sacrifice came from proprietors of Richmond's "hells" or gambling houses. These gentlemen met, and observed that Johnston's officers were spending too much time in the "hells," and agreed to close for the duration of the crisis.

None of this, of course, was going to stop McClellan's advance. The Union movement was slow but sure. By late May McClellan was approaching Richmond's suburbs. The General was unhappy that Lincoln and the War Department had cancelled McDowell's drive from the North (Washington must not be left defenseless). But despite rain and wretched roads McClellan was having things pretty much his own way. Then he made a mistake. Seeking to broaden his front, McClellan moved two corps of his army south of the Chickahominy River. Then the rains came and washed out the bridges over that normally sluggish stream. The two corps were momentarily isolated, and Johnston knew it.

On May 31 the Confederates struck near the little village of Seven Pines. They pushed the Federals back a bit, but could not get together for the coordinated assault which might have destroyed them. And in the process Johnston was severely wounded.

At this juncture Davis gave command of the army to his advisor Lee. The middle-aged Virginian had had a frustrating time in this war. Lee had led fruitless minor campaigns in western (now West) Virginia and in coastal South Carolina. Then as advisor to Davis he had to endure the military limbo of counseling rather than commanding. Now at last Lee had a major command—perhaps a bit too major; doubtless he realized that he could lose the war almost single-handedly in this command.

Amazingly it was McClellan who acted as though he were in grave danger. His spies (organized by Alan Pinkerton) told him that the Confederacy had 200,000 troops in Richmond, and Seven Pines tended to confirm the estimate. In mid-June General J. E. B. Stuart and his cavalry rode completely around the Federal army scouting, disrupting communications, and leaving the impression that the Rebels were everywhere. Then there was the matter of McDowell's army in Washington; McClellan became convinced that the President and the War Department were ignoring his needs and his requests for some of the troops covering the capital. The Union army of 105,000 inched toward Richmond, defended by between 65,000 and 70,000 men. The normally cautious "young Napoleon" began acting the paranoid.

Prime reason for Lincoln's insistence that McDowell stay at home was the presence of Stonewall Jackson in the Shenandoah Valley. Jackson, during May and June, had baffled and beaten Union armies whose strength totalled 40,000 men. The Confederates had less than half that number, but Lincoln could not know that. The valley was a natural invasion route to Washington, and nobody knew what Jackson and his "foot cavalry" would do next.

Seven Days

What Jackson would do next was join Lee before Richmond in a daring gamble. Lee positioned about 25,000 men in front of Richmond, between McClellan's army and the capital. The remainder of his army (47,000 men), he massed on the Union right. Jackson was to come in on McClellan's right rear and apply the crusher. Lee gambled Richmond for the chance to destroy all or a large part of the blue host.

On June 25 the two divisions in front of Richmond attacked; the idea was to make McClellan believe that a strong army was in front of him. McClellan believed. Then on June 26 the weight of the Rebel attack fell upon McClellan's right. The next day Jackson's men joined the assault. By the evening of June 27 McClellan had had enough; he decided to retreat to Harrison's Landing on the James where his gunboats could protect him (Sketch Map 6.4).

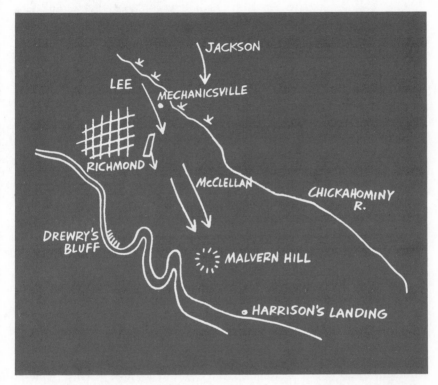

Sketch Map 6.4.

Still the Confederates came on. McClellan told the War Department that his army was threatened with annihilation and that if he were able to save it, it would be with no thanks to the government. "You have done your best to sacrifice this army."

The fighting went on during McClellan's retreat. At last in the afternoon of July 1, the armies reached Malvern Hill, the final chance for Lee to overrun the Federals before they reached sanctuary at Harrison's Landing. Lee had not been pleased these past few days. He was driving his enemy; but he was not destroying him. Malvern Hill was the last chance.

Lee had come too far and now stood too near total victory to turn back. In the late afternoon of July 1 three waves of gray infantry washed up Malvern Hill. Massed Union artillery and staunch blue riflemen turned them back with terrible carnage. Darkness fell. All night the wounded cried out for aid, for water, for death. The Seven Days Campaign was over. Both Richmond and McClellan's army were safe.

Confederate Offensives

McClellan remained at Harrison's Landing for over a month, licking his wounds and actually considering a march on Washington to set the government aright. Appropriately, a young bugler named Butterfield composed the bugle call "Taps" while there with "young Napoleon." In August the army began to sail away, back to northern Virginia. There a new savior was promising victory for the Union.

John Pope had won in the West and believed that he could do the same in Virginia. The Union War Office hoped he could. Pope got off on the wrong foot from the beginning; he belittled his men. There was nothing wrong with the Union's eastern army that a little leadership could not cure. Pope, however, questioned the very manhood of his new command. "I come from the West," he said in his address to his troops. "We are used to seeing the backs of our enemies." Then he added that he, Pope, was going to show them how to win a war. "My headquarters will be in the saddle," he said. Some wag remarked that Pope's headquarters were where his hindquarters should be. And before long Pope's troops came to believe that their general's headquarters and hindquarters were one and the same.

While McClellan's army was in transit from Harrison's Landing to northern Virginia where Pope was collecting strength, Lee and Davis decided to invade the North. What they envisioned was a limited offensive designed to take the pressure off Virginia and Tennessee, to allow Rebel sentiment to crystallize in Kentucky and Maryland, and perhaps to catch a Yankee army in an untenable position and destroy it. Lee would cross the Potomac into Maryland; Braxton Bragg would march into Kentucky. First, however, Lee would have to deal with John Pope, and Bragg would have to do something about Don Carlos Buell who was preparing to move against Chattanooga.

Lee and his army (by now officially styled The Army of Northern Virginia) defeated Pope at Manassas (August 30). Wilbur McLean's farm was again a battlefield, and in the aftermath of the battle McLean decided to move out of the path of this war. He went many miles south and west to the sleepy, county-seat town of Appomattox Court House. Second Manassas (Bull Run) was a battle of movement which showed Lee and Jackson at their best and Pope at his worst. Lee first deluded Pope, and then while

Pope was engaging Jackson's corps, James Longstreet's corps fell upon Pope's flank and almost destroyed his army (Sketch Map 6.5).

Lee then divided his army and sent three columns north into western Maryland. Washington reacted by dispatching poor Pope back to the West —way out West to the Department of the Platte in Minnesota—and recalling McClellan to command the Army of the Potomac (which had emerged as the Union's primary eastern army).

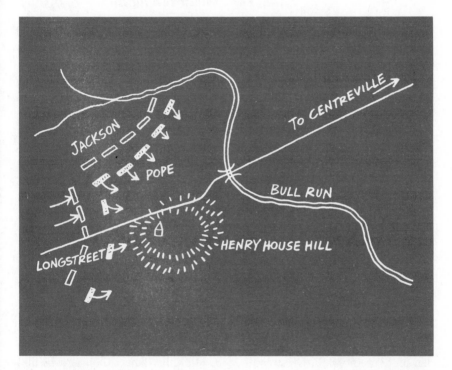

Sketch Map 6.5.

Braxton Bragg was a strange man. Most of the time he was a good administrator. All the time he was a stern disciplinarian. Some of the time he was a capable strategist. But never was he an aggressive battler. Bragg had the temperament of a "military Eeyore" (Winnie-the-Pooh's friend); he expected disaster everywhere.

Bragg's Kentucky campaign began hopefully enough in August. He dealt with Buell's longstanding threat to Chattanooga by not dealing with it. Bragg put his army on the railroad and moved north of Buell and into Kentucky. Buell then had no other choice but to abandon Tennessee and give chase. Bragg had his way in Kentucky for a while. He threatened Cincinnati and Louisville and occupied Lexington and Frankfort (where he installed a Confederate government).

Lee was in Maryland; Bragg in Kentucky. How different from the situation only a few months before. Now the Union was fighting for its life. This alteration was not overlooked in Europe.

"The American Question"—Reopened

During the fall of 1862 Britain came perhaps as close as she ever would to intervening in the American war. Confederate victories and the twin offensives in Maryland and Kentucky combined to make Palmerston's government reevaluate the situation. Napoleon III was saying encouraging things to John Slidell. Gladstone, on October 7, made a speech in which he said that the Confederates had "made a nation." Charles Francis Adams was worried and with good reason.

Letters passed between Russell and Palmerston. The government scheduled a Cabinet meeting to consider seriously some British response to the "American Question."

Some Tentative Answers

Antietam (Sharpsburg)

The Army of the Potomac cheered McClellan's reinstatement as its commander. McClellan had profited by the failures of rivals in his own army; now he was to profit from a lapse on the part of his enemy.

A Federal patrol happened upon a copy of Lee's complete movement order wrapped around three cigars and brought the document to McClellan on September 13. Lee was divided. McClellan knew that, and he also knew the location of each of Lee's dispersed columns. If he acted quickly, he could smash in turn each isolated element of the Army of Northern Virginia.

At first McClellan could not believe what he had. Then he suspected a trick. Finally he moved—*almost* fast enough.

Lee learned of the wayward order soon after its loss. He then did the only thing he could do. Frantically he tried to reassemble his army near Sharpsburg, Maryland (Sketch Map 6.6). Lee left troops guarding the mountain passes between Sharpsburg and the advancing Army of the Potomac. This delaying action allowed the Army of Northern Virginia, most of it at least, to concentrate and dig in on the west bank of Antietam

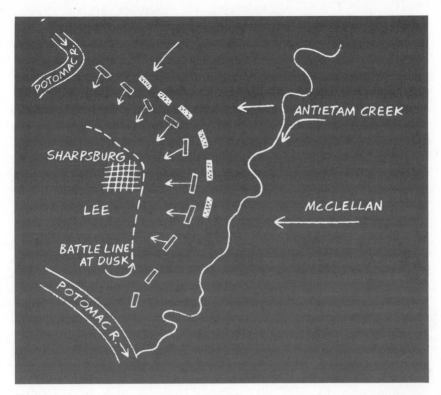

Sketch Map 6.6.

Creek during the day and night of September 16. More troops (Jackson's) were on the way from Harpers Ferry.

At dawn on September 17 McClellan attacked. The battle of Antietam began on the extreme northern edge of the field and sort of rolled south all day. The terrain was open; the combat fierce. Had McClellan been able to coordinate a general assault all along the line, he probably would have driven Lee into the Potomac River. As it was, the battle was a horrible, gory draw (the bloodiest single day of the entire war). When it was over the Army of Northern Virginia limped back across the Potomac to Virginia, and McClellan let them go.

Lincoln was furious. McClellan may have saved the Union at Antietam, but Lincoln, with the vision of an untutored Clausewitz, could see that his general had lost the opportunity to destroy Lee and win the war. While Lee rebuilt his shattered force, McClellan followed him into Virginia at a pace which could be charitably described as deliberate. The

President and War Department were not inclined to be charitable. McClellan was too slow; he would have to go.

Kentucky

Braxton Bragg could not march around northern Kentucky indefinitely. Buell finally caught up to the Rebels and offered battle. The decisive battle of Bragg's campaign took place at Perryville on October 8. Like Antietam the battle was bloody and, in itself, inconclusive. Nevertheless Bragg decided that he had had enough of conquering. Kentuckians had not exactly flocked to his banners. He took his army back to Tennessee to resume defending.

Buell, like McClellan, lost his job in the aftermath of the invasion. William Rosecrans (whom Southern newspapers consistently called Rosencrantz, Shakespeare's minor villain in *Hamlet*) took charge of Union forces in Tennessee and marched off from Nashville in search of Bragg. The armies collided at Murfreesboro (Stones River) on the last day of 1862. Bragg all but won the battle, then realized what he was doing and withdrew. He led his army out of the war into winter quarters at Tullahoma, Tennessee. In the West, Bragg, Buell, and Rosecrans had wrested stalemate from jaws of victory.

Fredericksburg

Ambrose E. Burnside was a good man and a good corps commander. When Lincoln made him commander of the Army of the Potomac, Burnside reportedly said, "I am not fit to command this army." Having made the statement, Burnside then proceeded to prove its validity.

He attacked Lee at Fredericksburg on December 13. The Army of the Potomac was spread over a wide front south of the town itself. But Burnside concentrated his assaults where Lee was strongest. Twelve times the Federals charged up Marye's Heights in the face of withering fire from the Confederate entrenchments. Each time the troops had to cross a drainage ditch and then about 500 yards of open ground up a hill. The Rebels were standing in a sunken road behind a stone wall on the front slope of the hill. Artillery near the crest fired over the heads of the defenders and into the face of the attackers. Twelve times the blue lines wavered and fell back. Lee had preserved the stalemate in the East.

London

News from the New World traveled rather slowly to Europe in 1862. Yet Palmerston and Russell were quite capable of evaluating the results of the Confederate twin offensives. Charles Francis Adams was correct when he said, "Great Britain always looks to her own interest as a paramount law of her action in foreign affairs." Britain needed Southern cotton desperately by the fall of 1862. But Britain did not need a losing cause.

Moreover the very definition of the cause had changed dramatically. On September 22 Lincoln had announced his intention to proclaim the emancipation of slaves. The "war for union" was for the most part an abstraction in Europe. A "crusade against slavery" was another matter entirely. British workingmen could and probably would make considerable trouble for a government which intervened against such a crusade.

Palmerston postponed indefinitely the cabinet meeting on the "American Question." Britain would wait and see some more.

HOMEFRONT WAR 7
IN THE NORTH

Wars and particularly revolutionary wars have a way of getting out of hand. This war, as we shall shortly see, transformed the South and forced Confederate Southerners to define themselves in highly novel ways. Even though the war did not threaten the very physical survival of the North, the war experience was transforming—in ways both dramatic and profound.

What began at Bull Run as a summertime excursion to quash a few rebels at Richmond became a war. Then the war became long and promised to become even longer. In the midst of all of this, Americans were forced to refine their goals and so to redefine themselves.

If we look closely at the pre-war North (Chapter 2), we can see two fundamental tendencies present in American life—(1) the drive toward material and economic growth (both for the nation and individual citizen), and (2) the optimistic commitment to reform ideals (both within the nation and as a national expression). These tendencies were vague, latent, and often intermingled in antebellum America. However, the trauma of war forced Northerners to come to grips with these moral and material aspirations and to define them more precisely.

To understand what the war meant in the North, we need to focus upon four major topics—(1) war aims, (2) war leadership, (3) the cost of the war, and (4) the profits of war. These topics gave meaning to the war which transcends its battlefields.

War Aims

During June of 1862, while McClellan was slogging his way up and down the Virginia Peninsula, Abraham Lincoln began doing some writing in the telegraph room of the War Department. Ostensibly he went to the telegraph room to check on war dispatches. But for a few weeks the President spent more time writing than reading. Lincoln worked at this office to have peace and quiet, all but impossible at the White House. Only after he had completed his labor did Lincoln tell the clerk in charge what he had been doing. The President said that he had drafted an order freeing Southern slaves. Charles Eckert, the clerk, was the first to know of the momentous step.

The President had not easily reached his decision. Lincoln had entered the war an abolitionist, but a very moderate one. He opposed slavery and was committed to its ultimate extinction. Still, in 1860 he only fought the expansion of bondage. During the first year of the war he faced the prospect of emancipation, but envisioned compensation to slaveholders and colonization for slaves.

All the while, advice and pressure came from various quarters. Charles Sumner, Senator from Massachusetts, Frederick Douglass, ex-slave abolitionist, and Horace Greeley, editor of the New York *Tribune* were among many who told the President in public and private to do his duty and free the slaves. Slaves themselves exerted pressure on the President by escaping to Union lines, expecting freedom. At the same time border-state men and some Republican Party chieftains counseled the President to do nothing about slavery. Emancipation might cost the Union Kentucky and Missouri. Undoubtedly it would inspire the South to greater exertions. And what would emancipation mean for Republicans in the upcoming Congressional elections in the fall? If the party lost Congress, not only emancipation, but the Administration's whole war policy might collapse.

Lincoln pondered this advice and resisted the pressure to act prematurely. When two of his army commanders in the South, Charles Frémont and David Hunter, took it upon themselves to free slaves under the authority of martial law, Lincoln restrained them, and countermanded the orders. The President's summum bonum was Union; slavery must go, but not at the expense of Union. Lincoln was above all else a consummate politician, and he was a militant moderate. He believed that the Union was the only vehicle through which emancipation, or anything else, was possible. On August 22, even after he had discussed his emancipation order with his cabinet, Lincoln wrote to Greeley in response to a *Tribune* editorial, "If I could save the Union without freeing *any* slave I would do it, and if I could save it by freeing *all* the slaves I would do it; and if I could save it by freeing some and leaving others alone I would also do that. What I do about slavery, and the colored race, I do because I believe it helps to save the Union; and what I forbear, I forbear because I do *not* believe it would help to save the Union."

But in the late spring of 1862 Lincoln believed the Union to be in desperate peril. He later said, "Things had gone on from bad to worse, until I felt that we had reached the end of our rope on the plan of operations we had been pursuing; that we had about played our last card, and must change our tactics, or lose the game!" To some people emancipation was indeed a change of tactics. Yet in a broad sense what Lincoln did was further define the concept of Union. If a concrete crusade against slavery inspired more people than an abstract war for Union, so be it. In terms of the Republican world-view, they were one and the same thing.

The President showed his draft proclamation to few men during June and July. His intentions remained a closely guarded secret from the public and even from some of Lincoln's friends. Then on July 22 Lincoln announced his decision to his Cabinet members, read them a draft of his proclamation, and asked for their comments. The document Lincoln read to the Cabinet declared that by authority of an act of Congress providing for confiscation of property belonging to rebels (passed July 17), the President would on January 1, 1863, proclaim the emancipation of all slaves held in rebel states.

Spirited discussion followed the reading. Secretary of the Treasury Salmon Chase liked the idea, but favored emancipation by military order as Union armies occupied rebel territory. Secretary of War Edwin M. Stanton thought Lincoln ought not only to free slaves, but also to arm them to fight for the Union, and do these things immediately. Montgomery Blair, the Postmaster General, argued against the proclamation. He believed that so radical an act would cost the party (and thus the war effort) the fall elections. Lincoln listened to all these points of view. However, the opinion of Secretary of State William H. Seward impressed him most. Seward was all for emancipation, but considered timing essential. The President, Seward contended, must proclaim emancipation from a position of strength, not weakness. Otherwise the whole scheme would assume a tone of desperation. Wait until Union arms have produced a victory, was Seward's counsel. And Lincoln adopted it.

To the dismay of the President a Union victory was a long time coming. Lincoln had to maintain his stoic silence on emancipation for two full months while Pope lost at Bull Run and Lee and Bragg invaded the North. In the interim he even argued *against* emancipation to individuals and groups who petitioned him to act on the matter.

Finally on September 17 came the slaughter at Antietam, and Lee's retreat back into Virginia. Had McClellan followed up his advantage, the victory would have been a great deal more impressive. As it was, Antietam was the only victory Lincoln had; it would have to do. Accordingly, the President called an emergency meeting of his Cabinet at noon on September 22 and read his proclamation. He told the Cabinet that he wished no comment. The decision was his, and he had made it. Lincoln merely wanted his Cabinet to know the decision before the public. That very afternoon the Preliminary Emancipation Proclamation (preliminary because it promised to proclaim actual emancipation on January 1, 1863) went to the Government Printing Office for publication and distribution. And on New Year's Day, 1863, the President proclaimed emancipation.

Was Lincoln the "Great Emancipator" that American folklore has made him? Probably not. As Lincoln's detractors have pointed out, the Emancipation Proclamation did not actually free one single slave. The final draft excluded from its provisions by name Union-held counties of Confederate states. Emancipation applied only to Rebel slaves—slaves over whose destiny the United States had no real control. Too, the Proclamation's political and diplomatic significance has tended to overshadow its humanitarianism. And, as we have seen, Lincoln seemed to be far more concerned with Union than he was for slaves.

Then was the whole thing a sham and Lincoln a cynical demagogue? No, again. The Emancipation Proclamation put Lincoln and his government on record for freedom. From this point, there was no turning back. Ultimately, the Proclamation freed four million people. From the moment the President issued the document, slavery was doomed.

More important was Lincoln's capacity for growth. The final draft of the Emancipation Proclamation officially sanctioned the enlistment of black men in the Army. Approximately 200,000 black soldiers did literally fight for black freedom before the war ended. Black troops in Lincoln's army had a hard time of it. They received less pay and had no black officers. Nevertheless the President insisted upon equality in matters of discipline and treatment. Lincoln went on to encourage free education for the freedmen in Southern states under Union control. He suggested civil and political equality for blacks who had served in the Army or who had education or property.

By the standards of late twentieth-century America, Lincoln might be judged a racist. He saw and recognized a great evil and did not act immediately to rectify that evil. Moreover he believed that "all men are created equal" and still he was willing to compromise on immediate, full equality for black people. But Lincoln lived in the mid-nineteenth century and, in the context of his time, he struck a blow for freedom and took a stand on equality. He grew in his humanity, and he translated convictions into effective action. Perhaps Charles Sumner and Frederick Douglass would have done more. But neither of these men were, or within the realm of political possibility could be, the President. And the vast majority of Americans in Lincoln's position would have done considerably less.

By the fall of 1862 the American people had three broad goals in this war:

1. to restore the Union, with all that the term implied;
2. to end slavery;
3. to defeat their enemies.

This last goal takes into account the war's dynamic. By the time Lincoln proclaimed emancipation, victory had become for many an end in itself.

War Leadership

We have seen a case study of Lincoln at work in the decision and execution of the Emancipation Proclamation. Because this war was so much Lincoln's war, we need to look further at the President as war leader. In the process we will of necessity deal with all phases of leadership and leaders in the wartime North.

Cabinet

Let us first examine Lincoln and his Cabinet. To do this, we will need a score card.

Lincoln's first Cabinet was a political construction. Cameron was the "weak sister." He soon proved incompetent to organize the war office, and many of his supply contracts had about them a foul odor of fraud. Lincoln removed Cameron by "kicking him upstairs" to the post of minister to Russia in January, 1862. Seward, we already know. Once he real-

Office	*Man*
Vice-President	Hannibal Hamlin, 1861–65
	Andrew Johnson, 1865
Secretary of State	William H. Seward, 1861–65
Secretary of War	Simon Cameron, 1861–62
	Edwin M. Stanton, 1862–65
Secretary of the Treasury	Salmon P. Chase, 1861–64
	William P. Fressenden, 1864–65
	Hugh McColloch, 1865
Secretary of the Navy	Gideon Welles, 1861–65
Attorney General	Edward Bates, 1861–63
	Titian J. Coffey, 1863–64
	James Speed, 1864–65
Postmaster General	Horatio King, 1861
	Montgomery Blair, 1861–64
	William Dennison, 1864–65
Secretary of the Interior	Caleb B. Smith, 1861–63
	John P. Usher, 1863–65

ized that he was not President, Seward did an outstanding job as Secretary of State and (as we have seen in the case of emancipation) often offered sound advice on domestic matters. Chase, too, was essentially capable. A strong abolitionist, he hated Seward as a political rival and because he believed Seward was "soft" on the slavery issue. Chase did not much care for Lincoln either; he never quite realized that Lincoln was a "bigger" man than he. We have already seen Blair in action (very timid on slavery), and we have met Welles, a former Democrat from Connecticut. Perhaps the greatest tribute to Lincoln's tact and political savoir faire was his ability to retain and use this "mixed bag" of ministers.

The War Office

In normal times the most influential Cabinet posts had been State and often Treasury. Now, however, the job of Secretary of War challenged these "plums." For a time Edwin M. Stanton tried to be both administrator and strategist. He failed. Lincoln in July, 1862, made Henry Halleck General-in-Chief and thereafter Stanton concentrated upon the more mundane but vital aspects of his job. Halleck was no genius, but he had the knack of translating the President's common sense to the military mind and vice versa. Indeed Lincoln, not much less than Jefferson Davis, took seriously his Constitutional role as "Commander-in-Chief." His fundamental problem was finding generals upon whom he could rely and with whom he had mutual trust. Lincoln's military talent search only ended in early 1864, when he made Ulysses S. Grant "Commander of the Armies of the United States." Halleck stayed on as a kind of chief of staff under Grant. The Commander of the Armies prescribed general policies and "turned loose" talented subordinates like William T. Sherman and Philip H. Sheridan. Grant himself, however, remained with the Army of the Potomac and personally directed operations against Lee. This was not quite a textbook model of military organization, but it worked. It worked because Lincoln relied upon people, not "decision-making flow charts."

Lincoln had virtually no military background. He learned quickly. Indeed Lincoln's military perception was more often correct than was that of the military establishment upon which he had to depend. He diagnosed McClellan as having a case of the "slows," and he asked "young Napoleon" if he could "borrow" his army since it was apparent McClellan was not going to use it. Lincoln appraised Grant simply and accurately, "I like that man; he fights." When someone reminded Lincoln that Grant was a "drinking man," the President asked, "What brand?" and suggested sending a case to all his generals. Both nations depended upon the established American tradition of the citizen-soldier—and Lincoln in a real sense was the foremost embodiment of that tradition.

Politics of Wartime

If "politics and wars make strange bedfellows," then what about wartime politics? The possibilities for "sleeping around" are boundless.

Let us consider for a moment the political situation which confronted Lincoln during this war. What of his "friends." Republican "radicals" sought to use the war to cleanse and remake American society. The ideologues often measured men in terms of their zeal, and Lincoln came up short. Conservatives, on the other hand, saw war and Union as agents of the status quo. To them Lincoln was dangerous and his or anyone else's social programs were visionary and bad for business. A third faction, the "War Democrats," supported the war, but not always the Administration. They also demanded consideration on matters of policy and patronage.

At one time or another just about everybody cursed the President for "going too far" or "not going far enough" or both. Lincoln often seemed no more than some Illinois bumpkin who had been in the right place at the right time. The Republican Party was born in opposition and to some degree was composed of opposites. The party might well follow the old Whig habit of winning an election and coming apart. Lincoln came to the presidency and the war with a highly volatile group of allies, many of whom distrusted each other and most of whom belittled the President.

And Lincoln had enemies, too. All along the border lived many Confederate sympathizers. Some were "Copperheads," potentially pro-Southern activists. Copperheads never became a bona fide "fifth column." But the threat of Copperhead activity hung always over the war effort. "Peace

Democrats," too, threatened the Administration with essentially neutral sentiments about the war. Immigrant communities whose members had fled Europe's wars wished no part of a conflict they did not understand in the New World.

Lincoln had to cope with all these factions and more among his political "friends" and enemies. Where he could not lead, he tried to neutralize. For example, he made few demands for troops and taxes on Kentucky and Missouri in an effort to ensure their good will toward the Union. He commissioned and retained "political generals" (like Ben Butler) whose primary claim to their positions lay in Republican zeal or zealous friends. He cajoled and temporized when he wished to act decisively. Very often he did nothing. As historian David Donald has pointed out, Lincoln was a master at listening patiently to a partisan tirade from some group or individual, then telling "a little story," and ushering his still guffawing guests to the door. And Lincoln kept a firm, even heavy, hand on the reins of patronage. Politicians might laugh at the "backwoods buffoon," but they rarely crossed him and escaped unscathed. By wit, skill, tact, patience, and a measure of political ruthlessness, Lincoln held on to the uneasy support of his friends and outlasted his enemies.

We shall deal with the crucial presidential election of 1864 later. Now it seems worthy to note that Montgomery Blair's dire predictions of political ruin in the Congressional elections of 1862 did not materialize. The Administration's working majority in the Senate and House slipped a bit as is usually the case in off-year elections. But for the most part the Administration coalition remained intact, even though many members won reelection by the skin of their teeth.

It would be comforting to believe that, even though the politicians gave Lincoln a hard time, the great mass of people in the United States loved and respected "Honest Abe." Unfortunately this was not quite true. Those who heard it in person, appreciated Lincoln's wit and homespun common sense. But we must remember that we are talking about a time before mass communications provided direct contact between people and leaders. Lincoln could have no "fireside chats" or televised messages. He made personal appearances. But more often the President's leadership was filtered out to the hinterland by newspapers and by local politicians. And newspaper editors and local politicians were not always friendly. Most of the major dailies in the country opposed Lincoln and referred to him with such charming phrases as "awful, woeful ass" and "mole-eyed monster." Of course Lincoln had his supporters and support. Few could hear or read his prose and not be moved. Consider for example the Gettysburg Address. Precious few war leaders (Winston Churchill?) have ever said as much to a people at war than did Lincoln in that brief statement. But his strongest claim to popular approval was the cause he sustained. Americans were willing to persevere for the Union, even though many of them were at best neutral about the Administration's ability to lead the crusade. As often happens the American people never quite realized Lincoln's greatness until he was dead.

The Cost of War

Wars cost people. This one cost approximately 600,000 people on both sides. This figure does not include those men who survived but who had to learn to work their farms with only one leg or arm. Total casualties numbered about one million men. This means that very roughly one man in three who fought in the war was a casualty.

Wars cost money, too. The United States levied taxes of all sorts, including an income tax. But the Union for the most part financed the war with loans (bonds) and inflated currency (greenbacks). Treasury Secretary Chase relied upon the banking house of Jay Cooke to promote and manage the government's bonds. Many people, Chase included, abhorred the Union's dependence upon Cooke for support. Yet there seemed no alternative.

Wars cost liberties, too, and especially civil war. The Union could never be sure who was for and who was against its cause. Lincoln's attitude was generous. He did not equate attacks upon the Administration with treason as some counseled. He did authorize the military to declare and enforce martial law. And some commanders were overzealous with this power. Let us look at two examples.

Ben Butler, commanding the occupation force in New Orleans, had a problem. The city had surrendered, but many of its residents still defied him. Ladies especially abused the occupation army verbally and otherwise. They spat upon Butler's officers and emptied their chamber pots from second-story windows onto the heads of troops passing beneath. Butler had a problem, but he overreacted. He issued a general order declaring that any female displaying disrespect to an officer or man of his army would be treated as a "lady of the town [prostitute] plying her trade." Butler's high-handedness earned the Union some embarrassment at home and abroad and won for him the sobriquet "Beast" in the South.

Far more serious was the case of Clement Vallandigham, member of the House of Representatives from Ohio. Vallandigham opposed not only the war policy of the government, but the war itself. Following an especially outspoken address by Vallandigham, the army commander in Ohio Ambrose E. Burnside placed him under arrest. The President regretted this action and commuted the sentence to exile. Burnside then dispatched his prisoner South through Rebel lines. Vallandigham subsequently returned to make more trouble for the Administration during the election campaign of 1864. Yet Lincoln did not disturb him. He reasoned, correctly, that Vallandigham was less dangerous making speeches than he was in prison a martyr.

Perhaps, to understand the full cost of this war, we need to look closely at New York City in the summer of 1863. During the first two years of war many WASP workingmen had volunteered to fight. Thus for a little while New York's Irish minority could enter the labor market without seeing the hated acronym NINA—No Irish Need Apply. But another minority group soon challenged the Irish for jobs in New York. Native and Southern black men gravitated to the city looking for the rewards of freedom. The new "immigrants" glutted the labor market and drove wages down. Clever employers used black men as strike breakers and kept wages at or below the subsistence level. Racial friction grew out of economic distress and helped neither black nor Irishman. Then came the draft.

In March of 1863 Congress passed its first conscription act. The law provided for enlistment quotas from each state, and whenever volunteers did not fill a state's quota, a random draft was to complete the job. Any man drafted could avoid service by paying $300 or hiring an acceptable substitute. Obviously poor men were going to fight, while middle- and upper-class men bought their way out of the war. New York fell behind its quota, and as Lee's Rebel army marched into Pennsylvania, New York's military establishment made preparations for conscription. The city's militia companies had left for Pennsylvania; no one expected trouble.

They should have. The Governor of New York, elected in the fall of 1862, was Horatio Seymour, a Democrat. He had openly opposed the draft on principle and quarreled with the War Department about New York's quota. Seymour's partisanship lent an air of respectability to resistance. And there was resistance aplenty in New York City. Workingmen, and particularly Irish workingmen, believed that they were being compelled to fight for the very people who threatened their livelihood, black people. The government was asking them to take a private's wage and the onus of "conscript" and risk their lives to free the very men who would take over their jobs back home. High prices and wartime inflation had been hard on working-class people all over. In New York economic distress had racial overtones and gave reason for one oppressed minority to hate another oppressed minority. The draft was the last straw.

Conscription began quietly enough on Saturday morning, July 11. 1863. Assistant provost marshals spun drums containing slips of paper on which enrollees' names were written. Apparently good-natured crowds saw the slips drawn and heard the names read. They even made "wisecracks" about the "lucky winners." On Saturday night and all day Sunday in the poorer quarters of the city, a weekend of bad whiskey produced sobering second thoughts about the draft. By Monday bitterness had replaced the grim humor of Saturday morning. Large numbers of workers stayed away from their jobs. Their mood was ominous.

On July 13 began four days of riots in New York. The original target of the rioters was the draft. But class and race soon became involved. Crowds of men, women, and boys first stopped the draft proceedings and then moved on to looting and burning.

On Monday large crowds burned one of the buildings in which the draft was being conducted. A mob beat Police Superintendent John A. Kennedy until he was nearly dead. Local militia, the "Invalid Corps," charged the mob but soon fled in terror before the crowd. A crowd burned the Colored Orphan Asylum (Fifth Avenue between 43rd and 44th Street). Police were powerless to stop looting and burning.

Next day amid battles with police and hastily formed militia units, the mob sacked the home of Mayor George Opdyke. The crowd continued looting and burning and built barricades to protect their territory. On this day individual acts of violence against black residents increased.

On Wednesday July 15 the City Council appropriated funds to buy exemptions from the draft for the poor. Governor Seymour and Mayor Opdyke delivered proclamations calling for order. The police and military took the offensive and made headway against the rioters. Still the violence continued.

William Henry Nichols was a young black man who lived at 147 East 28th Street. Nichols' mother had come to his house for safety. At about 3:00 on the afternoon of the fifteenth a mob attacked the house with bricks and stones. As they broke down the front door, Nichols and his mother retreated to the basement. Upstairs a member of the mob hurled a three-day-old baby from a window. Then the mob cut the water pipes, and the basement began to fill with water. Nichols, his mother, and several other residents fled to the yard. The mother tried to climb the fence and escape but could not. The mob fell upon her. Nichols threw himself between his mother and her assailants crying, "Save my mother, if you kill me." The men obeyed. Two of them seized his arms while a third crushed Nichols' skull with a crowbar. He died two days later.

Thursday the police and soldiers attacked the largest groups of barricaded rioters and disbursed, killed, or arrested large numbers. Roman Catholic Archbishop John Hughes personally appealed to the rioters to cease bringing discredit upon Ireland and Catholicism. A torrential summer rainstorm finished the job. In four days the riot had cost approximately 500 lives (estimates vary from several hundred to several thousand) and roughly one million dollars worth of property damage.

The draft sparked riots. Once underway, though, riots took on class overtones—poor men struck out blindly against symbols of economic power. And race, too, was involved. The mob attacked black New Yorkers with regularity and viciousness.

Confederate armies never reached New York. Most people in the United States never saw battles fought in their front yards. Nevertheless William Henry Nichols, and indeed his murderers, were casualties.

Profits of War

Secession scared the American business community. The nation was recovering from the financial Panic of 1857, and business leaders were not exactly confident during 1860–61. But when the revolution settled down and became a foreign war to the North, business confidence returned. Armies were and are voracious consumers. Government contracts for everything from cannon to morphine stimulated commerce and manufacturing.

Yet there is an apparent paradox here. The American economy, as a whole, did not grow at as rapid a rate as we might expect. Indeed some historians contend that the war actually retarded industrial growth. Still, a lot of people made a lot of money during the war. How can we account for a relatively moderate level of economic expansion and those newly rich men? The answer seems to lie in the concentration of wealth. For example, when ten shoemakers closed their shops and joined the army, one shoe factory replaced them. Sewing machines replaced workers who had marched off to war. The output in shoes produced might not have been drastically increased, but the profits from those shoes went into one pocket instead of ten. For the relatively few business leaders, war was good business.

Government policy aided business, too. Let us consider some wartime economic legislation.

  —*Morrill Tariff Act*, 1861. As they had promised during the election campaign of 1860, the Republicans raised the tariff and kept raising it in subsequent acts throughout the war.
  —*Contract Labor Law*, 1864. This act allowed employers to import workers from abroad and made those immigrants draft exempt.
  —*Homestead Act*, 1862. Congress, fulfilling another Republican campaign promise, offered unoccupied western land free to settlers who lived on it for five years. Another section of the act provided that any settler could purchase land after six months for $1.25 per acre. Speculators quickly became "settlers," bought up most of the prime acres, and sold them for up to $15 per acre.
  —*National Banking Act*, 1863. This act had the effect of standardizing currency by outlawing scrip of state banks.

In addition to these acts the government subsidized railroads and, of course, let contracts for the necessities of war.

In some cases the government sought to discourage economic activity —trade with the enemy. Yet studies indicate that trade with the South continued; its volume may have declined, but its profit margin increased. American merchants and shippers simply dusted off the old tricks learned by their forefathers before the revolution against the British. Bribery, smuggling, and fraudulent cargo manifests kept the trade alive. Along the extensive land border, too, cotton bales moved northward in spite of military patrols and roadblocks.

If we stand far back and look at the United States in wartime, we can see the shape of the "modern" nation emerging. The war meant heroism and sacrifice on the homefront as well as on the battlefield. But the war opened the way for what Americans would later call "progress."

1. Freed from the shackles of Southern influence, the Republicans could and did emancipate the slaves. The reform program went further to provide for black service in the army and confront at least the issue of political equality.

2. Wartime proved to be a catalyst to economic growth. The government was friendly, even solicitous, toward business. And wealth tended to concentrate as economic units tended to become larger in size and fewer in numbers.

During the emergency of wartime, if anyone asked whether this reforming impulse was compatible with this business activity, no one heard. Perhaps Lincoln the moderate might have kept these tendencies in perspective. But in 1865 Lincoln himself became a war casualty.

George B. McClellan.

Robert E. Lee.

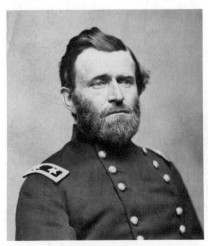

Ulysses S. Grant.

William T. Sherman.

Braxton Bragg.

Pickett's Charge at Gettysburg.

Spottsylvania.

Explosion of the powder charge at Petersburg.

Shiloh.

A cavalry charge.

THE 8
CONFEDERATE
SOUTH

To understand Confederate Southerners, we must first see them as they saw themselves—as revolutionaries. In 1776 their grandfathers had had all they could stand of Parliament and George III, and so they separated from the British Empire. They separated, ironically, to preserve the "rights of Englishmen" which during the revolutionary prologue the British themselves had threatened. Southerners in 1860–61 believed that their "way of life" (a rough equivalent of the "rights of Englishmen") was in peril. This time the Black Republicans and Abraham Lincoln were the villains, but essentially the situation was the same as it had been in 1776. The Confederacy represented a replay of that other Revolution. Southerners revolted against the Union, not to pursue any distant or visionary utopia, but simply to preserve their "way of life," the utopia they believed already at hand.

This is the way one Virginian remembered:

> It was a very beautiful and enjoyable life that the Virginians led in
> that ancient time, for it certainly seems ages ago, before the war came
> to turn ideas upside down and convert the picturesque Commonwealth
> into a commonplace, modern state. It was a soft, dreamy, deliciously quiet
> life, a life of repose, an old life, with all its sharp corners and rough sur-
> faces long ago worn round and smooth. Everything fitted everything else,
> and every point in it was so well settled as to leave no work of improve-
> ment for anybody to do. The Virginians were satisfied with things as they
> were, and if there were reformers born among them, they went elsewhere
> to work changes.

A bit oversentimental, certainly, but the writer believed his words. The
point is that Virginians and other Confederate Southerners thought they
were separating, violently if necessary, to conserve their ideology, that
"very beautiful and enjoyable life."

Confederate Southerners also believed they were involved in a revolution. It was no accident that the Great Seal of the Confederate States
featured George Washington on horseback and the motto "Deo Vindice"
(God our Defender). Throughout the war period letters and diaries often
referred to that other Revolution and compared the prospects of the
South's forces with those of the Continental Army. In fact when Howell
Cobb of Georgia took charge of his state's "home defense" troops, he asked
a correspondent to send him a copy of George Washington's military
manual so he would know what to do.

To achieve this "conservative revolution" Southerners constructed a
nation and fought a war. We have already discussed the war, and we will
again. Now we need to pay some attention to the nation. This nation was
supposed to be the ultimate expression of Southern ideology and to some
extent it was. But revolutions and wars, as we have seen, transform people.
The North in wartime found it necessary to refine its ideology and define
itself in the process of putting down the revolt. We might expect the experience of war and revolution to have an even greater impact upon the
South. Let us look, then, at the Confederate nation and see what happened
to the Southern world and world-view.

Politics—The Davis Administration

The very name "Confederacy" and the act of secession were expressions of
a State's rights political philosophy. Jefferson Davis, his Cabinet, and the
Congress were supposed to serve the interests of sovereign states. Had the
Confederacy lived in peace, they probably would have. But the Southern
nation existed for most of its life in a state of total war. And wars are

hard on confederations. Thus the Davis government, by accident and by design, pursued the politics of centralization and nationalization.

To discuss these politics of the Davis Administration, let us look over the cast of characters.

Office	Man
Vice-President	Alexander H. Stephens 1861–65
Secretary of State	Robert Toombs 1861
	R. M. T. Hunter 1861–62
	Judah P. Benjamin 1862–65
Secretary of War	Leroy Pope Walker 1861
	Judah P. Benjamin 1861–62
	George Wythe Randolph 1862
	Gustavus W. Smith 1862
	James A. Seddon 1862–1865
	John C. Breckinridge 1865
Secretary of the Treasury	Christopher G. Memminger 1861–64
	George A. Trenholm 1864–65
Secretary of the Navy	Stephen R. Mallory 1861–65
Attorney General	Judah P. Benjamin 1861
	Thomas Bragg 1861–62
	Thomas H. Watts 1862–63
	George Davis 1864–65
Postmaster General	John H. Reagan 1861

Both Cabinet and the Congress suffered to some degree from a talent drain in the direction of the military. Many of the South's established political leaders and some of her "bright young men" believed that they could better (and more conspicuously) serve the Confederacy in the army than in government. The Confederate government also suffered from the dissent inherent in the wartime transition from State's rights to nationalism. Southerners had been fighting the State's rights cause for too long to embrace nationalism, even Confederate nationalism, quickly or easily. We will examine the "not-always-loyal opposition" to the Davis Administration later. First let us look at the record of the wartime government in the South.

National Army Very early in the war Davis insisted that state troops muster into the Confederate Army and thus come under the centralized control of the War Department. The government had to haggle with state governors over men and material throughout the war. Nevertheless, the Administration usually got its way and kept state governors out of the army chain of command.

The Draft In the spring of 1862 the Confederate States enacted and enforced a draft law, the first ever in North America. Conscription was never popular in the South. Especially odious was the provision exempting anyone who had authority over 20 or more slaves. Like the $300 exemption in the North this "twenty-nigger law" inspired the cry, "Rich man's war, poor man's fight."

Martial Law   Because the South was in constant danger of invasion, the Confederate government invoked martial law (as prescribed by an Act of Congress) within its own territory. Military commanders could and did make arbitrary arrests, fix prices, and control travel (passports) in the name of national security.

Impressment   In March, 1863, Congress authorized the military to do what it had already been doing for some time—seizing property from private citizens. Slaves, food, forage, and horses needed by the armies were impressed, and former owners received only the government's promise to pay. In addition, the government impressed cotton with which to carry on foreign trade.

Monopoly on Foreign Trade   In early 1864 Congress created a government monopoly in blockade running. The Confederate government, with impressed cotton and a "commercial navy," attempted to manage all of the nation's foreign trade. In 1861 Southerners were unlikely prospects for an experiment in state socialism, but three years later they tried it.

Income Tax and Tax-in-Kind   The Confederacy, like the Union, tried to finance the war with loans (bonds) and inflated paper. By the spring of 1863 Congress recognized the necessity to tax. The solons passed a graduated income tax and an "agricultural tithe" (10 percent of each farmer's harvest in kind). The tax-in-kind (TIK) proved most unpopular in action, because the TIK men often used their authority to act more like brigands than government agents.

War Department Controls   The Confederate War Office maintained de facto control over raw materials, labor, and rail transportation in the name of military necessity. In practice this meant that if a man made wagons for the army, he usually received the necessary iron and draft-exempt workers. On the other hand, the manufacturer of women's corsets was unable to find steel for stays, could not ship it if he could find it, and lost all of his able-bodied workmen to the army. The War Office also could refuse draft exemptions to workers in firms whose profits exceeded a limit set by Congress.

Bureaucracy   A force of 70,000 civil servants (more than in the United States) kept these controls in effect. Naturally enforcement of the tax-in-kind and many of the War Department's regulations was often inefficient, sometimes selective. Nevertheless, 70,000 bureaucrats were a lot of Southern "big brothers."

The point of all this is that the Confederacy became quite a bit more than an extension of the South's antebellum State's rights political philosophy. The Confederate South experienced nationalism and centralization—to a degree perhaps greater than the Union North. And this unsouthern activity took place in spite of the heritage of State's rights individualism, in spite of diehard politicians, and, to some extent, in spite of the war leadership of Jefferson Davis.

War Leadership

Davis was a great man and a good president. Yet he is ever compared with Lincoln, and he always finishes a distant second. Davis deserves better. As we have seen, Davis had more than adequate credentials for his job. None of this experience, however, could prepare him or anyone else for the responsibilities of the Confederate President. Davis had to unlearn many lessons during the course of his administration, and the first of these involved State's rights. It was Davis who authored the policies of centralization and nationalism outlined above. Davis also pushed these measures through Congress and tried to oversee their execution. Thus, whatever else Davis was, he was an innovative, creative President and a better than average politician. His leadership dragged the Confederate South kicking and screaming into the nineteenth century.

Yet Davis had another side. He was far more at home with laws and battle plans than he was with people. With people he was or could be obstinate, vindictive, aloof, contentious, and plain nasty. He quarreled with his Vice-President, his generals, Cabinet members, and Congressmen. Perhaps much of the internal conflict was unavoidable, but Davis had the knack of making a disagreement over policy into a personal affront and then of keeping the clash alive and festering. Few men have ever been more loyal to their friends, but unfortunately for Davis some of his friends were of the likes of Braxton Bragg. Davis hated and loved too well. Davis, too, had difficulty delegating authority. He tried to run the government all by himself. Overwork made him tired and sick and did not exactly improve his disposition. If it is possible to be at the same time a creative statesman and a poor "war leader," Davis was.

Alexander H. Stephens was no help. The Vice-President was a legalist. He realized that the Administration's war measures mocked the Confederacy's State's rights origins and opposed the President's policies in public and private. After a time Stephens left Richmond, returned to Georgia, and offered the Confederacy nothing more than criticism.

Confederate Cabinet members varied in ability. Mallory as we have seen was capable. So was Postmaster General Reagan. Memminger probably did all he could with the treasury. Like Chase he resorted to bonds and paper to finance the war. Yet Memminger did not have the financial resources Chase did, and consequently Confederate paper money declined rapidly in value. The South did secure one large foreign loan from the French banking house of Erlanger. And the Confederacy sustained four years of total war with only about 27 million dollars of "hard" money.

The Attorneys General of the Confederacy offered advice and not much else. The South never created a supreme court and relied upon state courts to interpret the law. Significantly the state courts more often than not sustained the nationalist legislation of Davis' Congress.

Benjamin was important to the Davis Administration though not too popular in the country. Davis liked Benjamin and retained him even when it was impolitic to do so. Benjamin, a Jew, inspired none too subtle anti-Semitism in the press and too often was a scapegoat for the government's less popular policies. Yet the man was bright, witty, and competent. As Secretary of State, Benjamin realized that the South's diplomatic fate lay in the hands of the war gods. He had some minor successes—the Erlanger loan, the London *Index* edited by Henry Hotze which was a good propaganda organ, a near miss at recognition from France. Benjamin's primary value lay in his wide-ranging counsel and good humor.

Davis' Secretaries of War were supposed to be "yes men." Most of them were. Randolph was an exception. The Virginian tried to convince Davis of the importance of the Confederate West, and he tried to make the command structure more flexible. The Confederacy began the war by dividing the nation into military departments. Each departmental commander had his own little "empire" to defend. Trouble was that when Union armies came, the War Office had to shift troops from one department to another, and these shifts cost time and "red tape." Randolph in the fall of 1862 attempted in a very small way to make the structure less rigid. The resultant conflict makes a good case study of Davis as war leader.

All Randolph did was order some troops shifted from one departmental command to another. Unfortunately he did it without the knowledge and consent of the commander in chief. Davis sent Randolph an official rebuke. Randolph resigned. And Davis accepted the resignation with unseemly haste. But then Davis saw the wisdom of what Randolph had been trying to do. In the spring of 1863 Davis created a "theater of command" of the West, and made Joseph E. Johnston commander of the entire region and of two major armies. Johnston, however, was still smarting from quarrels with the President and suspected that Davis was trying to get rid of him. As a result Johnston spent most of his time thinking of reasons why his theater of command was unworkable and too little time commanding. Thus Davis lost the services of Randolph who called the Secretaryship of War a job for a "chief clerk." Davis did learn from Randolph; he created a flexible, independent western command and magnanimously bestowed that command upon Johnston. But the old enmity between Johnston and Davis blinded Johnston to his opportunities. This case represents an almost perfect object lesson in how to do the right thing and still lose a war.

Davis began his Administration with a friendly Congress. An opposition group developed and grew stronger after the Congressional elections of 1863. Nevertheless the Administration programs survived, and Congress by implication placed its stamp of approval on nationalism and centralization.

Davis' relation to the Southern people was something less than a love affair. It was natural for the people to look to generals rather than civilians for wartime salvation. And Davis' presidential "style" did not do much to alter that situation. He made two major "tours" of the Confederate hinterland, but during these trips he saw more generals than common people. In Richmond he remained cloistered with his work, and many Richmonders would probably not have recognized Davis had they passed him on the street.

In sum Davis probably did more politically creative things than Lincoln. Yet the Confederate President deserves the back seat he usually takes to Lincoln in the North and Robert E. Lee in the South. Davis' problem was people.

Economics—War on a "Shoestring"

A very old folk joke has a "mushmouth" Rebel colonel complaining between mint juleps, "We could have beaten the Yankees with cornstalks, suh! But they would not fight with cornstalks." From what we know of the Old South we might well believe that the colonel was right. The Confederate South had plenty of cornstalks and all too few guns and ammunition, right? Wrong! The South's agriculture failed the Confederacy, and the Confederates made fantastic strides toward an industrial revolution.

When we speak of antebellum Southern agriculture, what do we mean?—subsistence plots, staple crop plantations, and modestly commercial general farms. Subsistence farmers by definition feed only themselves, not armies and other non-farmers. The South's great staples were cotton, tobacco, rice, hemp, and sugar. Confederates could neither eat nor shoot cotton bales. Tobacco is not very nourishing. Hemp is worthless without rope factories. And Union troops occupied most of the South's primary rice and sugar producing areas. Staple crops, then, represented much potential but little actual wartime economic worth. The Confederacy depended upon commercial farmers and upon planters who turned to food crops for subsistence. Farmers and planters who joined the army were consumers instead of producers. Transportation facilities were inadequate to move large quantities of food to armies and urban areas. And from fields in or near the "war zone" or under Union control, the Confederacy reaped little or nothing. The point of this sad story is that whenever Confederates gathered together in armies or cities some or many of them were hungry. Southerners had boasted "a nation of farmers will never go hungry." Perhaps the farmers did not go hungry, but the nation did. Even if the Yankees had been willing to fight with cornstalks, the Rebels would probably have run out of cornstalks.

The most striking thing about the Confederate economy was its instant industrialization. This is not to suggest that the wartime South became an industrial giant, nor that the South even approached the industrial strength of the North. Rather, an overwhelmingly agricultural nation industrialized well enough, fast enough to sustain four years of total, "modern" war. This is a fairly safe statement; the war did demand the products of industry and it did last four years. It is significant, and not a little bit ironic, that the Confederacy achieved and sustained a level of industrialization. But an equally interesting point concerns the method or means of the Confederacy's industrial revolution.

The Confederacy began, continued, and controlled its drive to produce the necessary tools of war "from the top." The government, or more precisely the War Department, directed the effort. The Old South had no defined class of industrial capitalists. The Tredegar Iron Works in Richmond was just about the only large, heavy industrial manufacturer. Significantly, the master of the works, Joseph R. Anderson, joined the army for a time and ultimately tried to turn over his works to the government. If Anderson was a capitalist, he apparently suffered some kind of class identity crisis. In wartime the Confederacy, for the sake of speed and perhaps for the sake of planter-class interests, bypassed entrepreneurial industrialism. The government either did the manufacturing itself in arsenals and works scattered throughout the South, or controlled private manufacturing by means of draft exemptions, transportation and raw material priorities, and laws prescribing maximum profit margins and markets. As one historian has affirmed, "No country, since the Inca Empire down to Soviet Russia, had ever possessed a similar government-owned (or controlled) kind of economy."

The achievements of Confederate industry were substantial. Alabama was producing four times more iron by 1864 than any other state in the old union. The largest powder works on the continent was in Augusta,

Georgia. Selma, Alabama, became an industrial boom-town in which the Confederacy maintained a huge naval factory, five major iron works, and a powder work housed in a five-acre building. The architect of much of this development, Confederate Chief of Ordnance Josiah Gorgas, recorded his satisfaction in his diary (April, 1864): "Where three years ago we were not making a gun, a pistol nor a sabre, no shot nor shell (except at the Tredegar Works)—a pound of powder—we now make all these in quantities to meet the demands of our large armies."

Again, the wartime South had neither the time nor the resources to become an industrial nation. Nevertheless in one crucial area, war production, the Confederacy became industrially self-sufficient.

The Southern Body Social

Confederates felt the war more deeply than their Northern brethren. War ravaged their fields, threatened their homes, and killed a greater percentage of them. All this is obvious. But what was the impact of becoming so involved in the conflict upon people?

For one thing an agricultural people moved in large numbers into cities. Urban areas had for the most part been mere extensions of the countryside in the Old South. During the Confederate period cities not only grew in size and influence (as military objectives, refugee centers, industrial centers, and military gathering points); they also assumed urban identities distinct from the countryside. Vicksburg and Charleston under siege and Richmond and Atlanta in peril (to cite only four examples) developed an urban consciousness far exceeding anything which existed during the antebellum era.

The stress of war also went a long way toward breaking up the classless nature of Southern society. In life and death situations Confederate plain folk were less ready to do or die for the planter civilization. In the cities workingmen sometimes went on strike or threatened to do so. Women led "bread riots" in Mobile, Atlanta, Macon, Greensboro, High Point, and Richmond. In the backcountry farmers dodged the draft and evaded impressment agents and TIK men, sometimes in groups, with violence. In Jones County, Mississippi, pine-woods farmers backed by a band of deserters from the Confederate army seceded, for all practical purposes, from the Southern nation. This activity and more took place under the class aware slogan, "Rich Man's war, poor man's fight."

The planter class, too, felt the war. Land and slaves may have yielded status in the Old South, but in wartime military skill and valor was the prime source of prestige. Of course many of the old aristocracy retained and even increased their social and political standing as Confederates. But the war demanded that the old order undergo a testing and reconfirm its claim to aristocratic status. Wade Hampton of South Carolina was one of the richest planters in the South when the war began. During the conflict he led Rebel cavalry long and well. At the opposite extreme was Nathan Bedford Forrest. When the war started Forrest was a semi-literate slave trader (curiously many of the same Southerners who defended slavery as a "positive good" held nothing but contempt for these "dealers in human flesh" who served the "peculiar institution"). By means of talent and gall, Forrest rose to prominence as a cavalry general whose exploits are still legendary. Even Lee was "made" by this war. Lee, of course, had impeccable credentials at birth. But the family was not wealthy then, and in 1861 middle-aged colonels wielded no special political power and held little more than "comfortable" social standing. Demonstrably the experience of war did not result in the wholesale repudiation or displacement of the Southern aristocracy. War did kill large numbers of aristocrats. And it changed the "ground rules" of status in the South. As a consequence the Confederate "Who's Who" (had there been one) was a bit different from the Old South "Social Register" (had there been one of those).

What we are fundamentally talking about is ferment—the unsettling ways of war. Not surprisingly, this ferment affected economic status, too. Many Southern families now speak of a distant ancestor as having "lost everything in the war." The implication is that "everything" was land and slaves and that the Yankees took these away. In many cases this was true. But sometimes those who "lost everything in the war" lost it to fellow Rebels. In the commercial economy of the blockaded Confederacy countless established merchants found themselves unable to cope with shifting markets and closed sources of supply. Shrewder, hungrier men often displaced these old-line merchants in the market place. Had Confederate currency retained any value after 1865, perhaps some Southern families might be speaking of a distant relative who "made everything in the war."

This war, fought exclusively by men, had a profound effect upon Southern women. Women supported the war effort in innumerable ways. They ran hospitals, tended farms, served the governmental bureaucracy, worked in factories, spied upon the Federals, sewed uniforms, and brightened the lives of Southern soldiers for fun (at parties) and sometimes for profit (in houses of prostitution). Confederate women were more effective than the draft at recruiting armies, because it was the women who stigmatized those able-bodied men who did not fight.

All of this seems natural enough. Northern women had done many of the same things during the American Revolution and would have again had this war come to their doorsteps. After all it was Clara Barton who founded the American Red Cross during this conflict. The significance of the wartime experience of Southern women lay in its liberating tendencies. Wartime broke the mold of the Southern belle on her pedestal.

Let us take the example of hospital work. In the beginning social mores made it all right for women to tend wounded soldiers in their homes. But Southern doctors rejected the services of women as nurses in military hospitals. Indeed some doctors resented women coming into hospitals as visitors. Dirt and dying was man's business; women were supposed to be above all that. Very rapidly, however, the simple demand for nurses made women acceptable, even welcome in military hospitals. And before too long women were operating private hospitals and as matrons running wards of government facilities.

The belle had been more ideal than reality in the Old South. Yet as a social model the belle confined female roles and prescribed acceptable behavior and activities. Wartime changed this. The belle climbed down from her pedestal and assumed an active role in the "Cause." Confederate women did not do anything terribly startling like burning their whalebone corsets. They did not have to. Wartime provided enough new and challenging experiences; symbols did not matter much. A woman left alone to manage a farm did not necessarily like or embrace her liberation. But if she survived the experience, she was doubtless quite reluctant to resume the nineteenth-century pedestal pose.

As we might expect the experience of total war bent the Southern "mind" a bit. Confederates found their cherished individualism circumscribed by the government and by the military. Johnny Rebs deserved their reputation as some of the world's least disciplined soldiers. Nevertheless, military service did confine the Southerners' individualism. And the "Cause" gave Southerners, many of them for the first time, some sense of corporate identity.

Refugee life and army movements may not have been the most desirable ways to "see the world." But the war experience did tend to lessen the Southerners' traditional provincialism. And chains of command and proper bureaucratic channels challenged (usually unsuccessfully) the traditional Southern personalism.

Southerners, too, found out the hard way that many of their romantic notions about themselves were false. One Rebel under ordinary circumstances could not in fact lick ten Yankees.

The harsh realism of war even forced Confederate Southerners to ask whether God were still on their side. Southern religion underwent trial and question in wartime. Churches became far more socially conscious, and Protestant doctrine turned a bit from judgment toward saving providence.

When we speak of social change in the Confederacy, we are dealing with matters of emphasis and degree and with the inevitable unsettling of a losing war effort in an invaded nation. We expect to find flux, and we do. Politically, economically, and socially the old order changed in the Confederate South.

Slavery and the Confederacy

In perhaps his most famous speech, Alexander H. Stephens described slavery as the "cornerstone" of the Confederacy. After the war Southerners were fond of telling stories about the loyalty of their servants during the conflict. And a black folk parable told during the war suggested that when two dogs fight over a bone the way North and South were fighting over black people, the bone has no business joining the scrap. All of this would lead us to believe that behind Southern battle lines slavery went on as before, unaffected by the war. Not so. Just as antebellum slavery had a profound effect on both white and black Southerners, the war experience had a profound impact upon white and black Confederates.

Slavery, we have suggested, was more than an abstract institution. At its core, it was a human relationship with all of the individual variables inherent in a human relationship. Slavery the institution tended to degrade its victims and to corrupt the masters. Slavery the human relationship was less predictable; yet only in individual human terms can we account for kindly masters and whole, undegraded slaves.

What did the war experience mean to this system of relationships? We do not know completely. The body of historical scholarship about Confederate slavery is small. Yet there are some strong hints available.

The most obvious fact about the war and slavery was the mass exodus of masters. Also many slaves served for extended periods as impressed labor for various state governments or the army. And many slaveholders moved, sold, or rented their slaves during the war period. All of this adds up to alteration of the human relationship between master (or overseer) and slave. Masters acted less like masters. Sometimes wives, young boys, or old men of the master class were able to assume the role of master and continue the relationship. Sometimes white overseers remained at home. Often, however, the departure of the master or the physical dislocation of the slave dissolved the human relationship of slavery. And the institutional structures of slavery were not sufficient to sustain the system.

When masters acted less like masters, slave acted less like slaves. Black Confederates never revolted en masse. Yet as individuals black people responded to the ferment of war. Perhaps the most universal complaint read in the letters of soldiers' wives was the obstinacy of the slaves. They refused to work. They broke tools. They abused the stock. Even under pain, pleading, and punishment the slaves produced less harvest than previously. No doubt more than one farmwife converted to abolitionism after her experience of trying to play master. Many became bitter and spoke of "treacherous Negroes." Yet the black reaction was human and natural. A human relationship requires two humans; slavery requires a master and a slave. When the master abrogated his master role, so also did the slave abrogate his slave role.

Black Confederates also, by their deeds, removed any doubts about the supposed bliss of slavery. Whenever Federal armies came near slaves decamped. Black folk tales and songs had played upon the theme of freedom for years. When the opportunity presented itself in the form of Union soldiers, the great majority of black men, women, and children embraced freedom. They did so in many cases despite fantastic stories of the Yankees as diabolical monsters told them by their masters. That Southern blacks did not turn upon whites and slaughter them is perhaps the ultimate demonstration of the human (not humane) rather than institutional foundation of slavery and race in the Old South.

The Confederate experience affected the master class as well as the bondsmen. Slavery in 1861 was a major part of the ideology of the white South. Most whites expected the slave system to continue as before and most did not understand or recognize the subtle changes taking place in the master-slave relationship.

Some whites, however, saw the wartime Confederacy as an opportune vehicle for reforming slavery. Prominent clergymen James A. Lyon of Mississippi and Calvin H. Wiley of North Carolina led a modest movement for reform. The reformers sought to pass laws forbidding the separation of black families and providing some recourse for a slave when he was treated cruelly by an overseer. Indeed the Alabama legislature in 1864 did enact a law requiring masters to provide legal counsel for their slaves when indicted for any offense.

In the fall of 1863 General Patrick Cleburne, a brilliant division commander in the Army of Tennessee, wrote and circulated a paper advocating the employment of slaves as soldiers. Cleburne further proposed to set free any slave who served in the army. Jefferson Davis instructed Cleburne's superiors to suppress the paper, but Davis and others continued to consider the use of black troops. Black men, free and slaves, were already performing quasi-military service as nurses, cooks, teamsters, and laborers. A very few black men were already in the army. Nevertheless arming the slaves was a momentous step. Once the decision was made, slavery was doomed in the Confederacy.

Finally, in the winter of 1864–65, the Confederate Congress debated in earnest a bill to enroll black soldiers. Ultimately Davis and

Judah Benjamin led the campaign for the bill. Robert E. Lee expressed his favor and his conviction that black men would make good soldiers. In February, 1865, the Confederacy authorized arming the slaves. The final bill provided no promise of freedom; slavery was never abandoned by the Confederacy. But no one volunteered in the event of victory to be the person to tell a black company who had risked their lives and endured the hardships of war that they were to lay down their rifles, take up hoes, and return to slavery. There was no way for black troops ever to be slaves again, and most of the Confederate leaders knew it.

Then in March of 1865 Davis made the ultimate gesture. The sent Louisianan Duncan Kenner as emissary to Britain and France to offer emancipation in exchange for recognition. The Kenner mission, of course, failed. But here the point is that Davis and many who stood highest in the Confederacy were quite willing to give up slavery. A young Confederate officer probably summed up the South's (or at least a large part of the South's) thinking about slavery: "I must say that I think slavery is dead, and I say let the negroes go to the winds—we are not fighting for them, but for our independence and for our very lives."

Fred Fleet, the young officer, raises an interesting query. For what exactly were the Confederates fighting? Consciously or unconsciously Confederates had surrendered or altered major portions of that "way of life" they were supposedly battling to defend. The Davis Administration had severely undermined State's rights. The Southern economy had shifted directions so that its major thrust became industrial. Cities were for the first time significant in and of themselves. Social mores had changed drastically. And finally the government was willing to abandon slavery. The Confederacy, independence, had become an end in itself. And "independence" meant, more than anything else, a perpetuation of personal ties to people and place in the South.

The Confederates saw themselves as revolutionaries, and they were more right than they knew. The external revolt against the North produced an internal upheavel within the Confederacy. Revolutions have a way of spilling over into areas they are not meant to touch. And so it was with the Confederacy in wartime. Yet none of these things happened soon enough, to a sufficient enough degree, to save the Confederate nation and war. As historian Frank E. Vandiver has stated, "The Confederate States was first exhausted, then defeated." The pre-industrial South fought an industrial North in a "modern" war, and God, as usual, rode with the largest battalions.

TURNING TIDES— 9
THE WAR IN 1863

The campaigns of 1863 began in the mud. Federal commanders seemed determined to wallow in it. In the West, William T. Sherman hurled 25,000 men across a swamp near Vicksburg to no good purpose. And, in the East, Ambrose E. Burnside insisted that the Army of the Potomac conduct a winter campaign against the Army of Northern Virginia. While Robert E. Lee's troops were underfed and undersupplied but nonetheless snug in cabins, Burnside's men oozed a little way up the north bank of the Rappahannock watching whole cannon disappear beneath the morasses passing for roads.

Sherman's abortive attack in front of Chickasaw Bluffs occurred on December 28, 1862, and proved to be the beginning of the campaign for Vicksburg. Ulysses S. Grant ultimately directed the operation. Vicksburg, as every schoolboy knows, was by this time the last major Confederate citadel on the Mississippi. The city was atop high bluffs on a bend in the river. Big guns, river obstacles, and the army of John C. Pemberton made Vicksburg a formidable objective. During the early spring of 1863 Grant made four attempts to seize the high ground north of Vicksburg east of the river. All of these maneuvers failed for one reason or another, and Grant was left with a dry canal, lots of marked-up maps, and an impatient War Department.

Burnside's "mud march" represented a dogged attempt on the General's part to save his job after the disaster of Fredericksburg. Both march and command slid to a cold, wet stall. The Army of the Potomac's "winter quarters" were tents in a veritable swamp, and Burnside proved himself no better administrator than he had been a tactician. His troops were miserable, and his subordinates insubordinate.

Burnside's officers, eight or ten of them anyway, were lobbying openly in Washington for his dismissal. Chief among the malcontents was Joseph H. "Fighting Joe" Hooker. Hooker was certainly the loudest, if not the most influential, troublemaker. Finally Burnside had had enough. He presented the President with an ultimatum: purge the army command or accept the resignation of the commander.

Lincoln did not ponder long over his decision. However much the President detested the backstairs maneuvers of Burnside's "brother officers," he was convinced that Burnside was not the man for the task of smashing Lee. Moreover Lincoln had only recently ridden out his own storm over command. In December, 1862, the so-called radicals in his party, represented by nine influential Republican Senators, had demanded that he purge the Cabinet by sacking Seward. Lincoln resisted the purists' steamroller and retained Seward and a moderate stance. The President believed that the Army of the Potomac, like the Administration, was in imminent danger of coming apart at the seams. Neither could successfully weather a purge. Exit Burnside; enter Joe Hooker.

The President decided to give Hooker the Army of the Potomac, but could not resist the impulse to let Hooker know what he thought of his conduct during the winter. Thus Hooker learned of his appointment:

> GENERAL: I have placed you at the head of the Army of the Potomac. Of course I have done this upon what appear to me to be sufficient reasons, and yet I think it best for you to know that there are some things in regard to which I am not quite satisfied with you. . . . I think that during General Burnside's command of the army you have taken counsel of your ambitions and thwarted him as much as you could, in which you did a great wrong to the country and to a most meritorious and honorable brother officer. I have heard . . . of your recently saying that both the army and the government needed a dictator. Of course it was not for this, but in spite of it, that I have given you the command. Only those generals who gain successes can set up dictators. What I ask

of you now is military success, and I will risk the dictatorship. The government will support you to the utmost of its ability. . . . I much fear that the spirit that you have aided to infuse into the army, of criticizing their commander and withholding confidence from him, will now turn upon you. I shall assist you as far as I can to put it down. Neither you nor Napoleon, if he were alive again, could get any good out of an army while such a spirit prevails in it. And now beware of rashness. Beware of rashness, but with energy and sleepless vigilance go forward and give us victories.

Yours very truly,
A. LINCOLN

With something less than a ringing vote of confidence, Hooker set out to revamp his army and have at Lee. The revamping went well. Hooker almost made his men believe that they were going to humble the Rebels. He was active and aggressive. When the roads dried and the winter broke, 94,000 men were ready to march on Lee's 60,000.

Meanwhile, in Richmond, Jefferson Davis had been doing some command juggling of his own. Lee of course was secure; his health faltered a bit during the winter, but as long as he could walk he would command the Army of Northern Virginia. The problem lay in the Confederate West. Davis determined to have overall direction west of the Appalachians and reluctantly decided to give an expanded command to Joseph E. Johnston late in 1862. Johnston was fully recovered from his wound (incurred at Seven Pines) and chafing for action. What Davis gave him was essentially a lot of territory and two major field armies: Pemberton's 30,000 at Vicksburg and Braxton Bragg's 40,000 facing Rosecrans from Tullahoma, Tennessee. Davis had thought to relieve Bragg, but Johnston dissuaded him. The problem was that Johnston wanted the Army of Northern Virginia and distrusted Davis. Consequently Johnston wrote plaintive letters to Texas Senator Louis T. Wigfall, and did not offer the unified direction Davis expected of him.

Both combatants began 1863 with new commanders and guarded optimism. Both nations believed that they could win in 1863.

Chancellorsville

Joe Hooker convinced himself that Lee was going to sit on top of Marye's Heights at Fredericksburg. Therefore, the Army of the Potomac could cross the Rappahannock and either strike Lee's rear or attack Lee's flank when he retreated toward Richmond. Hooker's idea was good, but it rested upon a fatal underestimation of Lee.

In late April Hooker dispatched his cavalry under George Stoneman into the Rebel rear to disrupt communications and supply. Then

Hooker made ready to deliver the coup de grâce with his infantry. He left 40,000 men in front of Fredericksburg and put 54,000 on the road west. The army crossed the Rappahannock and began moving parallel to the river along the south bank toward the Confederates. On April 30 at a place called Chancellorsville Hooker encountered a Confederate division, drove it off, and called for reinforcements.

To call Chancellorsville a village magnified its significance. Actually the place was a crossroads and one house. The surrounding countryside had the descriptive name the Wilderness—second-growth trees and almost impenetrable undergrowth. Hooker waited in this place until on May 1 his strength swelled to about 73,000 men. Then he proceeded down two roughly parallel roads and collided with elements of Lee's army (Sketch Map 9.1).

Lee had left Jubal Early and 10,000 troops at Fredericksburg and had advanced on Hooker with 43,000. Jeb Stuart's cavalry screened the Confederates' movement; Hooker, with Stoneman off raiding, had few

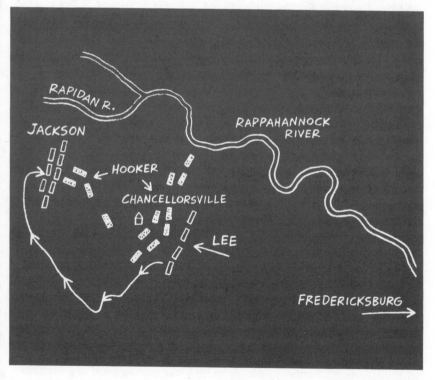

Sketch Map 9.1.

horsemen to help him. When the opposing columns clashed on May 1, each commander tried to determine the size and intentions of the other. Lee came to the conclusion that the Federals were there in strength and asked himself the perennial question, how to "get at those people." For his part Hooker came to no real conclusion; he fortified his front around Chancellorsville and relied on his original assumption that Lee would have to retreat or launch a desperate and surely disastrous assault on the Federal works.

Stuart provided Lee with crucial news on May 1—the Union flank and rear were wide open, "in the air." Lee and Stonewall Jackson met and discussed the situation. Lee asked Jackson what he wanted to do.

"Go around there," said Jackson pointing on a map to the Federal rear.

"With what force?"

"With my entire corps."

And Lee agreed. This meant that the Army of Northern Virginia would split into thirds: Early's 10,000 at Fredericksburg, Jackson's 26,000 on a day-long flank march, and Lee's remaining 17,000 in front of Hooker. The risk was enormous, but the rewards were rich if the scheme worked, and really the alternatives were few.

Jackson had his men on the road early on May 2. The march was about 14 miles, and it took nearly all day. Stuart's cavalry did its best to keep Union patrols from discovering the movement. Lee, facing 73,000 with 17,000, kept his people active. Hooker on May 2 could not make up his mind whether Lee was going to attack or retreat. Either way, he believed, victory was his.

The Union XI Corps commanded by Oliver Otis Howard endured another day of war's boredom on May 2. Howard was a good general, but his troops were green and many of them were immigrants and thus vulnerable to the taunts of native-born veterans. In the late afternoon supper fires were burning and about the only activity going on was the slaughtering and butchering of cattle. Suddenly Rebel artillery pieces emerged from the woods, and a battle line of gray infantry followed. Jackson's corps swept down upon Howard's astonished troops and drove them pellmell toward Chancellorsville.

As dusk drew on Hooker's army was fighting for its life within a narrowing perimeter. Hooker himself suffered the ultimate indignity of being knocked silly by a spent artillery shell. The Union commander was partially paralyzed; his command totally so.

Jackson had no plans to stop at dark. The moon would be full that night, and Jackson was determined to press the advantage in half-light. He rode forward in the gloom to survey the terrain and the defenses hastily being prepared by the enemy. As he returned to regroup and order the resumption of the attack, a small knot of Rebels mistook their general for enemy cavalry and fired. Jackson fell. His wounds were painful, but not believed to be serious. Dodging artillery fire Jackson's staff carried their chief to the rear. The moon rose, and the Confederate attack began, but became confused and stalled.

Next morning Jeb Stuart took command of Jackson's corps. The dashing horsesoldier tried to close the gap between himself and Lee and to complete the encirclement of Hooker. The Federals withdrew to a defensive perimeter, and Hooker saved his army, if not his pride. Later in the month the Army of the Potomac recrossed the Rappahannock, and the eastern armies were roughly where they had been when the campaigning season began.

As May drew on Lee added troops, but he had lost the man whom he called his "right arm." Jackson died of pneumonia on May 10. If we had to choose a time to designate as the "high tide" of the Confederacy, June of 1863 would probably be the best choice. The Army of Northern Virginia believed itself invincible. Bragg and Rosecrans still held a stalemate in Middle Tennessee. Vicksburg still held. And with each month the Confederate government seemed more "normal," less makeshift. But appearances were deceiving. The Confederate "high tide" was in reality a *nova*—that period in the life of a star in which it flares brightest before burning out.

Vicksburg

Grant, despairing of taking Vicksburg from the north, decided in late March to try from the south. Accordingly he put his troops on the road (or rather made roads) for the month of April. By May, Grant had three corps (commanded by Sherman, James B. McPherson, and John A. McClernand) across the Mississippi south of Vicksburg. His immediate target was the Jackson Railroad, Pemberton's major supply line (Sketch Map 9.2).

Pemberton marched out to meet Grant. And Johnston began collecting troops to help. The logical thing to do was for Johnston and Pemberton to join forces and attack Grant at or near Jackson. Johnston ordered Pemberton to join him (May 14) and the comedy of Confederate western command began. Jefferson Davis had written Pemberton not to abandon Vicksburg "for a single day." So Pemberton was caught between his commander and his commander in chief. Grant brushed Johnston aside and took Jackson. Pemberton took his army in search of Grant's supply line. Again (May 16) Johnston ordered Pemberton to join him. However, Grant was squarely between the two Southern

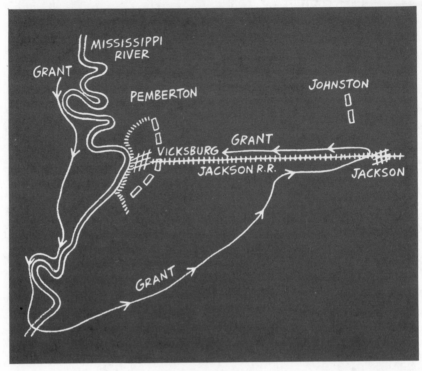

Sketch Map 9.2.

armies. On May 17 after a fight on the Big Black River, Pemberton in-
formed Johnston that he intended to withdraw to Vicksburg. Johnston
telegraphed an order to Pemberton to evacuate the city and save his
army. Once again Pemberton weighed his responsibilities and decided
that he had to stay in Vicksburg. Johnston replied that he would try
to help, and he set about collecting more troops.

Grant tried to assault Vicksburg before the Confederates could dig
in. After two days' fighting, the two armies settled down to a siege.
Grant's force ultimately numbered 71,000, half of whom were keeping
an eye on Johnston. Pemberton defended and Johnston scraped together
an army. Civilians in Vicksburg began living like moles, underground
to avoid shells from the gunboats on the river and artillery from the
land. Food ran short. Grant kept the pressure on.

Gettysburg

Vicksburg's peril made a strong impression on Richmond's government
and generals. Davis still hoped that Johnston would be able to relieve

Pemberton. But the President agreed with Lee that a decisive campaign in the East might be the best way to stave off disaster in the West. The Army of Northern Virginia, at the peak of its power, would again venture north of the Potomac.

With three corps (commanded by Richard S. Ewell, A. P. Hill, and James Longstreet) Lee slipped 76,000 men by Hooker's right and marched into Pennsylvania. Hooker with 115,000 followed cautiously, always staying between Lee and Washington. Lee's force was spread widely; Hooker overestimated its strength and pleaded for more troops. The Union War Department complied, up to a point. At that point Hooker offered his resignation. Lincoln accepted it, and on June 28 with the enemy roaming almost at will through Southern Pennsylvania the President made George G. Meade commander of the Army of the Potomac.

Meade had been a corps commander, so he knew the army. He was an "old army man" who had stayed out of army politics and performed capably, if unspectacularly. Meade's task was enormous. He had to stop Lee, save the Union, and adapt to his new command—all in a matter of days. He began by concentrating the army around Frederick, Maryland, and then he set out to locate Lee and give battle.

To understand what the Confederates eventually did or did not do at Gettysburg, we need to get inside the heads of two of Lee's principal subordinates, Longstreet and Stuart. Longstreet was not in the Chancellorsville campaign. He brought his corps north from the Virginia Tidewater and did not even talk with Lee during the advance. He did see Davis on his way through Richmond, and he left the President with the impression that this was to be a limited offensive. True enough, it was supposed to be. But Longstreet had in mind a replay of Fredericksburg—go north, dig in, and slaughter the Federals when they attack. Lee had more aggressive inclinations, perhaps a replay of Chancellorsville. If he could do such a thing on Northern soil, it just might win the war.

Jeb Stuart began the Gettysburg campaign under a cloud. He had arranged a grand review and ball after Chancellorsville, and Lee, the guest of honor, was unable to attend. Then Lee showed up a day later, and Stuart had his troopers go through the review all over again. They had performed with something less than precision and enthusiasm. Lee did not say anything uncomplimentary, but then he rarely did. Then the next day in the midst of Stuart's social disgrace, the war intruded. On June 9 Union General Alfred Pleasanton swooped down upon Stuart's force at Brandy Station and forced the surprised Rebels to fight for their lives. The Confederates drove off the Yankee horsemen, but with difficulty. Richmond newspapers roasted Stuart, and his ego reached a wartime low.

As the Army of Northern Virginia moved northward, Lee's instructions to Stuart were characteristically vague. Stuart was supposed to keep an eye on Hooker, send word of Federal movements, and join the army in time for the eventual showdown. Stuart believed he could recover his reputation within the latitude allowed by these instructions. Consequently, while Lee was feeling his way through Pennsylvania, never quite sure of what strength opposed him, Stuart was riding about in search of adventure. It came in the form of a Federal wagon train. Stuart captured 150 wagons, lost contact with the Army of the Potomac and moved north at whatever speed the 150 wagons could manage. He rejoined the army after the battle had been joined at Gettysburg. Stuart gave Lee the 150 wagons and no firm notion of Meade's strength.

Lead elements of the two armies met at Gettysburg; both Lee and Meade concentrated there. Ironically Lee's army converged on the town from the north, Meade from the south. Richard S. "Bald Dick" Ewell, leading Jackson's old corps, arrived to meet Abner Doubleday's corps on July 1. The first day the battle was for the town itself. Ewell won. But Gettysburg alone was not enough. The critical terrain feature in the area was a ridge line running north-south: Cemetery Ridge, anchored by Cemetery Hill nearest Gettysburg and the Round Tops (Big and Little) approximately a mile to the south (Sketch Map 9.3). Ewell was content to hold Gettysburg and wait. His subordinates pleaded with him to press on; a staff officer begged for a brigade with which to take Cemetery Hill. Ewell was intransigent.

By the morning of July 2 the Confederates were gathered around the ridge line in the shape of a huge fishhook. Ewell was the top of the hook, halfway around Cemetery and Culp's Hills, A. P. Hill was in the center, and Longstreet at the end. Action on the second day focused upon each flank. Lee ordered Longstreet to attack the Round Tops; in the early morning they were free for the taking. But Longstreet delayed. The Confederates had their own ridge line, Seminary Ridge on the other side of the Emmitsburg Road. Why not dig in on Seminary Ridge and wait for Meade's attack? Longstreet finally attacked the Round Tops in the mid-afternoon; by then they bristled with Union troops. The Rebels got to the Round Tops but failed to take them. Meanwhile to the north Ewell was struggling for the ground which could have been his the previous day. The Confederates snaked around Cemetery and Culp's Hills, but did not secure the high ground.

As night came after two days of hard fighting Lee was in a quandary. He could not know how many men Meade had; though he could see more arriving every hour. His options were few and hard. He could stay where he was. But how would he find supplies? And surely Meade was not becoming weaker as time passed. He could try to break off and

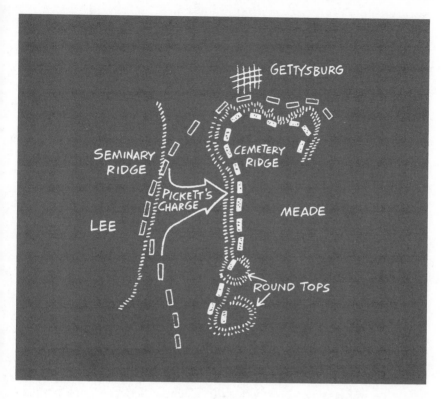

Sketch Map 9.3.

retreat or dash toward Washington. Maybe Meade would allow the Confederates to retreat; probably not. Certainly Meade would welcome the opportunity to strike the Army of Northern Virginia while it was on the march and strung out. The remaining alternative was to attack Meade where he was. Well, Lee had probed the Federal flanks as far as he could. Why not attack the center? He had not come all this way and risked this much to shrink from the moment of truth. There was so much to win, if he could break through in the center. Lee believed in his army. Afterwards he said that he had thought it invincible. Lee would attack!

July 3 was hot. Soldiers on both sides were tired and very nervous. Nothing much happened in the morning, but no one could rest. Then at around one o'clock, it began—one continuous "sheet of noise" from Union and Confederate artillery. The Southerners raked the top and back side of Cemetery Ridge. Most of the Union combat troops were entrenched on the front slope, but the rear elements felt the full fury of the barrage. Federal guns responded in kind. After more than an hour the firing stopped.

The Confederates came forward in the quiet. Longstreet gave (reluctantly) the order. George Pickett's division led the way. Shoulder to shoulder, flags flying, bands playing, they went, 15,000 Rebels. For long moments both armies watched as the Confederates marched, down to the Emmitsburg Road, across it, and up the long slope of Cemetery Ridge. It was grand, terrible, and insane, all at the same time.

Then the Federal artillery opened, and it was merely terrible. The blue riflemen began firing. The Rebels, many fewer now, came on, running, closing ranks. Then it was clearly insane. Longstreet saw the carnage coming and held up the supporting troops. Still the gray remnants plunged forward. A handful reached the crest, and Meade threw in his reserves. It was over. Pickett's Charge faded into nothing, and the living limped back over the fallen bodies of their comrades.

Lee was honest. "It's all my fault," he said, and he was right. Meade had outnerved Lee less than a week after assuming command. On July 4 the two armies rested and watched each other. Then Lee moved—south toward home. Meade all but let him go free.

Vicksburg

The city was a maze of caves and trenches. Besiegers and besieged lived close to the ground enduring constant danger beneath the hot June sun. Night brought little relief; shells and hungry rats interrupted fitful attempts at sleep. For 47 days the siege went on.

In the east Johnston assembled 31,000 effectives and moved cautiously toward Vicksburg. When he reached the Big Black River (July 1), he stopped and began probing the Federal front. Secretary of War Seddon had counseled Johnston, "It is better to fail nobly than, through prudence even, to be inactive." But now Johnston found the Federals too strong. Grant's army had grown faster than Johnston's. So Johnston did not fight.

Pemberton had done his duty. He had held out as long as possible, and he could see no way to break out and no good purpose in enduring the siege any longer. Thus on July 3, as the Gettysburg campaign reached its climax. Pemberton met Grant to discuss surrender. Grant was generous; he allowed Vicksburg's defenders to accept a parole and go home. On July 4 Grant's army entered Vicksburg. Johnston retreated to Jackson and then further east.

In two days the Confederacy had all but lost the war. Lee lost nearly 28,000 men at Gettysburg, and Pemberton surrendered another 30,000 at Vicksburg (and on July 9 the Confederate garrison at Port

Hudson fell; 6,000 more surrendered). The Mississippi was clear; three Confederate states were cut off. The entire Mississippi Valley was open to Federal armies. Lee's army learned the hard way that it was vincible. The South also lost the tools of war, 85,000 stand of arms among other things. Probably Chief of Ordnance Josiah Gorgas said it best. "Yesterday," he wrote in his diary, "we rode on the pinnacle of success. Today absolute ruin seems our portion. The Confederacy totters to its destruction."

The loss of morale almost equaled the physical losses. Lee sent Davis a letter of resignation. Davis refused to consider it. Then the fur began to fly over Vicksburg. Johnston railed at Davis for his "do not abandon Vicksburg" instruction to Pemberton and at Pemberton for disobeying his direct orders. Davis responded in kind. When Gorgas lamely remarked that Vicksburg fell from want of provisions, Davis growled, "Yes, from want of provisions inside, and a general outside who wouldn't fight!"

Across the Potomac the Union smelled victory. Lincoln was upset that Meade had not pursued Lee more vigorously. He kept Meade in command, however, and urged him on. Grant was the man of the hour. No one remembered Shiloh or strong drink anymore. At last the United States had a bona fide hero.

Victory Abroad

Lincoln could reflect upon diplomatic, as well as military, triumphs. No incident as dramatic as the *Trent* affair occurred. Yet the United States could count a number of minor victories and smile at Confederate frustration.

In February, 1863, French minister to Washington Henri Mercier formally proposed a six month's truce during which North and South could discuss terms of peace. Seward rejected the proposal and France did not press the issue. Prime among reasons for France's ambivalence was the attitude of England. Napoleon III did not want to commit himself unilaterally, and the British grew increasingly cool toward any sort of interference. The British had weathered the worst of the "cotton famine" and still doubted the South's chances.

The closest France ever came to taking an active part in the American question was in June, 1863. Napoleon III needed Southern cotton and American allies. French soldiers were in Mexico (they captured Mexico City in June). They went originally as part of a joint expedition (with Britain and Spain) to collect debts. But when the debt question was settled and the other two nations pulled out (May, 1862), French forces remained. Napoleon III had in mind the same kind of New

World Empire his famous uncle had envisioned. Eventually he installed the Austrian Maximilian as Emperor of Mexico.

In desperation the Confederacy made overtures of friendship to France and Maximilian. Seward remained silent for a time about this overt threat to the Monroe Doctrine. Napoleon III still hoped for concert with the British and had some very frank discussions on the matter with two Members of Parliament, John A. Roebuck and William S. Lindsay. Then on June 30, 1863, Roebuck introduced in Parliament a motion to recognize the Confederacy in concert with France. In the course of debate Roebuck gave chapter and verse of his discussions (plotting?) with Napoleon III. The Cabinet was incensed. England was quite able to conduct her diplomacy without the aid of amateurs like Roebuck and Lindsay, thank you. Really, even without the faux pas, what did Britain stand to gain? Supporting France to the greater glory of France was hardly in Britain's best interest. If England were to provoke confrontation with the United States, there had to be more in it for England. Parliament was so hostile to the Roebuck motion that he withdrew it. Napoleon III ultimately decided not to go it alone. He could interpret the significance of Gettysburg and Vicksburg as well as anyone. Besides the Mexican adventure might not provoke a war-weary United States; whereas support for the South would all but assure conflict with the United States. And Napoleon III no doubt remembered the last time France backed some American revolutionaries. In 1783 they made a separate peace and left France with little more than an empty treasury.

By the fall of 1863 the diplomatic tide had obviously turned in favor of the North. After Gettysburg, both England and France withheld ships for which the Confederates had contracted. France might talk about intervention, but action was another matter entirely. England had watched and waited and apparently, barring some blunder on the part of the North, planned to support the status quo. In September Judah Benjamin directed his emissary to the British, James M. Mason, to abandon London and try his luck in Paris. A month later Benjamin expelled the British consuls from the Confederacy. Clearly Anglo-Confederate relations had reached an impasse. Thus in the fall of 1863, Seward felt secure enough to begin making threats to France over Mexico. He invoked the Monroe Doctrine, though not by name, and announced his nation's displeasure—an action only a fool would take unless he were confident of victory at home and safety abroad. Seward was no fool.

Chickamauga Campaign

Bragg and Rosecrans had in effect been waiting in the wings as the battles for Vicksburg and Gettysburg developed. The Confederates had about

44,000 against 65,000 Federals. After considerable prodding from the War Department, Rosecrans in late June began his move South from Murfrees-boro. In a few days he had maneuvered Bragg back to Chattanooga, but on July 4 he stopped. While the War Office all but screamed at Rosecrans to keep moving, the Union army collected food and repaired railroads. Bragg remained behind the Tennessee River at Chattanooga and dis-patched his men into the fields to harvest wheat.

Finally in mid-August Rosecrans was ready. He advanced on Chat-tanooga and occupied Bragg's attention by shelling the city from across the river. The Tennessee was the key. Bragg convinced himself that Rose-crans would try to cross north of the city. Rosecrans crossed to the south on September 4. This forced Bragg to pull back to protect his supply line, the Western and Atlantic Railroad, which linked Chattanooga with At-lanta.

Then it was Rosecrans' turn to fall for a deception. Reports reached his headquarters that Bragg was in full retreat toward Dalton, Georgia. Rosecrans believed the stories and spread his army for the pursuit. Bragg had a fantastic opportunity to attack and destroy the Federals piecemeal. The Confederates muffed it. It was not all Bragg's fault, he was unable to move his subordinates at the crucial times.

Still Bragg had a chance. While Rosecrans reconcentrated his army, Bragg moved. On September 20, just west of Chickamauga Creek, Bragg's army fell upon the Federal corps commanded by George H. Thomas and John S. Crittenden. The Confederates had been reinforced by Longstreet's corps from Virginia, and Bragg was hopeful for once. The Rebels tried to flank Rosecrans' left and met initial success, despite the fact that the Southern assaults were uncoordinated. Rosecrans shifted troops furiously in response to Thomas' cries for aid.

During the late morning one of Rosecrans' shifts resulted in disaster. An entire division pulled out of the battle line to comply with a confused instruction. About the same time Longstreet's troops attacked, found the gap, and exploited it. Rosecrans decided to retreat and led the withdrawal himself. Thomas was left to face Bragg's army. It was here that he earned the sobriquet "Rock of Chickamauga." Desperation and Thomas' leader-ship saved the day. The Federals held until dark and withdrew.

Rosecrans was sure he was beaten. He regrouped at Chattanooga and prepared to retreat further. Bragg was not quite sure he had won. When a Confederate soldier who had witnessed Rosecrans' flight was brought to Bragg to tell his story, Bragg doubted him. "Do you know what a retreat looks like?" he asked. The soldier then told his commanding general, "I ought to, general; I've been with you during your whole cam-paign." Rosecrans remained in Chattanooga, and Bragg occupied the high ground overlooking the city.

Chattanooga

Rosecrans was in a bad way. He held Chattanooga, true, but Bragg had him in a state of semi-siege. From the high ground around the city (Lookout Mountain and Missionary Ridge) Bragg's army controlled the Tennessee River. Rosecrans could get supplies only overland, and he could do that only with great difficulty. His horses began to die, and his men were hungry. Bragg grew confident that he had Rosecrans where he wanted him—so confident that he sent Longstreet's corps to Knoxville.

Meanwhile Lincoln made Grant overall western commander, a command similar to that Davis had given Johnston a year previously. Grant, however, was not Johnston. He went to work immediately coordinating troop movements and breaking the siege at Chattanooga. Thomas replaced Rosecrans. More troops poured in. Supply lines opened up. Then on November 21 the Federals fell upon Bragg's army (Sketch Map 9.4).

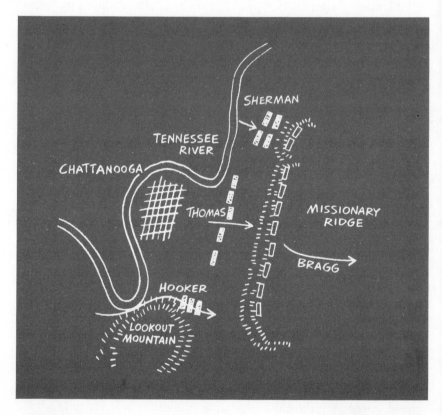

Sketch Map 9.4.

Grant planned the assault. He sent Joe Hooker and three divisions at Lookout Mountain on Bragg's left and Sherman's army (from Mississippi) at Bragg's right. Thomas went at Bragg's center, Missionary Ridge, head on. When Hooker threatened to get between Lookout Mountain and Missionary Ridge, the Rebels left the mountain and concentrated on the ridge.

Then on November 25 Thomas' troops broke through and swept up and down the trench line. The Army of Tennessee ran. For one of the few times in the war, virtually an entire army took to its heels and streamed to the rear. The Confederates stopped running at Dalton, Georgia. There Bragg went into winter quarters with a demoralized army and a disgruntled officer corps. The Union forces, too, settled in for the winter, and the campaigning season of 1863 was over.

Mine Run

Lee and Meade sparred with each other in Northern Virginia during the late summer and fall of 1863. Meade tried to turn Lee's flank. Lee tried to get between Meade and Washington. Late in November the two armies faced each other across the Rapidan River. Meade determined to have one more shot at Lee before winter set in. The Army of the Potomac crossed the Rapidan in an attempt to flank Lee's right. The Army of Northern Virginia hastily dug in along Mine Run and stopped the threat with trenches and determined men.

Having stopped and fixed Meade at his front, Lee then decided to strike his flank. On December 2, while trenches to the west contained Meade, Lee sought to strike him from the south. However, quite unaware of the danger, Meade had decided to withdraw into winter quarters across the Rapidan. Lee's attackers swept through the woods unopposed. Then Lee, too, settled down for the winter.

Winter Thoughts

The United States had come a long way from the mud of the previous winter. Victory, eventually, was probable. Still, the Administration was uneasy. The question was one of will. Would the people and the politicians, and the soldiers persevere long enough to win this probable victory? In the armies a lot of three-year enlistments were due to expire. Only months away was the presidential election, during which the Republicans would have to take their case and their conduct of the war to the people. Some Republican radicals were suggesting a "dump-Lincoln" move. Lincoln, it turned out, held the trump cards in his party—patronage, and the moderates' support—but the President had little control over the Democrats. The nation needed victories in 1864, and Lincoln needed them quickly.

Jefferson Davis would have gladly traded problems with Lincoln. Southerners had sacrificed and wondered whether any sacrifice would be enough. The South was hungry and tired. Optimism had given way to hope and then sometimes hope yielded to desperation. Congress was cantankerous; the anti-Administration ranks had grown in the previous fall's elections. Davis still got most of his major legislation, but with increasing difficulty and more compromise.

Both Presidents realized that the solutions to their problems lay on the battlefield. And so each analyzed his military posture and prospects. Lincoln at last had found a man upon whom he could depend, even though he had never met him—Grant. In late February, Congress made Grant a Lieutenant General and gave him overall command of the Union armies. Grant came east and visited Lincoln and Meade. He retained Meade in command and gave the prime command in the West to Sherman. Grant then urged all of his subordinates to press and keep pressing the Rebels, all together, all at the same time. He decided to stay with Meade and run the war from one of its battle fronts. The arrangement did not exactly delight Meade. But the system usually worked. Even with Grant in command the Union had not evolved a modern general staff structure. Victory was not yet in sight, but defeat was nowhere evident.

Davis had already found his general, Lee; so he was spared concern for the Virginia front. The fundamental command problem lay in the West (which was very rapidly moving east). Davis still liked Bragg and believed him to be a capable administrator. But even Bragg agreed that Bragg had to go. The general blamed everyone but himself for the disaster at Chattanooga. He called his troops cowards and his officers drunkards. Even so Davis kicked Bragg upstairs; he brought him to Richmond and made him military advisor to the President. Davis' question was, who could win in the West? Lee? Davis considered sending Lee west, but yielded to Lee's preference for Virginia. Beauregard? For some time Beauregard had been conducting a very resourceful defense of Charleston. At this juncture he asked for Bragg's command and 100,000 men and spoke dreamily of taking Cincinnati. Beauregard was just fine where he was. Unknowingly however, Beauregard had put his finger on the South's real problem. All the talent and system in the world could not take the place of resources—men and materiel. These the Confederacy did not have. The South made great strides in organization and industrialization, but in a long, industrial war, great strides were not enough. Davis could not know it, but the South had "shot its bolt." It was probably just as well that the President preoccupied himself with personnel matters. Finally Davis gave the Army of Tennessee to Joe Johnston. Davis did not like the choice particularly, but Johnston was popular with the troops, and in Davis' mind Johnston represented the least of evils. Maybe with Lee in front of Richmond and a revived Army of Tennessee—maybe the Confederacy could endure, and if not win, at least not lose, for a while.

Building a bridge under fire—Fredericksburg, 1862.

Black refugees seeking freedom and shelter in Union lines.

Kilpatrick's raiders move on Richmond.

154

Richmond in ruins, courtesy of the Virginia State Library.

Field hospital.

Wounded soldiers escaping the burning Wilderness.

After the battle.

The Stone Wall at foot of Marye's Heights, Fredericksburg, Va.

The trenches of Petersburg.

Unburied dead at Cold Harbor.

From a stereo photograph of the period. This Confederate's intestines were shown in countless parlors after the war.

FIGHT TO 10
THE FINISH—
THE WAR
IN 1864-65

Fort Pillow was almost as soft as its name. On April 12, 1864, Major William F. Bradford and 557 Federal troops held the place. The fort was not much more than an earthen mound on the Tennessee side of the Mississippi River about 40 miles north of Memphis. Black troops composed about half of the garrison, along with white Tennessee Unionists ("homemade Yankees").

Nathan Bedford Forrest and 1,500 Rebel horsemen swooped down upon Fort Pillow that day and demanded surrender. Bradford refused. Then the Confederates charged and carried the works with little difficulty. What happened next is open to question.

Bradford and the Federal survivors claimed that the Rebels slaughtered men who were trying to surrender. And indeed 231 killed and 100 wounded (Confederate losses, 14 killed, 86 wounded) was a rather high casualty rate in a command of only 557. Forrest claimed that the Yankees never surrendered and kept shooting as they retreated from their fallen fort. Thus the Confederates were overcoming a desperate rear-guard action when they killed all those men. No one now will ever learn exactly who was more truthful, Bradford or Forrest. The United States milked the Fort Pillow Massacre for considerable propaganda value. Bedford Forrest made his denials and kept on riding.

No matter where the truth lay, Fort Pillow underscored a trend which had been growing in this war. It was getting meaner. The whole thing began as a contest, with ground rules and notions of gallantry. By 1864, though, not much nobility remained. Still, although this war acquired the meanness of modern war, its antique aspects persisted.

Colonel Ulric Dahlgren was the son of a distinguished United States admiral. In March, 1864, Dahlgren led a column of Union cavalry on a daring raid against Richmond. Colonel Judson Kilpatrick commanded the operation which involved 3,500 cavalry. Kilpatrick divided his force and with the main body drove at Richmond from the east. Dahlgren with 500 troopers was supposed to cross the James River and enter Richmond from the south.

Dahlgren soon encountered difficulties. He stopped to rest at Sabbot Hill, home of Confederate Secretary of War John Seddon, upriver from Richmond. The colonel had known Mrs. Seddon before the war and accepted her invitation to drink some fine 1844 blackberry wine. While Dahlgren and Mrs. Seddon chatted, messengers sped to warn Richmond.

The gregarious Yankees were still on the north side of the James and needed to cross quickly if they were to coordinate their strike with Kilpatrick's. A black guide promised to lead Dahlgren to a ford. As it happened the river was up and the ford unfordable. Dahlgren was convinced that the guide had tricked him and had the man hanged on the spot with his own bridle reins. Then the blue column dashed for Richmond from the west.

Kilpatrick and Dahlgren missed each other by about six hours. Kilpatrick's force approached Richmond on the morning of March 1, met resistance instead of Dahlgren, and retired. Dahlgren's force advanced on the city in the late afternoon and in sleet and freezing rain turned back before a motley band of clerks and furloughed Southern soldiers.

Then the chase began. Dahlgren tried to circle north and follow Kilpatrick's escape route down the Virginia Peninsula. At a place called Mantapike, Confederate cavalry and "home guards" laid an ambush. The Federals fell into the trap, and Dahlgren was killed.

A young lad saw Dahlgren fall, and when it was safe dashed out to rifle his pockets. William Littlepage hoped to find a pocket watch for his schoolmaster. Instead he found a cigar case containing a copy of Dahl-gren's instructions to his men.

> We hope to release the prisoners from Belle Island [prison camp at Richmond] first, and, having seen them fairly started, we will cross the James River into Richmond, destroying the bridges after us, and exhorting the released prisoners to destroy and burn the hateful city, and do not allow the Rebel leader, Davis, and his traitorous crew to escape.

These instructions seem normal enough. Had Dahlgren succeeded, he might have shortened the war considerably. Burning cities and killing or capturing enemy political leaders is, to us, what war is all about. But in 1864 William Littlepage's discovery set off a storm of righteous indignation from both North and South.

Newspapers in Richmond demanded that the government hang the captives from Dahlgren's Raid. Robert E. Lee called the raid a "barbarous and inhuman plot." The Confederates buried Dahlgren secretly to prevent his body from being mutilated. Varina Davis (Mrs. Jefferson Davis) recalled old times in Washington when "little Ulric" in a velvet suit had sat upon her lap and could not reconcile her memory with this man who wanted to kill her husband. Lee finally demanded an explanation from Meade and sent photographs of Dahlgren's orders. Meade vigorously denied the whole thing and charged that the papers were a hoax. The implication was that the United States did not fight wars like that.

The "massacre" at Fort Pillow and Dahlgren's Raid are examples of how one war could be mean and high-minded, modern and antique, at the same time. In 1864, though, the meanness seemed to dominate. Bitterness mounted as the war became a fight to the finish.

Meanness was not the only new factor in this war. By 1864 the structure of war itself had changed. The conflict began with charges and bands and yells; by this time other things were more important. Bands still played and men still yelled. But the romance of war had gone; modernity had taken its place. Trenches and supply lines and impersonal numbers were the new factors. Industrial war between whole peoples, instead of just armies, was evolving.

The North Georgia Campaign

Joe Johnston joined his army at Dalton, Georgia, in December, 1863. Before he arrived Jefferson Davis had tried to convince Johnston and probably himself that Braxton Bragg had left the Army of Tennessee in good shape. Johnston soon learned differently. The army at Dalton was riddled with desertion and suffering through the North Georgia winter with inadequate supplies. Johnston began immediately to alter the situation; he announced amnesty for those who had deserted, restored order and discipline, and found supplies. For the first time in its existence the Army of Tennessee had a commander it could like and respect. By the time spring came Johnston had around 71,000 men spread among three infantry corps (commanded by William J. Hardee, John Bell Hood, and Leonidas Polk) and Joe Wheeler's cavalry.

In Richmond, Davis and his military advisor Bragg expected Johnston to take the offensive. They expected this even as they brought James Longstreet's corps back to Virginia from Georgia in April. Johnston believed that the best he could do was an offensive-defense, counterpunch in an effort to defend Atlanta, frustrate the Republican war effort, and destroy as much of William T. Sherman's army as possible.

At Chattanooga Sherman had three field armies totaling about 107,000 troops: Army of the Cumberland—65,000 commanded by George H. Thomas; Army of the Tennessee—25,000 commanded by James B. McPherson; Army of the Ohio—17,000 commanded by John M. Schofield. His intentions were offensive. Ulysses S. Grant, the General-in-Chief, called for the campaigns against Johnston and Lee to begin in May and continue relentlessly to the finish. We will of necessity have to follow one campaign at a time. But we must recall that the action in Georgia and Virginia was going on simultaneously.

Sherman established the pattern of his campaign early. Johnston and the Army of Tennessee were entrenched on Rocky Face Ridge in front of Dalton. On May 7 Sherman sent Schofield and Thomas at Johnston while McPherson headed around Johnston's left toward Resaca behind the Confederates on the Western and Atlantic Railroad.

Johnston withdrew to Resaca and gave battle on May 14. Again Sherman tried to pin down the Confederates and get behind them to their supply line, the Western and Atlantic Railroad. Again Johnston withdrew, this time to Cassville. Then the Rebels took the initiative. Johnston sent Polk's Corps and all the wagons in the army off toward the southwest. He hoped to make Sherman believe that Polk's dust was the entire Army of the Tennessee. Sherman believed. Thus Johnston with Hardee's and Hood's corps at Cassville had a golden opportunity to smash Schofield while Thomas and McPherson chased off after Polk. But Hood exposed the ruse. He attacked prematurely, giving away the Rebel strength at Cassville, and as Sherman reconcentrated, Hood and Hardee convinced Johnston to fall back.

Next Sherman sent his entire force west to Dallas, Georgia, in an effort to get around Johnston. The Federals found Johnston's army waiting for them at New Hope Church. Sherman then began fighting his way back toward the railroad. The two armies stayed at close quarters and dug trenches in each new position (Sketch Map 10.1).

Spring rains and frustration began to work on Sherman. The rain slowed his supplies, and frustration made him seek a decision. On June 27 he went at Johnston head-on at Kennesaw Mountain. It was a bad idea. In two hours the Federals sustained 3,000 casualties and did not dent the Confederate lines on the mountain.

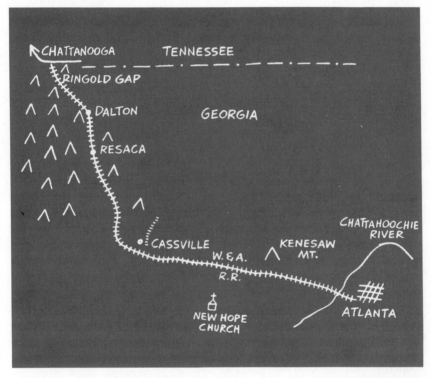

Sketch Map 10.1.

Sherman resumed his flanking tactics and Johnston withdrew in mid-July behind the Chattahoochee River to a defensive line along Peachtree Creek. At this point the North Georgia Campaign became the Atlanta Campaign. Sherman had moved 100 miles in 74 days and suffered 25,000 casualties. But the Union army was at the gates of Atlanta. Some military historians consider Johnston's effort against Sherman a masterpiece. Indeed the Army of the Tennessee had marched and fought well. Morale was high and the army had confidence in Johnston. But Richmond was unhappy.

Johnston had traded ground for time and Union casualties; but how long could this go on? Atlanta was not merely a political objective. The city was an important railroad juncture and as such was the link between the Atlantic and Gulf Coast States of the Confederacy. More important perhaps was the nature of Johnston's military mind. He was brilliant in strategic withdrawals; would he ever take the offensive? With these thoughts in mind Davis sent his military advisor Bragg to visit Johnston and to find out if "Retreating Joe" had any plans for defending Atlanta. Meanwhile Sherman gathered supplies and strength to move on the city.

The Richmond Campaign

On May 4, while Sherman was preparing to move on Johnston at Rocky Face Ridge, Grant and Meade launched their assault on Lee. The Federals were 119,000 strong—four infantry corps (commanded by Ambrose E. Burnside, G. K. Warren, John Sedgwick, and Winfield S. Hancock) and Philip Sheridan's 12,400 cavalry troopers. Lee's Army of Northern Virginia numbered about 64,000—three corps (commanded by Longstreet, "Bald Dick" Ewell, and A. P. Hill) and Jeb Stuart's cavalry.

The two armies had spent the winter on opposite sides of the Rapidan River. The Confederates were dug in, and so Grant decided to try to get on their right flank. The Federals crossed the Rapidan near its confluence with the Rappahannock not too far from Chancellorsville.

Lee did not contest the river crossing; he did concentrate his forces in the Wilderness, that tangle of trees and undergrowth in which he had baffled Joe Hooker the year before. On May 5 and 6 the armies of Lee and Grant grappled blindly. Wounded men fell and were never found in the thickets. Then the woods caught fire and burned those unable to flee the flames. At the end of two days of fighting, Grant saw he could not overrun Lee, and so he broke contact. In times past Federal commanders had limped backward after such carnage. Grant took his repulse at the Wilderness and pressed on.

Again Grant sought Lee's right flank, and again Lee raced south and east. The critical place was Spotsylvania Court House, and it was critical because two key roads leading south joined there. The Army of Northern Virginia arrived first, barely. Grant maneuvered and then attacked the hastily erected Rebel works in mass. The battle raged around a Confederate perimeter for three days. At one place, survivors claimed that they had fought hand-to-hand from dawn to dusk. The Confederates held, and Grant again put his columns on the road, south and east. Union cavalry under Sheridan had been raiding behind Lee's lines, and on May 11 at Yellow Tavern, Jeb Stuart stopped the threat but fell mortally wounded in the aftermath of battle.

Lee was waiting at North Anna on May 23–24. And Lee was waiting at Cold Harbor on June 3 (Sketch Map 10.2).

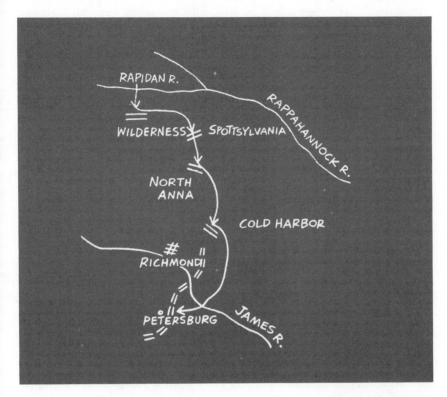

Sketch Map 10.2.

Like Sherman at Kennesaw Mountain, Grant had become impatient with his flank marches. Also, another flank march would send the Army of the Potomac farther away from Richmond, rather than nearer. Cold Harbor was another of those crossroads settlements whose significance was totally military. The ground had been a battlefield once before during McClellan's Peninsula Campaign. Lee's army occupied a long and rela-tively straight line of trenches squarely between Grant and Richmond. Grant decided to assault those trenches head-on, in the center. His imme-diate goal was a breakthrough. If the Army of the Potomac could blast a large enough hole in the center of the Confederate line, it could then roll up each half of Lee's army and end the campaign then and there.

The massed blue infantry charged on the morning of June 3. They charged for about an hour and sustained 7,000 casualties. Those who survived lay down where they were in front of the Rebel earthworks. No man could live in the open; instinct told them not to stand and retreat but to lie down and dig. The breakthrough attempt broke up.

For a solid month the two armies had been in almost continuous contact. Grant had lost an average of 2,000 men per day. Northern newspapers were calling him a butcher. Still he pressed on.

This time Grant broke contact completely. Lee, for a few critical days, had no idea where his enemy was. Actually Grant had done what Lee had hoped against hope McClellan would not do in 1862. The Army of the Potomac had crossed the James River below Richmond and headed for Petersburg. For one of the few times in the war Lee, the "Gray Fox," was outfoxed.

Petersburg was the "back door" to Richmond. The town, about 20 miles south of Richmond, was a rail center through which ran all but one of the rail lines connecting the Confederate capital with the South. At Petersburg as Grant's army approached on June 15 was P. G. T. Beauregard (up from Charleston) and 2,400 soldiers. On June 16 the odds were 4,000 Rebels against 48,000 Yankees. Beauregard's people were gallant; the Federals were úncoordinated. Petersburg held until Lee could reinforce its defenders.

Grant next decided to lay siege. Both armies dug trench networks, probed for weak points, and lobbed artillery shells at each other. The Federals extended their lines west reaching for railroads and north of the James toward Richmond. Lee was run to ground. His army could no longer maneuver. From mid-June, 1864, to the end of the war portions of the Army of Northern Virginia came out of their holes around Petersburg and Richmond in desperation. The entire army never again marched, except in the end when it fled.

Grant in the East, like Sherman in the West, had learned well the lessons of modern war. Both men realized that battle had become slaughter and that war was the ultimate expression of a whole people. The United States had the might and the will to win under these conditions; the Confederate States had not. In the South, Lee especially, knew these lessons, too. But knowing and being powerless to act only deepened his tragedy.

Finish in the West

Braxton Bragg was not exactly an impartial observer. When Davis sent Bragg to check on Joe Johnston in front of Atlanta, he must have realized the enmity between the former and incumbent commanders of the Army of Tennessee. Johnston with some reason felt that his fitness for command was being tried in a "kangaroo court." He revealed to Bragg none of his plans and no special confidence that he could save Atlanta. Davis heard Bragg's report, weighed the case, and decided to replace Johnston.

The next question was obvious; who could do the job? Since Sherman was poised to attack, the new commander must know the army and the situation. Among the corps commanders of the Army of the Tennessee, Polk was dead (at New Hope Church); Hardee was solid but not especially aggressive; Hood was a fighter, but inclined to be rash. Davis decided to gamble on Hood, even though Lee was cool to the whole idea and especially to the choice of Hood.

On July 17 Johnston received the President's telegram and briefed Hood on his new command. Hood knew very well why he had been chosen—to fight. And in truth he had been a bold fighter in the past. Now he had the government's mandate to risk everything in a showdown battle. Hood had personal reasons, too, for wanting to prove his gallantry. He had lost a leg in battle and his heart to a young "belle" during his convalescence. Whether he fought for Davis or for Sally "Buck" Preston, just 48 hours from the time he assumed command of the army, he committed it to battle.

As Sherman approached Atlanta he divided his army. He sent Thomas' force at Peachtree Creek and Schofield and McPherson to the east. Johnston had foreseen this move and had planned to attack Thomas with all the force he could muster. Hood adopted the plan and on July 20 struck the Federals as they crossed Peachtree Creek. However Hood committed his units piecemeal, and they could do no more than check Thomas. To win, Hood had to annihilate someone.

Next day (July 21) Hood attacked McPherson's flank as he approached from the east—again, no decision, although McPherson himself was killed in the action. On July 28 Hood attacked again, this time west of the city at Ezra Church—same result. The "Gallant Hood" had fought three major battles in one week and suffered a fantastic number of casualties, all to no good purpose. Sherman settled down to a siege and moved on Atlanta's railroads.

The siege lasted just about a month. Then on August 26 Sherman all but left town. The bulk of the Federal army just seemed to disappear. Hood was convinced that Sherman had given up and made plans for a victory dance. Then on August 28 he realized that Sherman was marching toward the Macon Railroad, Atlanta's last link with the "outside." Hood evacuated Atlanta and rushed to give battle. Hardee's corps attacked at Jonesboro but suffered a repulse. On September 2 Sherman occupied Atlanta; Hood's army was at Lovejoy's Station more than 12 miles away.

Hood had lost approximately 27,500 troops and Atlanta. Still he was ready to fight some more. Jefferson Davis visited the Army of the Tennessee while it licked its wounds and discussed with Hood prospects for the future. The two decided to march the army north to Chattanooga, cut Sherman's supply line, and lure the Federals into battle. Late in September the Confederates took the road north.

In Atlanta, Sherman, too, had been exchanging ideas with his superior, Grant. As Hood's strategy became clear, Sherman decided to follow the Rebels. The two armies fenced with each other through north Georgia and halfway across Alabama. Then in late October Sherman had had enough. He cut Thomas loose to chase Hood and headed for the Atlantic Ocean.

On November 12 Sherman drove his columns east from Atlanta. The Federals lived "off the country" and destroyed what they could not eat. Barns filled with the recent harvest went up in flames. Troopers drove livestock through broken fences. The Confederacy would not live this winter off this harvest. With Hood's army off in Tennessee, Sherman's men met little resistance. The work of destruction paused at Savannah (taken December 12) and then proceeded northward through the Carolinas.

Meanwhile Hood was still fighting, and losing. On November 30, with no artillery preparation, he sent 15,000 men across open ground against entrenched Federals near Franklin, Tennessee. When the smoke of battle cleared 6,000 Rebels were casualties. In the late evening the bodies of five Confederate generals were laid out on a single front porch.

Undaunted, Hood marched to Nashville to besiege Thomas' 48,000 with 31,000. Thomas came out of his trenches, and for one of the few times in the war one army destroyed another. In January, 1865, Hood asked to be relieved; Davis complied with the request. The survivors of the Army of Tennessee rejoined Joe Johnston who was then trying with little success to slow Sherman down in the Carolinas.

The Making of the President—1864

From hindsight Lincoln's reelection in 1864 seems a foregone conclusion. It did not seem so to Lincoln at the time. In August the President declared, "I am a beaten man, unless we can have some great victory." The issue was peace; the North was war weary. After nearly four years of fighting Grant was apparently no closer to Richmond than McClellan had been in 1862. Hood was loose in Tennessee. And Sherman was seemingly wandering about the Georgia countryside. The North believed it had paid in blood the price of victory. And yet victory had not come.

A resurgent Democratic Party talked peace and nominated a general —George Brinton McClellan. The peace talk was never unanimous; in fact McClellan was more than a little embarrassed by it. Nevertheless the

Democrats symbolized peace in 1864. The Democrats also hoped to attract votes from the men who had served in McClellan's army; the Army of the Potomac never loved another commander as much as "Little Mac."

Lincoln's problems began in his own party with Salmon Chase. The Treasury Secretary wanted the presidency and believed he deserved it. However, while Chase was being decorously coy and looking "available," Lincoln's managers were bagging delegates to the Republican Convention. Consequently the Chase candidacy never quite became more than a veiled threat. Lincoln did dump Hannibal Hamlin as Vice-President in favor of Andrew Johnson of Tennessee. Johnson was a very brave, very stubborn man. He began life poor in East Tennessee and worked his way up every rung of the political ladder, town councilman to Senator. When the Southerners departed Congress in 1861, Johnson watched them go. He was a Democrat and a Unionist; he despised the planter civilization. Lincoln had named Johnson governor of the Union-held portions of Tennessee, and now Vice-President. Of course Johnson's appeal in 1864 was his Southern origin and Democratic past. He would draw votes from the McClellan ticket, and so Lincoln wanted him.

Several factors helped to assure the Republican's victory. Perhaps none was more important than the underlying commitment to the Union shared by most Americans. They might talk peace and long for peace. But in the final analysis Americans were not willing to sacrifice the Union for peace. And when many people said peace they meant victory. For these the real issue was not so much the war as the Republican's prosecution of the war. The fall of Atlanta and the siege of Petersburg (frustrating though it was) made Lincoln look good, just in time.

Then, too, the soldier vote was heavy and heavily Republican. Even in the Army of the Potomac where McClellan was a magic word, the men could not bring themselves to vote against their record and their hopes for victory. Soldiers, on garrison duty around key cities like New York, helped to ensure a "fair" (sometimes translated "Republican") election.

Finally Lincoln himself left no stone unturned. The Republicans even changed their name to Union Party to sharpen the symbolism. As the election approached and Lincoln expected his margin of victory to be very small, the President hurried Nevada into the Union to add electoral votes and Republican/Union Senators.

As it turned out, Lincoln's fears were phantoms. McClellan carried only three Northern states (Kentucky, Delaware, and New Jersey) and lost the electoral contest 12–212. Lincoln's popular vote majority was about 400,000; he gathered 55 percent of the ballots cast. In addition, the Republicans increased their voting strength in Congress. Lincoln had his mandate to continue the war to the finish.

Finish in the East

The trenches at Petersburg foreshadowed the Western Front in France during World War I. Both armies used intricate networks of trenches. Felled trees with branches facing the enemy (abatis) added to the defensive barriers. There were chevaux-de-frise, poles with a series of sharpened stakes set in them at all angles to give the appearance and effect of porcupines. Artillery positions commanded both front and flanks of these fortifications.

Life in the trenches was hard. Men were always dirty, ever smelly. And danger was constant. Sometimes the enemies arranged a truce and traded newspapers, coffee, and tobacco. More often sharpshooters kept vigilance over the opposing works. Since in some places the lines were no more than 100 yards (even 50) apart, riflemen usually hit their targets.

Lee's predicament was obvious—how to break out of this grinding campaign of attrition which he had not the resources to win. Ultimately the Confederates out of necessity opted to remain in their trenches and hoped that the Union would weary, or that Grant would blunder.

Grant's situation was less sanguine than it looked. He could wait and probe and stretch the Rebels to their breaking point. But that would take time, and time was not on the Union side in the summer of 1864. Political objectives were not supposed to impede military minds. Grant and Lincoln knew that well. However, the nation might well repudiate the entire war at the polls in November unless Grant could achieve a victory, or at least the semblance of one.

In late June, Lee responded to his predicament by sending Jubal Early and about 12,000 troops into the Shenandoah Valley. Early dealt first with a threat to Lynchburg and then marched down the valley, crossed the Potomac, and drove for Washington in mid-July. Visions of Stonewall Jackson appeared in the collective mind of the capital. Early, however, was not Jackson and, more important, he did not have the strength to do more than scare Washington. He did do that. Grant had to rush troops to the defense of Washington. The Lincoln Administration suffered the embarrassment of having to make frantic efforts to defend its capital at the very time it was predicting the fall of Richmond. Indeed some of Early's troops actually shot at Lincoln as he inspected the city's defenses.

Early realized that Washington was too strong to take. Thus he retreated the way he had come and eluded Federal efforts to trap his force. But Early never returned to Richmond. He stayed in the Shenandoah Valley and faced with some initial success the hard-riding troopers of Phil Sheridan. Grant and Lincoln determined to do in the valley what

Sherman did in Georgia. In the fall of 1864 Sheridan with infantry and cavalry campaigned with increasing strength against Early and in the end all but annihilated the Confederates in the valley. Sheridan unleashed his men to burn and destroy the rich valley harvest. As in Sherman's case, Sheridan's inverse "scorched earth" policy made the war meaner, but relentlessly closer to a finish.

Meanwhile back in the trenches, Grant in late July tried to break the impasse. Lieutenant Colonel Henry Pleasants had the idea. Pleasants commanded a regiment composed largely of Pennsylvania coal miners. What Pleasants wanted to do was tunnel under the Confederate works, plant a very large explosive charge, and literally blow a hole in the trench system. Burnside, Pleasants' corps commander, liked the scheme and convinced Meade and Grant to adopt it.

Pleasants' miners dug beneath the Southern lines, and planted 8,000 pounds of powder. The task was incredibly difficult because of the necessity for silence and the lack of adequate ventilation. By the time the miners had completed their labors, the operation had assumed major proportions. Grant made a demonstration north of Burnside's front to draw off Rebel defenders. He also massed artillery and reinforcements to support the breakthrough attempt.

General Edward Ferrero's division was supposed to lead the charge. Ferrero's division was composed of black troops. These men, like other black soldiers, often had a hard time in the Union army. They received less pay than white troops, and there were no black officers. More often than not black units did the war's dirty work—digging trenches, burying dead, and such. This time, though, it was going to be different. Ferrero's men were enthusiastic about their assignment. They trained eagerly and rehearsed their role in the attack. They knew that the key to success lay in getting into the gap quickly and rolling up the Confederate flanks to widen the hole. Then the rest of Burnside's corps and the reinforcements would be able to pour through into the Rebel rear.

At the last minute Meade had second thoughts. What if the "blow-through" becomes a fiasco? How would it look in Washington to send in black troops as cannon fodder for a doomed attack? A white division must go first. General James H. Ledlie's division "won" a drawing of lots and made ready in haste.

The powder went off at 4:40 on the morning of July 30. The explosion had the effect Pleasants had promised; a 500-yard hole in the Confederate lines. Then the chaos began. Meade had given instructions for his engineers to stand ready to cut through the Federal defense system. Apparently someone forgot, because the assault troops became hung up in their own works. They eventually picked their way into the gloom of the still smoking "crater" in small bunches instead of as a massed division. Their commander, Ledlie, spent his time hiding in a dugout swilling rum. After two hours the Yankees were still in the crater. No one tried or was able to do what Ferrero's troops had been trained to do—press on and exploit the gap. Ferrero himself had joined Ledlie and was busy drinking his courage. Still more men poured into the crater.

Then the Confederates recovered. They had the rare opportunity to "shoot fish in a barrel," and they did it vigorously. The disaster cost 4,400 casualties.

Grant resumed his probing and the static war ground on. Trench warfare was hard in the summer heat; it was all but unbearable in the winter cold. The networks of earthworks eventually extended 50 miles around Richmond and Petersburg.

During the winter Lee's army became weaker. Men received letters from home telling of Sherman's or Sheridan's destruction. Wives asked their husbands what their children were to eat, and their men quit the war and went home. Desertion plagued Lee's army and alarmed the government.

Grant's army grew stronger. Reinforcements and supplies poured in. By early spring the veterans could smell victory. Sherman was in North Carolina, and Johnston could do nothing about it. Lee's lines were stretched to the breaking point.

Then it happened. Sheridan trapped and destroyed an entire Confederate division (Pickett's) on April 1, 1865, at a place called Five Forks. All of a sudden Lee's position was untenable. He telegraphed Davis that he hoped to hold out until the evening of April 2. The Confederacy made frantic haste to evacuate its capital. Lee hurried to save his army.

Davis put the government on wheels and fled by train from Richmond to Danville. Lee got his army on the road and headed west. His last hope was to outdistance Grant's army, turn south, and unite with Johnston.

Grant was happy to have Richmond. But he knew it was time to go for the jugular, to make the kill. Sheridan told Grant that he could cut off Lee's retreat, and Grant encouraged him to go to it. The pursuit was relentless. The Confederates reached for the railroad to Danville; Sheridan was there first. Lee plunged west toward Lynchburg, and Sheridan outdistanced him.

On April 9 the Army of Northern Virginia approached Appomattox Court House. The men had had no food supply for days. Of the 57,000 who manned the trenches of Richmond and Petersburg on April 1, only about 8,000 reached Appomattox with Lee. In the morning the Confederates drove off Sheridan's cavalry and then discovered that masses of blue infantry were in front and behind them. Lee had had enough.

Wilbur McLean found the war was again in his yard. He had moved from Manassas to Appomattox Court House after the second battle in

1862 hoping to find tranquility. Now the armies had again sought him out. This time, though, the conflict came into his very parlor. But the soldiers were Lee and Grant, and they met in peace.

Grant's terms were generous. He paroled Lee and his army. In so doing he gave the word of the General-in-Chief that no one would turn the surrender into a lynching bee.

Finish

Davis remained at Danville for a matter of days and then visited Joe Johnston near Raleigh, North Carolina. He knew Lee had surrendered. But even though the Confederate Congress had made Lee Commander-in-Chief, he only surrendered his own army. Davis asked Johnston about his prospects, and Johnston reflected gloom.

Then Davis ordered Johnston to let the government have his cavalry. The President wanted the infantry to disband under orders to rendezvous at a future time to fight on. What Davis proposed, of course, was guerrilla warfare. The Confederacy would live as long as one man was alive and willing to kill Yankees. The option was available. There were precedents; the Spanish for example had wrested their country from Napoleon with guerrilla tactics. Davis had been talking about partisan war for some months. Now was the time to make the commitment.

But Johnston refused. On April 28 he surrendered his army to Sherman near Raleigh. In fact Lee had had the guerrilla option and discarded it. He explained in a letter to Davis on April 20, that heading for the hills would not achieve independence. Johnston explained in his memoirs that partisan operations would have only bled the South more to no good purpose. Still we must ask, why? The Confederacy had given up much of its Old South ideology for the sake of independence. Why not carry on war to the knife?

Part of the answer lies in the nature of the men involved in the decision. Lee and Johnston were "regular" soldiers; they thought of partisan warfare as dirty and beneath them. Part of the answer lay in the condition of the Confederate troops; they were bone weary and fought out. Maybe, though, there was something in the Southern mind that prohibited a resort to guerrilla war. Southerners had sacrificed just about everything for which they once stood. But they never relinquished their attachment to people and place. Guerrillas by definition, must be nomads. They must forsake family, friends, and place for their cause. Perhaps this was the one feature of the Southern way of life, the surviving remnant of the Southern world-view, that the Rebels would not give up.

In a way Grant and Lincoln sustained this attachment to people and place. Grant had allowed Confederates who owned horses to take them home and get on with the spring plowing. Lincoln was preoccupied with reunion and a larger concept of kinship when he visited Richmond only days after the Rebels left. The commander of occupation forces Godfrey Weitzel escorted the President around his prize. Weitzel was having problems, he said, deciding what to do about hungry people and discipline in this occupied city. Lincoln would make no formal policy statement, but he looked Weitzel in the eye and told him, "If I were in your place, I'd let them up easy—let them up easy."

For whatever reason, the Confederate field armies surrendered and melted away, and Davis continued his flight. Finally on May 10 at Irwinville, Georgia, a squad of Union cavalry captured the "official family," by then shrunken to about the size of a family. On May 26 Edmund Kirby Smith surrendered the Confederacy's trans-Mississippi army, and it was over. Peace broke out.

RESTORATION, 11
RESURRECTION,
RECONSTRUCTION

Abraham Lincoln did not want to attend Ford's Theater on Good Friday (April 14) 1865. Nevertheless he went; his wife wanted to go, and unmaking the evening's plans seemed more trouble than going ahead with them.

At 10:15 P.M. John Wilkes Booth, a brilliant actor turned Southern zealot, shot the President in the back of the head. Lincoln never regained consciousness. He died early the next morning, and his apotheosis began.

Reconstruction Mythology

The assassination of Lincoln had a lot to do with the process and period known as Reconstruction (1865–1877). The assassination also has had a crucial impact upon what historian Kenneth M. Stampp calls the "tragic legend of Reconstruction." Lincoln's death, at the height of his power and prestige, begins the mythic tale of Reconstruction too long accepted and acted upon by Americans. Had Lincoln lived, the story opens, it would all have been different.

Lincoln would have been kind to the defeated South. His announced plans for Reconstruction rested on the premise that Southern states had never really left the Union. It followed that no one could impose harsh conditions upon these states to rejoin a Union from which they never separated. Thus Lincoln proposed that as soon as 10 percent of the qualified voters in a Southern state should take an oath of allegiance to the Union, then that state would be free to reorganize itself, write slavery out of its constitution, and accept full equality with the other states in the Union. Lincoln planned to be liberal with amnesty and to hang no traitors.

Booth's bullet ended the South's hopes for magnanimity. Andrew Johnson accepted the fundamentals of Lincoln's moderate plan and tried to make it work. But Congress, dominated by vindictive, "bad men" called Radical Republicans frustrated Johnson's efforts. Lacking the prestige of Lincoln, Johnson was no match for the Radicals. And, the myth continues, the evils of Radical Reconstruction began.

Congress refused to seat duly elected Southern members and refused to recognize legally constituted Southern state governments. Congress sent the army back into the South to enforce its malignant will. Congress created the Freedmen's Bureau, ostensibly to help the freedmen, but really to stir up racial trouble and to provide opportunities for graft. Congress imposed upon the Southern states nearly impossible conditions for reentering the Union and disenfranchised the South's natural leaders.

Reconstruction in the South was the lowest point in the region's history. Yankee "carpetbaggers" poured into the South, intent only upon filling their pockets. Southern traitors, "scalawags," joined this Northern ilk in an orgy of misrule. Mindless freedmen, duped by these "leaders," voted in farcical state governments which rode roughshod over "good" people. The combination of military-carpetbagger-scalawag-black rule taxed decent people into bankruptcy, deprived them of self-government, and left "uppity" black people free to work all manner of mischief.

The sordid story almost has a happy ending, however; long suffering white Southerners "redeemed" their states. They outlasted Yankee vengeance and finally by a variety of means succeeded in restoring black Southerners to their "place." Thus in a sense the South did "rise again."

Now of course myths and legends like the one just recounted do not originate in vacuums. There is truth in the mythology of Reconstruction. Lincoln did have a moderate program for restoring the Union. Johnson was an inept presidential politician. Some Radical Republicans were vindictive. Some Reconstruction governments were shamelessly corrupt. And many from the Old South's ruling caste did have a difficult time. All this is true enough. The issue, however, is one of perspective and emphasis. What has happened, it seems, is that historians and others have dealt with Reconstruction from the perspective of upper-crust white Southerners. From this point of view Reconstruction was about very sad things done to some upper-crust white Southerners.

More recently historians have revised the perspective and emphasis and looked at the period from the point of view of black Southerners. Reconstruction, argue the revisionists, was more than anything else about fulfilling the promise of freedom and equality to black Americans. Thus the period produced noble efforts on the part of Northern idealists to achieve racial justice. Its tangible results, specifically the Thirteenth, Fourteenth, and Fifteenth Amendments to the Constitution, were no small achievements. Yet ultimately Reconstruction failed as a program, not because of injustices done to Southern whites, but because of injustices done to Southern blacks, and because of the larger failure to face up to the challenge of racial pluralism. Still, Reconstruction laid some foundation for the so-called Second Reconstruction about 100 years too late.

Now, if we had to choose between the classical Reconstruction mythology and the revisionist reinterpretation, we would have little difficulty electing the latter. Southerners, after all, did lose the war. Comparatively speaking, Reconstruction was an easy peace. Most wars and especially civil wars end in bitterness and executions; this did not happen in 1865. Freedom and civil equality for black people were legitimate extensions of the Union's war aims, and thus if we are to pass judgment on the peace, we can use black Americans' civil rights as a criterion.

But must we choose? Is there not a third alternative available? Both the classical mythology and the revisionist works have in common the implied goal of passing judgment upon Reconstruction. Passing judgment of the past is one viable, indeed unavoidable, function of written history. Yet judging is a risky business. Historian Kenneth M. Stampp has shown how "the Tragic Legend of Reconstruction" ill conditioned the racial and political attitudes of generations of Americans. And however valid the revisionist's judgment of Reconstruction seems now, as part of the movement for racial justice, it sometimes implies condemnation and perhaps too little understanding of those same generations. The best of recent writings on Reconstruction has focused upon explanations, as opposed to blame.

When we discussed the historiography of the causes of the war, we found that "cause" usually implied blame. Thus we tried to explain how the war came, rather than proclaim why it started. And we spoke in terms of ideology and world view. Judging was involved, but it grew out of explanation instead of the other way around. Why not explain Reconstruction in terms of ideology also? If the war was about world views, then the peace, too, would logically seem to be about ideologies—perceptions of reality to some extent redefined by the war experience.

Situation—1865—South

The South lost the war, and Southerners knew it. Richmond, Charleston, Atlanta, especially, along with other Southern cities and towns were in ruins. In the countryside livestock roamed at will. Fences were down; barns empty or burned. These conditions existed not only in the wake of Sherman's and Sheridan's marches. Wherever armies had been, Union or Confederate, they had robbed chicken houses and corncribs. They had confiscated livestock and had used fence rails for campfires. And these were only the more obvious signs of defeat.

Roughly 260,000 men, 4 percent of the population, were dead. Some of the "lucky" survivors were missing arms and legs. The Confederate money and securities were worthless. Schools were closed. Banks were broke. Some white Southerners by hook or crook emerged from the war well-heeled; most, however, were down and out.

Black people in the South were no longer slaves. But freedom on an empty stomach is likely to be a hollow thing indeed. The freedmen had little or no property or money. Some freedmen returned to their former masters and asked for work. Others crowded into cities and towns seeking work and wages. Still others wandered aimlessly in search of relatives, or food, or both. While abolitionists, black and white, discussed suffrage and civil equality, evidence indicates that average freedmen were most concerned about land and economic opportunity.

For the most part white Southerners accepted military defeat. They credited themselves with a gallant effort, but realized that the South had expended every resource and lost completely on the battlefield. Southern independence was no longer possible.

Relatively few ex-Confederates fled the United States. Some government officials left the country out of fear, and a few of these like Judah Benjamin never returned. A few Southerners left for Mexico and Brazil; however, these were the exceptions. Most ex-Confederates were resigned to live with the military verdict and to become American Southerners once more.

Unlike many defeated nations, the South did not repudiate its wartime leadership. Generals, for years after the war, wrangled among themselves about who did or did not do what when. But for the most part Southerners venerated the old aristocracy and expected it to play a part in the restored Union. Even Jefferson Davis eventually became a hero. In the last days of the Confederacy Davis absorbed much of the blame for the collapse of the Southern nation. Then he went to prison at Fort Monroe, Virginia, for two years, and had the threat of a trial for treason held over him. In a sense Davis became a Christ-figure in the South, suffering not for the South's sins exactly, but more taking upon himself the shame of the vanquished at the hands of the victors. Davis bore the conqueror's wrath alone. Even though people talked of trials and hangings, only Henry Wirz, commander of Andersonville Prison, was tried and executed.

That Southerners did not vilify the old leadership says something crucial about their response to the war. The military decision would stand; the Confederacy was gone and independence with it. But the South's acceptance of defeat and reunion with the North did not signal the end of the South's ideology. Military and political decisions were one thing; social, economic, and cultural matters were something else entirely. As we shall see, the South as a whole was willing to live with defeat and reunion, but was unprepared to accept the ideological consequences.

Amid the ruins and rubble of defeat most Southerners were content, even anxious, to get on with the restoration of the Old Union. And therein lay the rub. The Old Union was no longer possible. Restoration was not reconstruction.

Situation—1865—North

In contrast with the South, Northern sacrifice in the war seemed slight. Battles for the most part had been fought far away from Northern soil, and in terms of percentages many fewer families mourned the death or maiming of a loved one. Nevertheless the Union had paid a dear price for its victory. More than 300,000 men were dead. Economic energy expended upon wartime production had slowed the nation's material progress, at least for the short range. The war, which was originally supposed to be a summertime excursion to Richmond, had become long and mean. Surely all this death and sacrifice must yield a proper peace. Surely some greater good must come from this heinous war and the glorious victory.

Those people most directly involved with the nation's aspirations for peacetime were the Republicans. In time they defined their peace goals as they had set forth their war aims. In both cases they reflected long-standing ideological preconceptions. The Union was essential. Slavery must go. Labor must be free. Hard work brought success. Society must be made as nearly perfect as possible; the nation must strive for high ideals. The United States was the hope and bastion for liberty-loving people everywhere.

This sort of thinking did not have in mind the mere restoration of the Old Union. The Republican/Northern ideology demanded reconstruction —reordering—remolding—of the defeated South. Nothing less would compensate for the price of Union victory. Victory was a mandate for remaking the South. The only question involved how to accomplish it.

Lincoln's Answer

Lincoln gave the eventual problem of restoring the fractured nation considerable thought while the war progressed. Perhaps the most ironic thing among many Lincoln ironies, was the fact that although Lincoln stood at the head of an ideologically oriented party and nation, all the while he was himself a profound pragmatist.

The President had insisted from the beginning that secession was not only illegal, but also impossible. It followed therefore that the Union was at war with some rebels, not a nation. To restore the Union it was necessary to defeat the rebels and allow the non-rebels and only-halfway-rebels to take the lead in regularizing Federal-state relations in the South. This process was primarily a military-executive function, and thus the President, not Congress, was responsible for reunion. The President had all the latitude and leverage he needed to do this, because after all these people were rebels and potentially subject to trial for treason.

Lincoln never convinced Congress that he, and not it, would be responsible for restoring the Union. He did, in his own mind, accomplish Presidential restoration during the war in portions of Virginia, Arkansas, Louisiana, and Tennessee. And in 1864 when Congress passed the Wade-Davis Bill, setting down its conditions of reunion, Lincoln pocket-vetoed the measure.

Although it was evident that he would have to treat Congress with kid gloves, Lincoln's program for restoration had become almost firm by the time of his death. He planned to restore the wayward Southern states as soon as 10 percent of the 1860 electorate had taken the oath of allegiance to the Union. Of course each state must forbid slavery in its constitution. Lincoln was disposed to be liberal with pardons and amnesty for Confederate leaders, although he privately hoped that many of them would leave the country. About race Lincoln was ambiguous; nevertheless, he seemed firm on the principle of full civil rights for blacks who had served in his army or who possessed a high standard of education.

In the secession crisis Lincoln had hoped that Southern nonplanters, old Whigs, and Unionists would assert the strength of their numbers and class interest. They had disappointed him. Once again Lincoln seemed to be convinced that Southerners would desert the planter cause and take the lead in restoring the Union. Thus Lincoln tried to make it easy for them. He tried to be magnanimous and shrewd at the same time. He had saved the Union. Now if he could salve the bitterness and realize the potential of those Southern Whigs, Unionists, and nonplanters, everything else just might fall into place.

Whether Lincoln's plan would have worked or not is of course a hypothetical query. Before Lincoln ever had the chance to try it out, John Wilkes Booth intervened. One thing is certain. Andrew Johnson took the essentials of Lincoln's program and made an awful mess of the whole thing. Lincoln's program in Johnson's hands was a near classic case of the baby dying and the afterbirth living.

Johnson's Answer

Andrew Johnson took the oath of office as President of the United States on April 15, 1865. He was President because a half-crazed assassin had shot the man who had needed a "loyal" Southerner to balance an election ticket in 1864. Johnson was indeed loyal. He breathed hatred of rebels and made casual remarks about hanging traitors. For a time the Republicans believed that Johnson was the man for the hour. The Tennessean was crude of manner, but then, so had Lincoln been. And Johnson like Lincoln was a living embodiment of the "work ethic." He was a Southerner with deep-seated resentment for the planter class and slavery. Johnson had risen from a tailor shop in Greenville, Tennessee, to the offices of alderman, mayor, state representative, state senator, governor, United States Representative, United States Senator, military governor, Vice-President, and now President. Political education Johnson had.

Not immediately apparent were the qualities which doomed his Administration. The new President had a finely tuned sense of righteousness, and he proved to be not merely stubborn, but intransigent, when his conception of right was challenged. Johnson, too, revered the Constitution and even in so novel a situation as Reconstruction tended to construe the Constitution strictly. Finally Johnson's personal manner seemed calculated to win enemies. He was fond of bombastic speeches and spread invective freely in public and private.

Johnson, the President, appropriated the essentials of Lincoln's program for Reconstruction. In a series of proclamations Johnson offered amnesty to common ex-Confederates who took the oath of allegiance and promised liberality toward those leaders, civil and military, whom he required to petition directly to him for pardon. Johnson did add one category to Lincoln's list of those who had to petition for pardon—anyone owning property worth more than $20,000. Theoretically this gave the President authority to strike a blow at the Old South's economic elite and potentially to redistribute Southern wealth and power. Yet Johnson was content with a symbolic blow to planter pride and issued pardons freely to those who seemed contrite enough to ask for them.

Like Lincoln, Johnson expected the Southern states in convention to renounce secession, accept all Federal legislation passed since 1860, abolish slavery, and repudiate Confederate currency and debts. Until these conventions were held, Johnson appointed provisional governments. And after the conventions, the states were to ratify their work by popular referendum. Then the Southern states could elect their own executives, legislators, and representatives to the Federal Congress. The legislatures were then to ratify the Thirteenth Amendment (forbidding slavery) and resume normal relations with the rest of the Union.

The President alone assumed responsibility for seeing that Southerners acted in good faith. And indeed good faith was all Johnson asked. He convinced himself that the "good people," the common white folk (like himself), would set things right. And about the black South the President seemed to care little, if at all. Slavery was dead, and that was sufficient. If white Southerners rejected equality for black Southerners, that was their prerogative. Indeed Johnson shared may of the racist assumptions soon to surface in the South and elsewhere.

Johnson and his restoration formula had their chance. From April 15, when Johnson became President, until December, 1865, Congress was in recess. During that period every Southern state except Texas complied with Johnson's program. When Congress reassembled the President announced that Reconstruction was complete. Despite Johnson's pronouncement, questions remained.

Had the South in fact reconstructed itself?

Would Congress accept the fait accompli?

The South's Answer

Travelers and Federal officials in the South confirmed the fact that Southerners had in 1865 accepted defeat. Many farmers and planters hired freedmen to make the 1865 crop. Chaos there was. But to some degree the old order reasserted itself. "Hard times" for one Richmond belle consisted of "company, and no extra servants—for one entire month we had no dining-room servant, and we girls had to change the soup and fish plates etc. I tell you I would never be a Yankee woman, were I to try."

Southerners swore allegiance to the Union in droves, and by September, 1867, President Johnson had issued 13,500 special pardons. Southern states, too, held their conventions and did the prescribed constitution-rewriting. It was all so swift and orderly; and that was the problem.

For the most part wealth remained in the hands of the same class (and some of the same individuals) as before. Political leadership went to some Old Whigs, some Democrats; white conservatives all. Service to the Confederacy was the common denominator in this "new" leadership. Georgia even returned Confederate Vice-President Alexander H. Stephens to the United States Senate.

State legislatures worked quietly to restore the old racial patterns. "Black codes," as they were called, strongly resembled the old slave codes and in some cases all but reinstituted the "peculiar institution." Vagrancy laws provided fines and imprisonment for a long list of "criminals" such as those who "misspend what they earn" or "neglect all lawful business." If this were not enough, the Mississippi legislature made vagrants of all freedmen without a job on the second Monday of January, 1866. Labor contract laws and apprentice laws had the effect of restoring slavery in all but name. Penal codes worked to keep the freedmen in their pre-war "place." "Convicts" were liable for hire to anyone who would pay their fine for the shortest period of service. Some states were less crass than others; but all made legal concessions to white superiority.

Under Johnson's Reconstruction the South indeed rejoined the Union. But contrition was rare. There is an old story of one of Stonewall Jackson's veterans who asked when he took the oath of allegiance to the Union, "Does that make me a Yankee?" Told it did, the man winked and said, "Boy, didn't Old Jack beat hell out of us in the Valley of Virginia?" Economic, political, and racial mores remained. And Southerners were proud, rather than guilty, about their rebellion. All of this seemed calculated to raise the wrath of Congress.

Yet however bigoted white Southerners were toward the freedmen, and however foolish they were to elect ex-Confederate generals to political office, these actions were predictable, even natural. Racial phobias were general in nineteenth-century America. The large numbers of black Southerners fed the fears and threatened the dominance of white Southerners. To reject Confederate memories, Southerners would have had to admit a massive guilt and ignore the blood sacrifice of war. Planters continued to plant because planting was what they knew. And the planter civilization, with its trappings, however, tattered and defeated, could hardly be expected to commit suicide.

Congress' Answer

On December 4, 1865, Congress assembled for the first time in nearly nine months. The legislative branch of government had, like the executive branch, given considerable attention to the problem of restoring and reconstructing the South. Charles Sumner, Senator from Massachusetts, had long ago contended that Congress, not the President, should have charge of the reconstruction process. Sumner argued that the Confederate states had "committed suicide" in regard to their status in the Union. Thus Congress could and should have control of these states in the same way that Congress dealt with territories of the United States. Pennsylvania Representative Thaddeus Stevens, wartime Chairman of the House Ways and Means Committee, argued that the Southern states were "conquered provinces." As such they were solely at the mercy of Congress, and the most merciful thing Congress could do was overturn the entire social, economic, and political bases of Southern civilization.

The views of Sumner and Stevens were extreme even in wartime. Nevertheless Congress in July, 1864, adopted its own Reconstruction program in the form of a bill sponsored by Senator Benjamin F. Wade of Ohio and Representative Henry Winter Davis of Maryland. The Wade-Davis Bill gave Congress direction over the reconstruction process and required that a majority of each Southern state's electorate take a loyalty oath before the state could hold a convention or elect state officials. Lincoln, as we have seen, gave the Wade-Davis Bill a pocket veto (i.e., took no action upon the bill and therefore it died). At the time of Lincoln's assassination, the question of who should control the reconstruction process was still unanswered.

Johnson, acting in Congress' absence, hoped he had settled the matter once and for all. He probably fretted a bit about the South's response to his terms; "his people," common Southern men, had not exactly asserted themselves and wrested leadership from the old aristocracy. Nevertheless Johnson had announced his terms, and Southerners had responded. The President was not disposed to repudiate the results of his own program. Congress had different ideas. Before the legislators even heard Johnson's opening message, they took up the matter of the Southern delegations and refused to seat them. Congress then appointed a Joint Committee on Reconstruction (or Joint Committee of Fifteen) to investigate the would-be Southern representatives and by extension the entire fabric of Johnsonian Reconstruction in the South.

American folklore has it that the Radical Republicans soon took charge of Reconstruction and acted in a highhanded manner toward the South for motives of greed or meanness or both. In truth, the first Reconstruction Congress contained a small minority of "card-carrying" Radicals. Stevens, Sumner, Wade, and Senator Zachariah Chandler of Michigan were the best known among them. Democrats and Conservative Republicans were small factions. The great majority of legislators were moderate Republicans who wanted nothing so much as to do the "right thing." And in December 1865, the "right thing" seemed to be anything but what the President and the Southerners were doing.

If the South's reaction to Johnson's reconstruction plan was natural, the North's response in turn was predictable. The President's "reconstructed" South jeopardized Union war aims and all but sneered at Union peace hopes. This was not a reconstructed but a resurrected South. The Southern delegates to Congress were ready to reopen the old sectional issues of the 1850s. The Southern states had made a mockery of the letter and spirit of emancipation. The South seemingly had not even considered the question of the rights of free black people, save in the negative. Under the "black codes" the freedmen appeared anything but free. Those people even had the gall to take pride in their late treason.

Accordingly the moderate majority in Congress dealt with the Johnson scheme of Reconstruction. The Joint Committee on Reconstruction called witnesses, and those witnesses described the Southern scene for the most part in biased, but not altogether untrue, terms. While the South's dirty linen was being displayed in the committee room and newspaper accounts, Congress attempted to legislate on behalf of the freedmen.

In February, 1866, Congress passed a new Freedmen's Bureau Bill. The bureau began nearly a year earlier as a temporary body designed to assist black Southerners in their transition from slavery to freedom. The new bill proposed to give the bureau power to try cases in which blacks were denied their rights as free men. The idea was to combat abuses associated with the "black codes" and to assure the freedmen of such elementary rights as protection from false arrest and just payment of wages. President Johnson vetoed the bill on the grounds that Southerners were not represented in Congress and that the process of trial by military commission prescribed by the bill violated "due process." Eventually (July, 1866) Congress overrode the President's veto.

To make clearer the status of freedom, Congress in March passed a Civil Rights Act which granted citizenship and equal rights to all native Americans (except, ironically enough, Indians). Federal courts, Freedmen's Bureau officials, and other government officers were responsible for enforcement of the bill. Once again Johnson exercised his veto prerogative, again explaining that Southern states were unrepresented in Congress and that Congress had no power to define citizenship and rights in the states.

Then in June the Joint Committee on Reconstruction had its say. Southern delegations to Congress were formally denied seats, and Reconstruction was declared the province of Congress. The committee also framed the Fourteenth Amendment to the Constitution. The Fourteenth Amendment ensured the citizenship of all persons born in the United States and guaranteed due process equal protection of law to all citizens. The second section undid the "three-fifths" method of counting slaves for the determination of state representation in Congress. It also provided for a reduction of a state's representation should that state deny the right to vote (except for a crime) to any male over 21 years old. The third section barred ex-Confederates from Federal or state office-holding (but permitted them to vote) unless two-thirds of each house of Congress should lift the bar. Finally the fourth section recognized the validity of the Union's war debt and pension promises, forbade payment of Confederate or Confederate state debts, and invalidated any claims for compensation for slave property.

The Fourteenth Amendment put the Union on record for civil rights and black suffrage. The section barring ex-Confederates from political office sounds vindictive and was to some degree. Yet it was also a compromise with those who would have denied suffrage to the rebels. The amendment, like the Freedmen's Bureau Bill and the Civil Rights Act, rested upon political assumptions. Make sure that the freedmen get "fair play" at the ballot box and in the court house. Keep the "bad men," ex-Confederates, out of leadership positions. Then all will be well for the nation's moral stance and for the Republican Party—so the majority in Congress hoped. These measures all but guaranteed a Republican South for some time to come.

The Peoples' Answer

Soon after the Fourteenth Amendment passed both Houses and went to the states for ratification, Congress adjourned. Then in the summer and fall of 1866 the battle over Reconstruction began in earnest. The off-year elections provided the test. A prudent President might have framed a compromise among the South, Congress, and himself. As historian Rembert Patrick suggests, Johnson might have convinced the South to accept the Fourteenth Amendment and Congress to receive this acceptance as proof of good faith. Such a compromise might have brought an end to Reconstruction then and there. But the President was piqued by the tactics of the radicals, angry that the moderates were deserting him and convinced that he had been right all along. Therefore he chose to take his case to the people and make the Congressional elections his vindication.

The South, too, was in no mood for compromise. Fearing black suffrage and feeling no shame over the Lost Cause, Southern legislatures (except in Tennessee) rejected the Fourteenth Amendment out of hand. To well-meaning people in the North the rejection of the Fourteenth Amendment looked like just what it was, defiance on the part of the vanquished. Yet Southerners were not the only ones opposed to the amendment. The President also, loudly and publicly, was denouncing the amendment and its framers.

More dramatic than the South's rejection of Congress' terms were the major black-white confrontations which occurred in southern cities. In Memphis an altercation between black troops and white police ended in three days of white rioting. The whites swarmed into black neighborhoods and burned and killed. When troops finally halted the violence, 47 blacks were dead and 80 injured. Only one white man was injured. Some Southern newspapers gloated over the "victory," and, many Northern editors filled their columns with stories of raped black women and murdered black children.

New Orleans, too, was a scene of racial violence in July. White policemen and a white mob attacked a political meeting of blacks and white Unionists. Relentless, vicious attacks on the part of the police and their allies killed about 40 people and wounded 200 more. Again national publicity convinced Northerners that mob violence was the South's answer to black aspirations for justice.

The conduct of the President did nothing to alleviate the growing bitterness. Johnson took the stump from one end of the country to the other defending his Reconstruction. For a little while he kept making the same speech at each stop. But the campaign techniques which had worked in antebellum Tennessee were ludicrous when major newspapers printed his speech, and his hearers knew that he had said the same thing many times before. Johnson's audiences turned sour, and the President responded in kind. He ceased merely to explain and defend his policies; he began attacking his enemies in such clever ways as suggesting the hanging of Thaddeus Stevens. Johnson simply could not rise above the rough and tumble brand of politics which had served him so well in another time and place. His tour and his campaign on behalf of his Reconstruction all but doomed his program.

When the votes were counted, the North had given Congress a mandate to proceed. The Republicans had better than a two-third's majority in both houses and the governorship of every Northern State.

The Radical view of reconstruction was ascendent in the hands of the Moderates; the President on the run. When the new Congress met in early 1867, Reconstruction would begin in earnest.

Many Southerners wondered in the coming months why the Yankees still hated them so. And they were sincere in their wonderment. Believing that black people were biologically inferior to white; like the majority of nineteenth-century Americans, they looked upon black suffrage and civil rights as punishment and degradation. They could not repudiate the Lost Cause without destroying themselves in their own eyes. And the old aristocracy clung to economic and political power for the same reasons any class does. Southerners simply did not realize the consequences of their defeat. They believed that they had been beaten in a struggle for separation. That was only part of the answer.

In the North people saw Reconstruction as their opportunity to reap the fruits of the war effort. The Union was not just an amalgam of states. Just bringing Southerners back into Congress and delivering mail to Yazoo City, Mississippi, did not constitute Reconstruction. The Union was ideals and reform. The South must become like the North, a place where honest toil yields reward. The "American dream" must become a Southern dream, too. The planter civilization, the sick chivalry, and "phony" ideas of honor must go. Put the idle rich to work, for their own good. Rebellion was sin; Southerners must realize that. The nation must unite in more than name.

Just as slavery had been a part of nearly every issue before the war, the condition of the freedmen, either substantively or symbolically, pervaded the Northern mind in Reconstruction. Freedmen were in a sense wards of the Union. Although few whites cared deeply about black suffrage and equal rights, they came to believe abstractly in the basic justice of these goals (for the South, at least). Uplifting black people somewhere else was the duty of a reforming people and a method of making basic changes in Southern society.

Victory was the mandate for restructuring the South in the North's image. If Northern people needed any proof of need to reorder Southern civilization, Southerners themselves supplied that proof in 1865–66. Consequently, Northern voters gave to Congress and the Radical Republicans the mandate to get on with the work of Reconstruction.

Abraham Lincoln visits conquered Richmond.

Black troops muster out.

Freedom! Black family reaches Union lines.

Andrew Johnson.

Charles Sumner, Massachusetts Senator.

Hiram Revels, Mississippi Senator.

John R. Lynch, Mississippi Congressman.

Thaddeus Stevens, Pennsylvania Congressman.

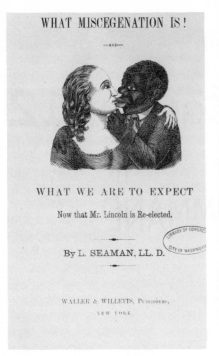

"What miscegenation is" (Racist cartoon).

"This is White Man's Government."

"The Union as it was."

"Shall we call home our troops?"

189

CONGRESS 12 IN COMMAND

Thad Stevens was in a hurry. Stevens was an old man in poor health, and he had a dream. His dream was a South made over. When Congress reassembled in January, 1867, Stevens knew that the Radicals in coalition with the moderates had the votes and hoped that Congress had the will to punish treason and to remold the South from the ground up. His fear was that he would not live to see his dream become reality. Thus he pursued his dream with the zeal of a man possessed.

Reconstruction Acts

Congress listened to President Johnson's opening address, a long ramble defending his actions on Reconstruction, and then got down to the business of putting the unrepentant South and the impotent President in their respective places. Thaddeus Stevens introduced in the House a bill to impose martial law in the South until such time as the states rewrote their constitutions, provided for universal male suffrage, and ceased attacking black people. He argued that troops were essential to preserve the lives and property of blacks and loyal whites in the South. The moderate Republicans first balked at military rule, but Democrats switched sides on moderating amendments in an effort to produce a bill so harsh that it was certain to fail. Then the House moderates responded to the call to action and passed the bill of Indianan George Julian providing for military rule in the South. In the Senate, passage of a similar bill produced a Republican caucus and a compromise committee headed by moderate Senator John Sherman of Ohio. Sherman, brother of General William T., hammered out an acceptable compromise.

The First Reconstruction Act became law on March 2, after Congress went through the formality of overriding the President's veto. The act began with the assumption that no legal governments existed in the South and thus divided the region into five military districts. Each district commander had the obligation and authority to preserve law, order, and property. Each Southern state was to call a constitutional convention. The convention was to draft a state constitution which enfranchised all male citizens regardless of race. Then the state was to elect governors and legislators. The new legislature at its first meetings had to ratify the Fourteenth Amendment. Only after the Fourteenth Amendment was a part of the Constitution would Congress declare the state reconstructed by admitting its Senators and Representatives. At this time the troops would leave, and normal relations with the rest of the Union would commence.

Two supplemental Reconstruction Acts passed in March and July clarified the authority of the military and spelled out the meaning of "ex-Confederate." The intent of Congress was to remove from the constitution-making process all Southerners who in any way, actively or passively, supported the Rebellion. Nevertheless, Congress did not presume to deny the vote to ex-Confederates once the new state constitutions went into effect.

One very good reason for imposing military rule on the South by law was the action of the Supreme Court in the case *Ex parte Milligan.* The court held that martial law was invalid while civil courts were operative. When Southerners hastened to test the constitutionality of military rule, the Court retreated, at least from the letter of *Ex parte Milligan,* by refusing to hear the cases (*Mississippi* v. *Johnson* and *Georgia* v. *Stanton*). And in *Texas* v. *White* the Court affirmed that the Union was perpetual and that secession had never in fact happened.

Predictably Johnson vetoed the Reconstruction Acts and despaired at what he considered the submission of the Supreme Court to the will of Congress. The President was indeed as skillful in his opposition to Congressional Reconstruction as he had been inept at Presidential Reconstruction. His veto messages made embarrassing points. Many Northern states still denied suffrage to black men. Thus Congress was operating a double standard by making black suffrage a condition for reconstruction. The North needed to set its house in order before attempting to cleanse the South. As a result of the President's barbs, some Northern legislatures did hasten to comply with the conditions imposed upon the South.

Johnson also maintained his constitutional integrity by living up to the letter of the Reconstruction Acts (as he interpreted them). He dispatched 20,000 troops into the South and appointed generally capable officers to command the five military districts. Yet the President sniped at Congressional policy whenever possible. There was no way in which the President could heal the breach between himself and the moderate/radical majority in Congress.

Economic Reconstruction

As we have seen a number of Radical Republicans collaborated in the fight for black suffrage and civil rights. Stevens was only one among several (Sumner, Wade, Julian and others) who sought to purify Southern politics and give the black man power with which to protect his interests. Stevens, however, almost single-handedly championed the cause of economic restructuring in the South. He pressed for high tariffs and taxes on exported cotton. His idea was to break the planters and force the South into a more diversified economy. Congress as a whole probably had less exalted motives. The South as a colonial appendage of the Northern economy was not the kind of goal one could talk about. Still, this was the way things worked out.

In March of 1867 Stevens introduced a bill providing for the confiscation of all Southern estates worth more than $5,000. He proposed to divide these lands among the freedmen (40 acres each) and sell any excess to give each freedmen $100 with which to build a house. If there were money left over Stevens proposed to use it to pay damage claims of loyal Southern whites and then the pensions of Northern soldiers.

Significantly, Steven's confiscation scheme never received serious consideration in Congress. He sought to punish the South, and that was all right. He wanted to remake Southern society, and that was fine, too, up to a point. But Stevens overstepped the North's ideological bounds when he demanded wholesale tampering with private property. The Republicans were willing to demand judgment for sin and to reform the

South (as long as the South continued to serve the interests of Northern industrial capitalism). They were not willing to undermine free enterprise and laissez-faire capitalism. If the Southern black is to have land, said the North in essence, let him earn it in the open marketplace.

Congress had in June, 1866, opened public lands in the South to black homesteaders. This far Congress would go. But confiscation was too much. In fact the black people who settled on abandoned acres at Port Royal, South Carolina, and on the plantations of Jefferson Davis and his brother Joseph, at Davis Bend, Mississippi, were soon to lose their titles in one way or another. When the ideals of the Puritan conflicted with those of the Yankee in Reconstruction, the morality of capitalism usually triumphed. Nor should this be surprising. We have long realized that the Northern world-view combined commitments to the work ethic, laissez-faire capitalism, romantic reform, and national righteousness. We cannot expect Reconstruction, a summary statement of this world view, to repudiate any one part of this ideology to accomplish another.

Impeachment

Southerners were not the only people in need of redemption at the hand of Congress. Once the Republican Radicals had dealt with the South, they turned their attention to President Johnson. Stevens especially pursued the President's downfall. Johnson was no longer any kind of obstruction to Republican legislation; the majority in Congress had the votes to override his vetoes. Some in Congress did believe that the President had tried to undermine the military rule in the South. One of Johnson's major crimes was pride. The President was down; but he refused to quit. And he kept denouncing Congressional policies and leaders. He continued vetoing bills and undermining the spirit of the law. How could the government carry out so major a reform as Reconstruction with so recalcitrant an executive? The man was in the way and out of step; he must be brought low and removed. If there were no substance involved, symbol would suffice.

The Tenue of Office Act provided the excuse. The Act passed, over Johnson's veto, the same day as the First Reconstruction Act, March 2, 1867. Even before that time a number of men and committees had been investigating the President in search of grounds for impeachment (Ben Butler spent considerable time trying to uncover a link between Johnson and John Wilkes Booth). The Tenue of Office Act said that the Senate must pass on the dismissal of any official whose appointment required the confirmation of that body. This, of course, applied to Cabinet members. But the act specifically excluded Cabinet holdovers from a previous

Administration (except during the first month of the new Administration).

Johnson decided to test the act's constitutionality and rid himself of an odious Cabinet officer at the same time. In August, 1867, the President suspended Edwin M. Stanton. As Secretary of War, Stanton had served Lincoln well; for a time, too, Stanton worked harmoniously with Johnson. However, Stanton was irascible at best, and when he "went over" to the Radicals, Johnson decided to replace him. The President appointed Ulysses S. Grant ad interim to Stanton's post. Grant, however, soon realized that he was caught in the middle of a potential showdown between the President and Congress and bowed out. Johnson then offered the War Office to a number of other men before he found one, General Lorenzo Thomas, who would take it. Stanton barricaded himself in his office and had Thomas arrested. Ultimately the Radicals convinced Stanton to submit to removal so that Congress could act on the matter before Johnson got it into the courts.

Accordingly, on February 24, 1868, John Covode of Pennsylvania offered a resolution in the House impeaching the President. The House, which acts as a grand jury in Presidential impeachment proceedings, passed the Covode Resolution 126–47. About a week later the House adopted 11 specific articles on impeachment. Presented by George S. Boutwell of Massachusetts, the charges boiled down to two issues: Johnson had violated the Tenue of Office Act (as well as the Command of the Army Act—a law requiring the President to communicate with the army only through the general in chief), and the President had displayed open contempt for Congress by not enforcing the First Reconstruction Act properly and by attacking Congressmen in his speeches.

These charges were strained at best. The President was attempting to test the constitutionality of the Tenue of Office Act. Indeed he had not even broken that law. Stanton was a Lincoln appointee and thus exempt from the provisions of the act. True, Johnson had said some nasty things about his political enemies; but his invective seldom equaled that of the last Tennessean President, Andrew Jackson. And Johnson, consciously at least, was meticulous about enforcing the First Reconstruction Act. The impeachment added up to an open political vendetta; the Radicals were going to "get" Johnson. And they almost did.

The Constitution provides that after a President is impeached by the House, he be tried before the Senate. Only if two-thirds of the Senate vote to convict him, shall he be removed from office. On March 7, 1868, the Senate chamber became in essence a courtroom. Chief Justice of the Supreme Court Salmon Chase presided as judge. To Chase's credit, he acted with considerably more impartiality than the Radicals would have liked.

The Senators took the prescribed oath to "do impartial justice"—Ben Wade, who as President pro tem of the Senate would have assumed the Presidency in case of conviction, along with the rest. Wade was so confident about the result of the trial, he had even picked part of his Cabinet. Ben Butler, who held the "shadow" portfolio of Secretary of State, also swore to "do impartial justice." In contrast with the cynicism of Wade and Butler, Charles Sumner viewed the proceeding as a political act, yes, but an act which was the last great blow against slavery.

Whether individual senators favored ideals, or "place" or some combination of the two, the decision depended upon votes. William M. Evarts, the President's chief council, made a good case for acquittal. Still, the Republican Party had the votes to convict; 42 of the 54 Senators were Republicans, and 36 votes would do it. The "jury" voted on the eleventh article of impeachment on May 16; the result was 35–19 for conviction, one vote short. Immediately the Senate recessed, and the Radicals went to work on the seven recalcitrant Republicans (Nathan F. Dixon, James R. Doolittle, William P. Fessenden, Joseph S. Fowler, James W. Grimes, Edmund G. Ross, and Lyman Trumbull). When the Senate sat again on May 26, Justice Chase called the vote on the first article of impeachment. The seven renegades held firm, again the count was 35–19, still one vote short of conviction. The Radicals tried again on the second article with identical results and then moved to adjourn.

Johnson had escaped the ignominy of removal. From hindsight the impeachment seems vindictive and not a little shabby. At the time, however, political passions ruled. That such a man as Sumner should favor impeachment, provides a clear index of the emotional temper of the time.

In the months which followed the impeachment trial, the principal protagonists made ready to leave the scene. Stevens had been in declining health for some time. During the trial he was ill, but attended the sessions faithfully, as though he hoped his sheer intensity might aid the prosecution. In August he died. Nevertheless, in the fall elections the voters of Stevens' district returned his corpse to Congress. Andrew Johnson served his time quietly and gratefully returned to Tennessee in March of 1869. He, too, was returned to national office, the Senate in 1874.

Congressional Reconstruction in the South

The first problem in dealing with the South during Reconstruction is that of time. We generally think of the Reconstruction period as lasting from 1865 to 1877. However, as we have seen military rule did not begin until March, 1867. And several states fulfilled the conditions for readmission in just over a year. No Southern state remained out of the Union beyond 1870. Perhaps the crucial factor was the return of "home rule"— defined as the re-establishment of white, conservative power. Again, several states had "redeemed" themselves by 1870, and only three retained Republican governments to 1877.

State	Restored to Union	Return of White Conservative Rule
Tennessee	1866	1869
North Carolina	1868	1870
South Carolina	1868	1877
Georgia	1868, 1870 *	1871
Florida	1868	1877
Alabama	1868	1874
Louisiana	1868	1877
Arkansas	1868	1874
Virginia	1870	1870
Mississippi	1870	1876
Texas	1870	1874

* Georgia was restored then removed again when whites expelled blacks from the state legislature.

The point of all this is that in many ex-Confederate states Radical Reconstruction was a relatively brief period. As it happened Radical Reconstruction lasted long enough to foster lasting bitterness among whites, but not long enough to spawn sufficient political power among blacks.

The degree of military rule also needs clarification. Only 20,000 troops went into the South. Obviously these were not enough to garrison every street corner and country crossroad. And many of the white soldiers displayed racial prejudice toward freedmen whose rights and lives they were supposed to be protecting. The "army of occupation" was spread rather thin, and its influence was decidedly mixed.

"Black Reconstruction," too, requires comment. The freedmen, as we have seen, did not as many whites feared seek wholesale reprisals against their former masters. Indeed most instances of violence (like the riots in Memphis and New Orleans) were cases of whites attacking blacks.

Black Southerners saw Reconstruction as their opportunity to enter the American mainstream, and many dreamed the "American dream." Education was the essential first step, and Southern blacks embraced any chance to become literate. Public education had not made much headway in the Old South. Thus schools were important priorities of Reconstruction legislatures and of the Freedmen's Bureau. Indeed many of the "carpetbaggers" (Northerners who went South after the war) were Yankee school marms, bent on teaching the "three R's" to black Southerners.

"Black Reconstruction" implies black political power in the South. Yet in only one state, South Carolina, did blacks ever outnumber whites in the legislature. Blacks did band together in the Union League to strive for concerted action. And black voters placed many Reconstruction legislators, black and white, in power. Nevertheless, racially the South remained for the most part under white leadership. Moreover the assumption that black voters represented a single-minded bloc is oversimplified. Where the Republican Party dominated in the South, black men opposed each other, as well as whites, in primary races. Getting elected was possible for black men during Radical Reconstruction. But it involved more than herding fellow blacks to the polls to rubber-stamp a candidacy.

The power of black votes gave political office to some very naive men in the South, and to some knaves as well. Yet the opportunity afforded by Reconstruction for black men to hold high office uncovered talented black leaders. Blanche K. Bruce, elected to the United States Senate from Mississippi in 1875, was a black cotton planter educated at Oberlin College. He served his full term in the Senate and held appointive positions in Republican administrations long after the party had need of *visible* black officials. Hiram R. Revels was another black Mississippi Senator. He served an unexpired term in 1870–71 and then broke with the Mississippi Republican organization. In contrast to the racial stereotype, Revels was instrumental in returning the Democrats to power in Mississippi. He criticized the Republicans as "unprincipled adventurers" and was proud that blacks had cast many of the ballots which expelled them from office in 1875. In Revels' case at least, a black Southerner asserted his Southernness as well as his blackness.

A number of black men served in the House of Representatives during Reconstruction, and many more in state governments. For the most part the black leadership in the South was no better and no worse than white leadership. Reconstruction simply brought men of ability to the fore without the political handicap of race. Francis L. Cardozo for example was a man of ability and integrity educated at the University of Glasgow. He was Secretary of State and Treasurer of South Carolina. Significantly, Cardozo was an honest man in one of the two blatantly corrupt Reconstruction state governments. Such a man would hardly have risen to prominence in "normal" times.

Reconstruction brought many "new people" into positions of power in the South. Some fit the stereotypical image of "carpetbagger." They came South for personal gain and used a unique political situation to gain power and pelf. Henry Clay Warmoth, Governor of Louisiana, defended his administration by noting, "corruption is the fashion down here." Warmoth left the governorship with a comfortable "stake," settled down in his adopted state and became a sugar planter. In contrast, Mississippi Governor Adelbert Ames was scrupulously honest, but fled the state as soon as his term ended. The problem with the label "carpetbagger" is one of definition. Many Northern people looked upon the South as a land of opportunity (for honest as well as shady enterprise). And many moved South as "missionaries" of the Yankee ideology. In fact those Northerners who did not have selfish or cynical motives in moving South (the majority) were in a real sense trying to spread the gospel of Yankeeism.

The institutional outpost of the North's hopes for Reconstruction was the Freedmen's Bureau, headed by General Oliver Otis Howard. The bureau was supposed to help ex-slaves through the first years of freedom. Howard began his work with high hopes. He planned to use the bureau to redistribute Southern land, to educate black people, and to keep a watchful eye on white employers of black labor. Howard's ambitions were not consistent with reality. Congress never appropriated enough money to carry out land reform. The bureau did build schools, and it distributed food and clothing to destitute blacks. But in the end the Freedmen's Bureau served more as an agency of pacification. It served the ultimate interests of white paternalism and by putting its stamp of approval on labor contracts and sharecropping arrangements helped to bind many black Southerners again to the land. The bureau was defunct by 1871 and on the way down from 1868. Investigations ordered by President Johnson charged that some officers of the bureau were guilty of graft. Some were. Yet Howard, scrupulously honest himself, was faced with a "no-win" situation. He never had enough funds to do the job he set out to do. And his staff too often spent their time doing such things as— registering voters and paying the pensions due black soldiers—important tasks, but something less than restructuring Southern society. Finally the Freedmen's Saving Bank failed, and its depositers lost the money they had hoped to use to buy land and achieve economic freedom. Once again the free labor capitalism of Yankeedom came up short. The North, Congress in the case of the Freedmen's Bureau, was willing to sponsor political reform and education, but when pressed the Radicals could not endorse economic radicalism.

What about the Southerners who held power during Reconstruction—the "scalawags." Reconstruction mythology holds that Southerners who took part in the Republican governments of the South were apostates and traitors. Indeed some were. But once again the stereotype is inadequate. Perhaps the most incredible Southern politician, ever, was Joseph E. Brown of Georgia. Brown was a power in Georgia before the war and governor during the Confederacy. When the war ended Brown joined the Republicans and filled his pockets during the period of Republican rule (as superintendent of a state-owned railroad). Then in

1871 Brown forsook the Republicans, rejoined the Democrats, and shared credit for "redeeming" the state for white conservatives.

Other prominent "scalawags" were a little more consistent. James Lusk Alcorn (Mississippi) had been a leading Whig and thus was somewhat at home with Republicans. Yet Alcorn had served in the Confederate army and fought for the old "cause." North Carolinian William W. Holden had been a Democrat but boarded the Republican bandwagon during Reconstruction and ran a competent administration. His "apostasy" consisted primarily of trying to combat the Ku Klux Klan with the state militia. Parson Brownlow of Tennessee was an old Unionist whose hatred of the Confederacy was only exceeded by his hatred of blacks. The point is that "scalawags" were a mixed bag at best.

The sum total of all these elements in Southern Reconstruction—blacks, "carpetbaggers," Freedmen's Bureau, and "scalawags"—varied from state to state. In South Carolina the legislature was a very bad joke. It incurred a fantastic state debt and made some people very rich. The Louisiana regime, too, was corrupt almost to the core. In contrast, Viriginia never had bona fide Republican rule; the white conservatives regained control of the state as soon as Congress restored Virginia to the Union. Republican legislatures did build schools and introduce widespread public education to the South. They also financed vitally needed railroad construction. The cost of these advances was high. The tax burden involved in paying for rebuilt public facilities, schools, railroads and such lay heavy upon the already destitute South. Corruption and waste added to the financial woes of Southern states. Nevertheless, historians have recently made the point that corruption in Southern states was petty in comparison to operations like the Tweed Ring in New York City. Too, the "redeemer" governments in the post-Reconstruction South were not exactly distinguished for their honesty.

To understate enormously, the majority of white Southerners resented Reconstruction. More often than not black people were the chief objects of white resentment and frustrations. These frustrations involved more than race, but the black presence became a symbol of all that was wrong in the Reconstruction South. Resentment of Yankee "meddling" in Southern affairs found a convenient outlet in racism. And the ultimate expression of Southern racism was the Ku Klux Klan.

Confederate General Nathan Bedford Forrest and a few friends founded the Klan in 1866 in Pulaski, Tennessee. The Klan began as a social club whose members adopted regalia and ritual more or less as a joke. The organization spread and very soon used the mumbo jumbo and anonimity of Klan costumes to frighten and intimidate the blacks. Actually the Klan was only the largest and best known of a number of organizations whose members committed racial intimidation and violence for fun and profit. In 1869 Forrest, concerned that he had created a monster, disbanded the Klan and decried the violence of some of its "Klaverns." Unfortunately the Klan and similar organizations were already out of hand. Night riding, threats, and racial violence became weapons with which Southern whites struck back at Reconstruction—a kind of guerrilla warfare once rejected by the Confederacy. Most Southern whites probably disapproved of such tactics. Nevertheless the Klan seemed to many people an unpleasant but necessary method of restoring "home rule." Indeed the Klan did influence elections by frightening black voters away from the polls. And the mystique of Klansmen as agents of the old order and protectors of white womanhood still persists. The facts were that the Klan was an organization of terror and violence. Whatever was good about the Old South suffered mean perversion at the hands of its hooded "defenders."

In 1870 and 1871 Congress heard testimony about Southern terrorism and passed Ku Klux Klan Acts. These acts attacked the Klan and similar organizations because they threatened the enforcement of the Thirteenth and Fourteenth Amendments. Clearly, to maim or kill a person deprives him of his civil rights as defined by those amendments. Yet the Supreme Court eventually ruled that these acts interfered with the police powers of the states.

In the end Southerners "redeemed" themselves from Radical Reconstruction at the ballot box. Congress in 1872 passed the Amnesty Act which allowed all but a few hundred ex-Confederates to resume the right to vote and hold office. It then became a matter of time before white conservatives again seized political power. The bitterness of the white majority in the South about Reconstruction was deep and persistent. In the long run it proved tragic.

State-by-State Summary

In addition to the general comments made above on Congressional Reconstruction as a whole in the South, we need to take a quick look at each Southern state to examine Radical Reconstruction in action. Keep in mind that for the most part Southern states from 1865–1867 were in white conservative hands as a result of Presidential Reconstruction. The period of Radical/Congressional Reconstruction, which concerns us here, begins with the First Reconstruction Act, passed in March, 1867.

Tennessee

"Parson" William Gannaway Brownlow controlled the reconstruction process in Tennessee. He became provisional governor of the state when his predecessor, Andrew Johnson became Vice-President in 1865. Brownlow was an East Tennessee Unionist whose attitude toward black Tennesseeans was less than charitable. Indeed it would be difficult to say whom Brownlow hated more, Rebels or blacks.

Tennessee's reconstruction was the only Johnson reconstruction which survived Congressional scrutiny in 1867. Under Brownlow's guidance the legislature ratified the Fourteenth Amendment and provided for black suffrage without completely rewriting the state constitution. Conflict between Radicals and Conservatives in Tennessee was not so much social or racial, as it was political. Whigs and Unionists in the state used Reconstruction as a vehicle for carrying out a political vendetta against their old enemies, the Democrats and secessionists. "Brownlow's Militia," a kind of political army, controlled elections and enraged ex-Confederates. Somehow, amid this partisan wrangling, black Tennesseeans were left in the lurch.

In 1868 Brownlow resigned the governorship to enter the United States Senate. His successor De Witt C. Senter bolted the Brownlow-Radical party and joined with white conservatives to "redeem" the state.

North Carolina

In May, 1865, President Johnson appointed William W. Holden provisional governor of North Carolina. Like Brownlow in Tennessee Holden was a Union man and not inclined to look kindly upon opposition to his administration by ex-Confederates. And as in Tennessee, the primary political issue during Reconstruction was the governor's use of the state militia as a private army. Holden, however, used his militia to suppress activities of the Ku Klux Klan. Under Colonel George W. Kirk the militia was zealous to the point of sparking what came to be known as the "Holden-Kirk war," sporadic bushwacking between the militia and white conservatives.

Although Holden himself was an honest man, some around him used political office and favors to dishonest advantage. For example, Milton S. Littlefield of Maine and native North Carolinian George W. Swepson managed to bribe their way into $17,500,000 worth of state railroad bonds. When the pair were indicted in North Carolina, they fled to Florida and began railroad manipulations anew.

Congress restored North Carolina to the Union in June, 1868. In 1870 the Conservative Democrats secured control of the legislature and impeached Governor Holden for his use of the state militia. At this point Lieutenant Governor Todd R. Caldwell became Governor and simultaneously a Conservative. By 1876 Zebulon B. Vance, North Carolina's Confederate Governor, was again in the executive mansion.

Virginia

During the latter stages of the war Francis Pierpoint maintained a Unionist state government behind Federal lines in Alexandria. In 1865 the Pierpoint government moved to Richmond and functioned as the legitimate state regime. When Congress took over the reconstruction process in 1867, John M. Schofield, commander of Military District Number One, replaced Pierpoint with H. H. Wells. Virginia's constitutional convention met in 1868 and framed a Radical constitution; it enfranchised black Virginians and denied suffrage to anyone who had given aid or assent to the Confederacy. This disqualification clause caused enough resentment to defeat the constitution at the polls. Then in April, 1869, Congress authorized voters to reject a portion of their proposed constitution without defeating the entire document. Virginians voted again in July, 1869, and ratified the constitution without the disqualification clause. In January, 1870, Congress restored the state to the Union.

To understand what happened next, we need to examine the machinations of William Mahone. Mahone had served in the Confederate army and won the sobriquet "Hero of the Crater" for his leadership in that battle. When the war ended Mahone became involved in the Southside Railroad and in Republican politics. More precisely, he joined the Radicals in Virginia and used his influence to battle for state railroad subsidies against John W. Garrett and the Baltimore and Ohio. In 1868 Mahone supported Wells' election to the governorship; then in 1870 he sabotaged Wells' candidacy by nominating a black candidate to be Wells' running mate. Next Mahone switched sides and supported the conservative Democratic candidate Gilbert C. Walker.

Thus the gubernatorial election in 1870 became a battle of railroad interests as well as political philosophies. When the smoke cleared Walker, Mahone, the Southside Railroad, and the white conservatives had won. Virginia's "redemption" demonstrated the potential of combining economic self-interest and conservative rhetoric in Southern politics, an object lesson not lost on New South politicians.

Georgia

In June, 1868, Congress readmitted Georgia to the Union and George G. Meade withdrew Federal troops from the state. However, when the legislature met, white conservatives proceeded to expel black members on the grounds that the right of suffrage granted blacks in the new constitution did not extend to office-holding. Ex-Confederates replaced the blacks. Congress then took a hand in the situation, restored the black legislators, removed Georgians from Congress, and sent Meade and his troops back into Georgia. The state re-entered the Union for good in 1870. In the same year the white conservatives won control of both houses of the legislature, and in 1871 Radical Governor Rufus B. Bullock resigned in the face of impeachment proceedings over some ill-gotten railroad bonds.

Georgia's experience with so-called Radical Reconstruction, then, lasted only two years. In that time only one black man went to Congress from the state, and black Georgians in general made little or no headway in their quest for lasting political power. Georgia's "redeemers" used race and railroads, among other things, to usher in the New (?) South.

Texas

Texas voters, like Virginians, first rejected their rewritten constitution of 1868, then ratified the document without a clause disenfranchising ex-Confederates. Congress re-admitted the state to the Union in March, 1870. The Radical governor of Texas from 1869–1874 was E. J. Davis, an honest Unionist. Davis' fellow Republicans in the legislature were not so virtuous; nevertheless, amid some corruption the Texas legislature built roads, schools, and railroads and passed a state homestead law to benefit settlers (and speculators). Davis employed the state police with a heavy hand "to protect Union men" or "to harrass ex-Confederates" depending upon who told the story.

Upset over the activities of the police and over the stiff tax bills necessary to finance the legislature's program, white Conservatives in Texas struck back. A taxpayers' convention came to Austin in 1871 to vent its wrath. In 1872 the Democrats recaptured control of the legislature. And in 1873 Democrat Richard Coke defeated Davis in the gubernatorial election.

Davis contested the election, won in the courts, but lost in Washington. Coke assumed the governorship in 1874, and President Grant advised Davis to drop his challenge. Davis bowed to Coke's fait accompli and Grant's advice; Texas was "redeemed."

Arkansas

Congress restored Arkansas to the Union in June, 1868. Arkansans had framed a constitution which made black suffrage rights perpetual and required voters to take an oath acknowledging the "Civil and political equality of all men." President Johnson vetoed the restoration bill on the grounds that most Northerners could not in good conscience sign the Arkansas voters' oath. Congress overrode the veto.

Governor of Arkansas from 1868 to 1872 was Powell Clayton, a former cavalry general in the Union army. Clayton's regime became known for its excessive railroad bonds and repressive militia tactics. In 1872 open war (almost) broke out between supporters of the two candidates for governorship—reform-minded Republican moderate Joseph Brooks and Radical Republican Elisha Baxter. The "Brooks-Baxter war" ended when Baxter won the election; but the new governor then denied his supporters their expected spoils by opposing the issuance of any more railroad bonds. In 1874 white conservatives revived the Democratic Party and elected Augustus H. Garland governor. Garland and the Democrats "redeemed" Arkansas.

Alabama

Radical Reconstruction in Alabama turned upon race, legislative appropriations (for schools, primarily), and upon railroads. Of the three issues, railroad subsidization was perhaps the most significant. The North and South road, subsidiary of the Louisville and Nashville (L&N) Railroad, backed by August Belmont and Democratic financiers, did battle with the Alabama and Chattanooga Railroad, supported by Jay Cooke and Republican capital. The prize was iron ore in North Alabama around Birmingham, and both Republican and Democratic legislators sold their favors to eager bidders.

Amid the railroad wrangling, social concerns and political philosophy were largely rhetorical. In the aftermath of the Panic of 1873, began by the failure of Cooke's bank, the North and South line (L&N) won the railroad war and conservative Democrats won lasting control of the state government (Democrats captured the legislature in 1872). Thus Alabama "redemption" occurred in 1874.

Mississippi

Federal troops in Mississippi acquired more reputation for repressing the black majority than for restraining white Mississippians. In addition some white Mississippians found the military authority surprisingly accomodating; Edmund Richardson, for example, operated his enormous cotton plantations with the labor of Mississippi convicts and received $30,000 to cover the expense of "caring" for his errant fellow citizens.

Mississippi's Radical constitution first failed ratification by the voters then passed without a clause disfranchising ex-Confederates. Congress restored Mississippi to the Union in February, 1870.

The State's first Republican governor was James L. Alcorn, ex-Whig, delta planter. Alcorn tried to build an enduring Republican organization from white ex-Whigs like himself (estimates are that 25–30% of Mississippi's white voters joined the Republicans) and black moderates. As governor, Alcorn was progressive and "safe." The administration built and integrated public schools, founded a black university, sponsored a civil rights act, and opened state hospitals and asylums. Mississippi sent black men to Congress, and the legislature elected John R. Lynch Speaker of the House. Yet only 35 of 140 members of the first Reconstruction legislature were black, and Governor Alcorn relegated black men to relatively unimportant posts in his administration.

Alcorn's strategy foundered in the gubernatorial election of 1873. Black Mississippians resented their lack of real power; white Mississippians resented taxes needed to finance Alcorn's legislative program. Accordingly "carpetbagger" Adelbert Ames defeated Alcorn for the governorship and began trying to find jobs for blacks and to cut state spending at the same time. Ames was sincere and honest, but his well-intentioned administration was unpopular. Racial violence flared, and Ames' economy drive stalled. Even Mississippi's black United States Senator Hiram Revels decried the "adventurers" in his state.

By 1875 white conservatives were ready and able to assert their strength. Eschewing open violence (which when tried previously had led to the return of Federal troops), whites adopted what came to be called the "Mississippi Plan"—a blatant show of armed strength which usually stopped short of violence. Armed bands of whites paraded in the streets and engaged in target practice near black homes and farms. Taunts and threats heightened the intimidation of black and white Republicans. Economic coercion also swelled the Democratic count. Such tactics "redeemed" the state in the election of 1875, and the Democrats took control of Mississippi's government in 1876.

Florida

The racial climate in post-war Florida was especially volatile. Substantial black migration into the underpopulated state scared resident whites. As a result Florida's "black codes" were stringent, and white violence directed against blacks pervaded the entire Reconstruction era.

Harrison Reed, a "carpetbagger" from Wisconsin, was Florida's first Republican governor. Reed was an honest, naïve, moderate man. His regime was more conservative than anything else. Reed reserved the "plums" of state patronage for whites and assigned blacks near-menial tasks in his administration. Moreover Reed refused to suppress, or even to investigate outbreaks of white racial violence. He fell victim to Littlefield and Swepson's railroad schemes (the pair secured railroads valued at $1,500,000 for just over $300,000 and then floated $4,000,000 worth of state bonds) and persisted in his belief that they were basically honest men. Reed survived four attempts by the legislature to impeach him and retired from the governorship virtually broke in 1872.

Reed's successors were both moderate Republicans, Ossian B. Hart and Marcellus L. Stearns. When conservative Democrats won power in 1876, Florida was "redeemed;" it is doubtful whether most black Floridians noted the difference.

Louisiana

Louisiana was the only Southern state to disfranchise ex-Confederates. As a consequence white conservatives had greater difficulty regaining political control. Politics in the Bayou State have always been somewhat bizarre; Louisiana politics during Radical Reconstruction were downright incredible. Henry Clay Warmoth of Illinois was elected Governor in 1868. In league with President Grant's son-in-law, James F. Casey, and Federal Marshal Stephen B. Packard, Warmoth filled his own pockets and those of his political allies from a state lottery, among other things. Conflict during Warmoth's administration developed between blacks and whites in the state and between rival factions within the Republican Party. White conservatives encouraged both battles and tried to form an opposition party made up of ex-Whigs and moderate blacks. The Unification movement, as it was known, resembled Alcorn's coalition in Mississippi and suffered the same fate.

In 1872 Warmoth attempted to switch sides and supported a Democrat for governor. The Radical Republicans then impeached Warmoth, bought more vote counters than the ex-Governor, and "elected" William P. Kellog of Vermont as Governor. Violence, political and racial, continued; Kellog's militia, the United States army, and bands of men belonging to the White League fought pitched battles throughout the state.

Finally in 1876 both Packard and Democrat Francis R. T. Nicholls claimed the governorship and led rival administrations in the same state. When Federal troops left Louisiana in 1877, Packard's government fell, and the Democratic "redeemers" had the state to themselves. Amid corruption and violence in Reconstruction, Louisiana politics was an exciting and lucrative, if hazardous, profession. Yet, to understate, somehow Louisiana Republicans lost sight of the vision of a South made over.

South Carolina

South Carolina's Radical constitution was a model; it included such enlightened provisions as manhood suffrage, public schools, equal civil rights for all, and even a liberal divorce section. Unfortunately two of three Radical administrations in South Carolina were also models—of graft and corruption. Black South Carolinians made use of their new-found political power. A strong Union League organization mobilized black voters and elected black candidates (two Lieutenant Governors, two Senators, and seven Congressmen). Yet the Republican regimes spawned political corruption along with tangible achievements (roads, schools, and the like) and established no lasting basis of black economic power or civil equality.

The first Radical Governor, Robert K. Scott of Ohio, was impeached for corruption and inefficiency, and the second, F. J. Moses, was even worse. In 1874 Daniel H. Chamberlain of Massachusetts won the governorship and ran an honest administration. However white conservatives, following Mississippi's example, struck back. "Rifle clubs" and "Red Shirts" led by Wade Hampton and Martin Gary intimidated Republican voters and promised "protection" to black men who "voted right." In 1876 Hampton, once the state's richest planter and Confederate cavalry general, ran against Chamberlain for governor. Both men claimed victory and a Federal court decided in Chamberlain's favor. Nevertheless when Federal troops left South Carolina, so did Chamberlain. Hampton and the "redeemers" had won.

In light of the sketches of the Reconstruction process presented above, we can now add one more general observation about Radical rule in the South. In many instances the rhetoric of race and politics formed a rather thin veneer to cover a more fundamental issue—economic power. Some white Southerners seemed to have learned well the crasser lessons of Yankee capitalism. Perhaps Congress' Reconstruction policy was never more immediately successful than when it gave Southern entrepreneurs opportunities to wheel and deal with the new order of industrial capitalists. This, of course, was not exactly what the original Radical Republicans had in mind. Nevertheless some of those who met the challenge of rebuilding the Southern economy appropriated Yankee (in the pejorative sense of the word) business ethics and methods. And many of the Southern "redeemers" had more in common with Northern business/political interests then with the remnants of the ante bellum agrarian ideology in the South.

Reconstruction Winds Down

Congress in early 1869 tried to insure black suffrage in the South by passing the Fifteenth Amendment which forbade any state from depriving citizens of the vote because of race. Ratification of this amendment became a condition of reconstruction in those Southern states still outside the Union at that time.

The last gasp of Congressional Reconstruction came in 1875. Charles Sumner, trying to salvage some of the program's original idealism, sponsored the Civil Rights Act. The law forbade discrimination because of race in public places and on juries. By this time much of the original enthusiasm for remaking the South had waned, and many of the original ideologues had left the stage. Summer's bill became law, but the law became a dead letter at the hands of the Supreme Court in 1883. The Court ruled that the law applied to states, not individuals. After that civil rights became a farce at the hands of Southern state legislatures which passed the Jim Crow (segregation) laws denying equal rights in public accommodations and transportation.

The spirit and drive of Reconstruction as a crusade began to wane almost as soon as Congress had imposed its program and had its showdown with Andrew Johnson. The Republicans in 1868 elected Ulysses S. Grant President. Grant was a great general and a poor President. More important, he did not share the reforming zeal of some of the Radicals to cleanse the South. Perhaps a strong-willed President might have pressed the South; Grant had neither the motive nor the strength to lead the fight. He said many of the right things, but did little. He accepted the verdict rendered in Johnson's case and left Reconstruction mainly to Congress. However Congress was not equipped to supervise elections and stop night riding; these were tasks for the executive branch.

Grant's two terms in office are better remembered for their scandals than for anything else. The General was naïve and trusting. He looked upon the presidency as a reward and politics as alien territory. The same man who won the war by relentless, vigorous pressure on his enemies, was content to let things run their course in the South and pay little or no attention to the many hands in the public till.

The "age of enterprise" was in full flower. The energy of industrial capitalism broke free. Perhaps the North tired of trying to reform the South and took the South's word that it was reconstructed. Maybe the business of business absorbed the North's attention and energy. But also, the same ideological preconceptions which sparked the Reconstruction crusade in the final analysis dulled the effort to make the South over. Congress had rejected the notion of land reform and redistribution of wealth. The North was willing to dominate and exploit the South economically, but not to tamper with property rights. Work and wealth had moral connotations. The rhetoric of industry and capitalism made thrift and the work ethic a kind of secular gospel. Material success was evidence of secular "election." Later the Social Darwinists would codify the doctrine and speak of "natural selection" and "survival of the fittest." The point is that the same "mind" which demanded that men and labor be free, also insisted upon an unrestrained operation of the marketplace. And in the Reconstruction South of poor whites and penniless freedmen, laissez-faire capitalism, economic democracy, and racial justice proved mutually exclusive.

Formal Finale

Reconstruction died a political death. Perhaps it was only proper that blatant sectional hostility begin and end in presidential elections. In 1876 the Republicans were in serious trouble for the first time in a long time. The scandals associated with Grant's administrations had soured the public image of the party as savior of the Union. The liberal Republican faction and some old-line antagonisms within the party produced the nomination of Rutherford B. Hayes. The nominee was a new face with enough credentials (Hayes was an officer in the Federal army and Governor of Ohio) to claim the job. The Democrats nominated Samuel J. Tilden, Governor of New York, and based the rational level of their campaign upon reform and "clean" government. Both parties slung mud with reckless abandon and girded for a close finish.

When the returns came in, Tilden had apparently won a clear but close victory. He had 184 electoral votes for sure—one vote short of election. The Republicans, after almost conceding the election, then contested the validity of the vote count in four states, Florida, Oregon, Louisiana, and South Carolina. If Hayes could get all of the electoral votes involved, he would win. The issue then became, not how many votes each candidate received, but who should count those votes. The Constitution provided little guidance, and Congress agreed upon an Electoral Commission of 15 members to make the crucial counts. The Republicans controlled the Senate and ensured that party regulars filled three of the five positions on the commission allotted to that house. The Democrats, in control of the House of Representatives, filled the House quota with three Democrats and two Republicans. The remaining five members of the commission were to come from the Supreme Court. The understanding was that two Republicans and two Democrats on the Court would choose as the fifth justice (and fifteenth member of the commission) David Davis, an independent. Davis, however, was elected to the Senate in the interim, and Joseph P. Bradley, a Republican Justice, took Davis' place.

The Republicans had an eight to seven majority and used Bradley's vote to accept Republican results in each contested election and declare Hayes the winner. This could not happen, however, without cooperation from Southern Democrats; only their votes in concert with those of the Republicans could stop the threat of a filibuster and more from Northern Democrats. The Hayes managers worked overtime and reached a sectional-political rapprochement with the South. On March 2, 1877 (only three days before the inauguration) Congress in joint session endorsed the decision of the Electoral Commission and declared Hayes elected.

What was the nature of the deal between Hayes and the South? When the Republicans realized that they would need Southern support to remain in power, they fell back upon their common bond with the Redeemer Democrats of the South—economic self-interest. The Southerners wanted "home rule," no more "meddling" from Congress about reconstruction. Obviously the Southerners wanted Federal troops removed from South Carolina and Louisiana, the last two states in which they were stationed. And the Redeemers wanted still more. They wanted a Southerner in Hayes's Cabinet. They wanted a delayed share of the "pork barrel"—internal improvements for the South. Specifically, the Redeemers wanted Federal subsidies for the Texas and Pacific Railroad. They wanted repeal of the act opening up public lands in the South to homesteaders. They wanted levees built along the Mississippi River. Redeemers, who supposedly had restored the old order in the South, showed the depth of their conversion to "Yankee" ways of doing business.

Obviously the mass of white Southerners cared mostly about "home rule" and troop removal. Yet the men in a position to bargain for those things saw their opportunity and showed their mettle as "horsetraders." The compromise worked also because the North was willing to allow the South to take care of its own business concerning race relations. The zeal to reform and purify the South was all but burnt out.

Hayes was as good as his word. He appointed David M. Key of Tennessee Postmaster General and withdrew the troops. The South was back in the hands of white majorities. The Union was officially one again. Historian C. Vann Woodward has described the Compromise of 1877 as a thermidor—the cooling-off, conservative reaction to revolution. The New South was in many ways a throwback to the Old South. Racial subordination returned; agriculture persisted; and the Lost Cause almost won. Individuals became rich from mills and railroads and deluded themselves and others into believing that the South was indeed new. But the New South rhetoric was more or less a glaze to cover Northern economic exploitation, racial injustice, and a new class of "scalawags." In the "New" North the thermidor took the form of expanded industrial capitalism to the exclusion of "radical" ideals of reform and social justice. The crusade for Union and freedom moved on toward wealth and power.

EPILOGUE—
AMERICAN
UNIFICATION

Americans are accustomed to think of their national trauma as a totally American experience. Even the most popular name for the military conflict—the Civil War—implies an isolated, intramural struggle. Yet at roughly the same time other peoples experienced roughly the same kind of national unification. The two most obvious examples are Italy and Germany. In each case the most industrially developed section (three "norths," Prussia, Piedmont, and the American North) forged the union with "blood and iron." And in each case the social, economic, and cultural issues were raised to the level of ideology. Union or nation became an end in itself.

A comparative approach to these unifications adds scope and significance to the Civil War era in America. But it would be a mistake to stretch parallels too far. Nothing about the unification era in Western

Civilization suggests that nation-building was predetermined or inevitable. In fact a relatively few years after the American, Italian, and German unifications, Europe plunged into general war over an incident involving the deunification of Austria-Hungary.

Even more important is the uniquely American nature of the Civil War era and its aftermath. The issues and ideologies of North and South were peculiar to a time and place. The resultant union was firm—Southerners have not seriously considered secession since 1865. Yet beneath the facade of Union, Americans worked out and are still working out sectional solutions to mid-nineteenth-century problems. The nation as a whole adopted the world view of the winners and moved on to wealth and power. Yet amid the glory of "Yankee ingenuity," and "the Yanks are coming," has been the shame of national racism and the taint of the "Yankee dollars."

Perhaps the best way to assess the unique strength and weakness of American unification is to look at the losers. Some Southerners never gave up. Edmund Ruffin, for example, chose not to survive the Confederacy. Late in the war he returned to his plantation. The Yankees had been there; Ruffin read their obscene graffiti on the walls of his home. He cursed them and in his diary called down eternal damnation upon the entire "Yankee race." Then when he finished writing, Ruffin took up his shotgun and went for a stroll in his garden. There among his prized plants, Ruffin placed the muzzle of the gun in his mouth, put a forked stick to the trigger, and blew his brains out.

Characteristically Ruffin's response was extreme. Other Southerners acted out their continuing devotion to the "Cause" in other ways. There is an oft-told story about Georgian Robert Toombs and the great Chicago fire of 1871. Toombs heard about the fire and went to the local telegraph office to get the details. When friends asked him about the event, he reported that the Chicago fire department was doing its best to confine the flames and save the city. "But," he said, "the wind is in our favor."

Ruffin and Toombs bore witness to the strength and depth of the Southern ideology which lived on in defeat. And to the extent that the South is distinct from the rest of the nation, it lives even now—sometimes perverted and perverse, but more often often simply human and "different."

In the broad perspective, though, the sectional conflict resulted in the unification of the United States. Southerners had their own Reconstruction. They may have clung to the old culture, venerated the "Lost Cause," and codified racial subordination in the years after Appomattox; but paradoxically they also rejected the thought of independence and even the word "rebellion." There is more than irony in the fact that recently in the *United Daughters of the Confederacy Magazine* —an organization which exists to celebrate the long and bitter war *against* the United States—the U.D.C. President General exhorted her membership to observe Flag Day, "We are proud of our heritage, and as Americans all, let's show it."

mond, *Banks and Politics in America from the Revolution to the Civil War* (1957).

About the frontier West two books by Ray Allen Billington are standard, *Westward Expansion* (1949) and *The Far Western Frontier, 1830–1860* (1956). A crucial study of western attitudes about race is Eugene H. Berwanger, *The Frontier Against Slavery: Western Anti-Negro Prejudice and the Slavery Expansion Controversy* (1967).

The list of recent studies in the social and intellectual history of the "Old North" is long indeed. Perhaps the best beginning is with Vernon L. Parrington's *Main Currents in American Thought*, Vol. II, *The Romantic Revolution in America, 1800–1860* (1927). Parrington's work is biased toward his conception of Jeffersonian Democracy, but it still rewards reading. Merle E. Curti's *The Growth of American Thought* (1943) is good, and Irving H. Bartlett's *The American Mind in the Mid-Nineteenth Century* (1967) is an excellent short interpretation. James T. Flexner's *That Wilder Image* (1962) is a work of art in this period. Paul C. Nagel's *One Nation Indivisible: The Union in American Thought, 1776–1861* (1964), in a sense, complements Foner's study of political ideology cited earlier *(Free Soil, Free Labor, Free Men . . .)*.

On the subject of reform the best overview is still Alice Felt Tyler's *Freedom Ferment* (1944). Two books by C. S. Griffin, *Their Brothers' Keepers: Moral Stewardship in the United States, 1800–1865* (1960) and *The Ferment of Reform, 1830–1860,* offer a provocative interpretation that tends to portray the reformers as self-righteous do-gooders (and in the case of the nativists, for example, "do-badders").

The abolitionists have recently received much attention. Staughton Lynd in his *Intellectual Origins of American Radicalism* (1968) sees the antislavers as part of a long-standing radical tradition in America. Martin Duberman, ed., *The Antislavery Vanguard* (1965) is a collection of essays, some of which project the abolitionists into the present as forerunners to the civil rights movement. Eileen S. Kraditor's *Means and Ends in American Abolitionism: Garrison and His Critics on Strategy and Tactics* and David Donald's *Charles Sumner and the Coming of the Civil War* are thoughtful and thought-provoking studies. Louis Filler's *The Crusade against Slavery* (1960) is probably the best factual summary of the abolitionist movement. An intriguing look at the other side of the movement is Leonard L. Richards, *"Gentlemen of Property and Standing:" Anti-Abolition Mobs in Jacksonian America* (1970). Other significant aspects of race in mid-nineteenth century America are treated in Leon F. Litwack, *North of Slavery: The Negro in the Free States, 1790–1860* (1961), and Arthur Zilversmit, *The First Emancipation: the Abolition of Negro Slavery in the North* (1967).

The Old South

Clement Eaton has written the best summaries of the ante bellum South. His *History of the Old South,* revised edition (1966), *The Growth of Southern Civilization* (1961), and *The Mind of the Old South* (1964) are basic. So are Charles S. Sydnor's *The Development of Southern Sectionalism, 1819–1848* (1948) and Avery O. Craven's *The Growth of Southern Nationalism, 1848–1861* (1953).

For more interpretive studies, a student must begin with Wilbur J. Cash, *The Mind of the South* (1941). William R. Taylor's *Cavalier and Yankee: The Old South and the American National Character* (1961) is another classic attempt to discover the Old Southern soul. Important essays on the Southern experience are in David Potter, *The South and the Sectional Conflict* (1968); C. Vann Woodward, *The Burden of Southern History,* enlarged edition (1968); Frank E. Vandiver, ed., *The Idea of the South* (1964); and Charles Grier Sellers, Jr., *The Southerner as American* (1960). The most recent reinterpretation of the Old South is in the works of Eugene D. Genovese, *The Political Economy of Slavery* (1965), *The World the Slaveholders Made* (1967), and *In Red and Black* (1971).

Closely tied to views of Southern "civilization" are studies of the Southern economy. Significant recent contributions on this topic are Harold D. Woodman, *King Cotton and His Retainers* (1968), and Stuart Bruchey, ed., *Cotton and the Growth of the American Economy, 1790–1860* (1967). The "classic" on Southern agriculture is Lewis C. Gray, *History of Agriculture in the Southern United States to 1860,* 2 vols. (1933).

Two studies of social structure deserve mention: Anne Firor Scott, *The Southern Lady: From Pedestal to Politics* (1971), and Frank L. Owsley, *Plain Folk of the Old South* (1949).

About slavery the literature is vast. The best beginning point is still U. B. Phillips' *Life and Labor in the Old South* (1929) and *American Negro Slavery* (1918). Phillips' value judgments are dated, but his research is exhaustive. The standard revisionist summary is Kenneth M. Stampp's *The Peculiar Institution* (1956). Stanley M. Elkins' *Slavery: A Problem in American Institutional and Intellectual Life* (1959) is still provoking thought and debate about the effects of the slave experience on the black mind and personality.

One of the best ways to examine the Elkins thesis is to read William Styron's *Confessions of Nat Turner* (1967), a kind of restatement of Elkins in narrative fiction, and then read John Henrik Clarke, ed., *William Styron's Nat Turner: Ten Black Writers Respond* (1968). This case study of Nat Turner's life, William Styron's fiction, and Stanley Elkins' ideas is the subject of several anthologies including Eric Foner, ed., *Great Lives Observed: Nat Turner* (1971); John B. Duff and Peter M. Mitchell, ed., *The Nat Turner Rebellion: The Historical Event and the Modern Controversy* (1971); and Henry Irving Tragle, *The Southampton Slave Revolt of 1831: A Compilation of Source Material* (1971).

Two studies of urban slavery deserve mention, Richard C. Wade's *Slavery in the Cities: The South 1820–1860* (1964) and Robert S. Starobin's *Industrial Slavery in the Old South* (1970).

Slave narratives, accounts of slavery by those most involved, are vital to the literature. One of the best among many collections is Gilbert Osofsky, ed., *Puttin' on Ole Massa* (1961).

Another fruitful approach to the study of slavery and the Old South is that of comparing slave societies, thereby adding perspective to what has been a rather provincial enterprise. One of the leading advocates of the comparative approach is David Brion Davis in his *The Problem of Slavery in Western Culture* (1966). A good anthology of comparative studies is Laura Foner and Eugene D. Genovese, *Slavery in the New World: A Reader in Comparative History* (1969).

The War of the "Worlds"

The best narrative summaries of the 1850s are Allan Nevins, *Ordeal of the Union*, 2 vols. (1947), and *The Emergence of Lincoln*, 2 vols. (1950); Roy F. Nichols, *The Disruption of American Democracy* (1948); and Avery O. Craven, *The Coming of the Civil War*, revised edition (1957).

More emphasis on the structure of politics is in Joel H. Silbey, *The Shrine of Party* (1967). On the South U. B. Phillips, *The Course of the South to Secession*, ed. E. Merton Coulter (1939), is good; and Ralph A. Wooster's *The People in Power: Courthouse and Statehouse in the Lower South, 1850–1860* (1969) analyzes the "nuts and bolts" of Southern politics.

One way to unravel the politics of sectional crisis is to read the biographies of the politicians involved. On Lincoln in this period see especially Don E. Fehrenbacher, *Prelude to Greatness: Lincoln in the 1850's* (1970). The standard biography of Stephen A. Douglas is Gerald M. Capers, *Stephen A. Douglas: Defender of the Union* (1959); a fine recent study of Douglas' later career is Damon Wells, *Stephen Douglas: The Last Years, 1857–1861* (1971). Glyndon G. Van Deusen has written the standard work on Seward, *William Henry Seward* (1967). David Donald's study of Sumner, *Charles Sumner and the Coming of the Civil War* (1960), cited above, is incisive. The standard biographies of the Presidents during this period are Robert J. Rayback, *Millard Fillmore:*

Biography of a President (1959); Roy F. Nichols, *Franklin Pierce: Young Hickory of the Granite Hills,* new edition (1958); and Phillip S. Klein, *President James Buchanan* (1962). Works on leading Southern figures include Richard N. Current, *John C. Calhoun* (1963); Charles M. Wiltse, *John C. Calhoun,* 3 vols. (1944-51); Gerald N. Capers, *John C. Calhoun —Opportunist: A Reappraisal* (1960); Margaret L. Coit, *John C. Calhoun: American Portrait* (1950); Hudson Strode, *Jefferson Davis,* 3 vols. (1955-64); Avery O. Craven, *Edmond Ruffin, Southerner: A Study in Secession* (1932); Laura A. White, *Robert Barnwell Rhett, Father of Secession;* and William Y. Thompson, *Robert Toombs of Georgia* (1966). Among the Calhoun studies, Wiltse is perhaps still the best, Coit the most readable, Current the most analytical, and Capers the most critical. Strodes' work on Davis is extensive but uncritical and ponderous.

For the crises of the 1850s the best beginning is Holman Hamilton's work on the Compromise of 1850, *Prologue to Conflict: The Crisis and Compromise of 1850* (1964). Harriet Beecher Stowe, *Uncle Tom's Cabin,* and the literature of the entire war period are brilliantly discussed in Edmund Wilson, *Patriotic Gore: Studies of the Literature of the American Civil War* (1962). The Kansas-Nebraska Act is perhaps best summarized in Nevins' *Ordeal of the Union* and in Capers' biography of Douglas. On "Bleeding Kansas," see James A. Rawley, *Race and Politics: "Bleeding Kansas" and the Coming of the Civil War* (1969). Stephen B. Oates, *To Purge This Land with Blood: A Biography of John Brown* (1970), is excellent on Brown's career in Kansas.

About the diplomacy and international posture of the 1850s, two recent works are especially good, William H. Goetzmann's *When the Eagle Screamed* (1966) and Fred Somkin's *Unquiet Eagle* (1967). The classic study of the Dred Scott decision is Vincent C. Hopkins, *Dred Scott's Case* (1951). A good brief coverage of the Taney Court in perspective is R. Kent Newmyer's *The Supreme Court Under Marshall and Taney* (1963).

About Harpers Ferry, the Oates biography of Brown is outstanding. This most recent attempt to fathom Brown's mind and soul is the best yet.

The best general treatments of the election of 1860 are in Nevins' *Ordeal of the Union* and Lincoln biographies. Lincoln literature is vast. The best one-volume biography is still Benjamin P. Thomas, *Abraham Lincoln* (1952). Two longer studies are Carl Sandburg's six volumes, *Abraham Lincoln: The Prairie Years* (1926) and *Abraham Lincoln: The War Years* (1939), and James G. Randall's four volumes, *Lincoln the President* (1945-55) (Richard N. Current completed volume four). Three collections of essays about Lincoln are especially good, too: David Donald, *Lincoln Reconsidered* (1956); Norman Graebner, ed., *The Enduring Lincoln* (1959); and Richard N. Current, *The Lincoln Nobody*

Knows (1958). One more study of 1860 deserves mention, Norman Graebner, ed., *Politics and the Crisis of 1860* (1961). This is a collection of essays on the political crisis.

Among the many books on secession a few are "musts." Dwight L. Dummond's *The Secession Movement 1860–1861* (1931) and *Southern Editorials on Secession* (1931) are basic; Donald E. Reynolds, *Editors Make War: Southern Newspapers in the Secession Crisis* (1971) is a newer study of editorial attitudes in the South. Steven A. Channing's *Crisis of Fear: Secession in South Carolina* (1970) is a brilliant case study of revolution in South Carolina. Ralph A. Wooster's *Secession Conventions of the South* (1962) is a statistical study of the disunion process. Finally, George H. Knoles, ed., *The Crisis of the Union, 1860–1861* (1965) presents a selection of essays on the topic.

David M. Potter's *Lincoln and His Party in the Secession Crisis* (1942) is excellent on Northern action and reaction to secession and the Sumter crisis. Kenneth M. Stampp's *And the War Came* is also good on the immediate origins of the conflict. About Sumter, per se, Richard N. Current's *Lincoln and the First Shot* (1963) treats the issue of blame. W. A. Swanberg, *First Blood* (1958), and T. Harry Williams, *P. G. T. Beauregard: Napoleon in Gray* (1955), deal with the specifics of the Sumter confrontation.

Armed Mobs

Unfortunately no good general study of second-round secession exists. Wooster's *Secession Conventions of the South* covers some of the ground and state studies must fill in the rest.

To understand the process of war, several avenues are open. "Picture books" are indispensable to recapture the times. Among the dozens of pictorial presentations available, a good selection is Richard M. Ketchem, ed., *The American Heritage Picture History of the Civil War* (1960); Francis T. Miller, *The Photographic History of the Civil War*, 10 vols., new edition (1957); and David Donald, ed., *Divided We Fought* (1952). Vincent J. Esposito's, *The West Point Atlas of the Civil War* (1962) is an outstanding work of maps and commentaries.

Probably the best introduction to the military thought of the period are the appropriate sections of Lynn Montross, *War Through the Ages*, new and enlarged edition (1960), and T. Harry Williams' essay "The Military Leadership of North and South" in David Donald, ed., *Why the North Won the Civil War* (1960). Marcus Cunliffe, *Soldiers and Civilians: The Martial Spirit in America, 1775–1865* (1968) is an outstanding piece of intellectual history dealing with the place of war in the

American mind. Bruce Catton's *America Goes to War* (1958) is a brief analysis of this war's effect upon the participants, and vice versa.

The common soldiers of the period are the subject of two classics by Bell T. Wiley, *The Life of Johnny Reb* (1943) and *The Life of Billy Yank* (1952). The standard work on black soldiers is Dudley T. Cornish, *The Sable Arm* (1956).

On the Battle of First Manassas or Bull Run the standard account is Robert M. Johnston's *Bull Run* (1913). Volume I of Douglas S. Freeman's *Lee's Lieutenants: A Study in Command,* 3 vols. (1942–44) and Bruce Catton's *Mr. Lincoln's Army* (1951), the first of three volumes on the Army of the Potomac, treat Bull Run from Southern and Northern perspectives respectively. T. Harry Williams' biography of Beauregard is also good. Finally, Stephen Vincent Benet's narrative poem *John Brown's Body* (1928) presents incisive insight into the war period (especially the effect of the Manassas combat upon the combatants) in verse.

A Question of Union

The initial impact of the Civil War is perhaps best seen in studies of capitals and cabinets. Margaret Leech, *Reveille in Washington* (1941) is especially good on Washington's shock in the aftermath of First Manassas. Emory M. Thomas, *The Confederate State of Richmond: A Biography of the Capital* (1971) treats Richmond's response to wartime. Rembert W. Patrick's *Jefferson Davis and His Cabinet* (1944) is good on the Davis Administration and its early difficulties. Burton J. Hendrick's *Lincoln's War Cabinet* (1946) is the Union counterpart volume.

About the diplomacy of the war period no one work covers the ground. Van Deusen's biography of Seward, Jay Monaghan's *Diplomat in Carpet Slippers: Abraham Lincoln Deals with Foreign Affairs* (1945) and Frank L. Owsley's *King Cotton Diplomacy* (1959) perhaps compose as good a summary as any.

The standard work on European reaction to the American war is Donaldson Jordan and Edwin J. Pratt, *Europe and the American Civil War* (1931). A recent overview is Phillip Van Doren Stern, *When the Guns Roared: World Aspects of the American Civil War* (1965). An important book on Southern attempts to influence public opinion is Charles P. Cullop's *Confederate Propaganda in Europe, 1861–1865* (1969). And Harold Hyman, ed., *Heard Round the World: The Impact Abroad of the Civil War* (1969) is an excellent collection of essays.

On relations with individual nations the best works are Lynn M. Case and Warren F. Spencer, *The United States and France: Civil War Diplomacy* (1970); Ephraim D. Adams, *Great Britain and the American Civil*

War, 2 vols. (1925); Frank J. Merli, *Great Britain and the Confederate Navy* (1970); Stuart L. Bernath, *Squall Across the Atlantic: American Civil War Prize Cases and Diplomacy* (1970); Albert A. Woldman, *Lincoln and the Russians* (1952); Robin Winks, *Canada and the United States: The Civil War Years* (1960); and (on Latin America) Dexter Perkins, *The Monroe Doctrine, 1826–1867* (1933). In addition to Van Deusen's *Seward*, some biographies of key diplomatic figures include Martin B. Duberman, *Charles Francis Adams* (1961); Henry Adams, *The Education of Henry Adams: An Autobiography* (1918); Robert D. Meade, *Judah P. Benjamin: Confederate Statesman* (1943); and Daniel E. Carroll, *Henri Mercier and the American Civil War* (1971).

The naval war has not inspired nearly as much literature as the land war. The best summary is Virgil Carrington Jones, *The Civil War at Sea*, 3 vols. (1960–62). Standard biographies of the Navy secretaries are Joseph T. Durkin, *Stephen R. Mallory: Confederate Navy Chief* (1954) and Richard S. West, Jr., *Gideon Welles: Lincoln's Navy Department* (1943). Good works with a Union orientation include H. Allen Cornell, *Guns on the Western Waters: The Story of River Gunboats in the Civil War* (1949) and James M. Merrill, *The Rebel Shore: The Story of Union Sea Power in the Civil War* (1957). Good studies of Confederate operations are William M. Still, Jr., *Iron Afloat: The Story of the Confederate Ironclads* (1971); William N. Still, Jr., *Confederate Shipbuilding* (1969); Milton F. Perry, *Infernal Machines: The Story of Confederate Submarine and Mine Warfare* (1965); and Tom H. Wells, *The Confederate Navy: A Study in Organization* (1971). Of course the definitive collection of sources for the water war is the *Official Records of the Union and Confederate Navies in the War of the Rebellion*, 30 vols. (1894–1922).

For the land war there are the *Official Records of the Union and Confederate Armies*, 128 vols. (1880–1901). About the war in 1862 (and after, too) there are excellent works on three major field armies. Douglas S. Freeman's *Lee's Lieutenants: A Study in Command*, 3 vols. (1942–44) on the Army of Northern Virginia is a classic; as is Bruce Catton's trilogy on the Army of the Potomac, *Mr. Lincoln's Army* (1951), *Glory Road: The Bloody Route from Fredericksburg to Gettysburg* (1952); and *A Stillness at Appomattox* (1953). Thomas L. Connelly has two fine volumes on the Confederacy's western army, *Army of the Heartland: The Army of Tennessee, 1861–1862* (1967) and *Autumn of Glory: The Army of Tennessee, 1863–1865* (1971). Bruce Catton's *Terrible Swift Sword* (1963) covers the military events of 1862 well and spiritedly.

Biographies of leading warriors include Warren W. Hassler, Jr., *General George B. McClellan: Shield of the Union* (1957); Gilbert E. Govan and James W. Livingood, *A Different Valor: The Story of General Joseph E. Johnston, C.S.A.* (1956); Douglas S. Freeman, *R. E. Lee: A*

Biography, 4 vols. (1934–35); Frank E. Vandiver, *Mighty Stonewall* (1957); Grady McWhiney, *Braxton Bragg and Confederate Defeat,* 2 vols. (1968–69); and three volumes on Grant begun by Lloyd Lewis (*Captain Sam Grant,* 1950) and completed by Bruce Catton (*Grant Moves South,* 1960, and *Grant Takes Command,* 1969). On the campaigns themselves some good studies are Clifford Dowdey's *The Seven Days: The Emergence of Lee* (1964) and Edward P. Stackpole's *From Cedar Mountain to Antietam* (1959). Archer Jones's *Confederate Strategy from Shiloh to Vicksburg* (1961) is a challenging work on the "big picture" in the West.

Homefront War in the North

The literature of the homefront North revolves around Abraham Lincoln. Yet a number of good studies exist in addition to Lincolniana. About politics Leonard P. Curry, *Blueprint for Modern America: Nonmilitary Legislation of the First Civil War Congress* (1968) is important, as is Herman Belz, *Reconstructing the Union: Theory and Policy During the Civil War* (1969). Hans L. Trefousse, *The Radical Republicans: Lincoln's Vanguard for Racial Justice* (1969) is a good interpretative work. On the same subject T. Harry Williams' *Lincoln and the Radicals* (1941) is standard. William B. Hesseltine's *Lincoln and Civil War Politics* (1969) is a collection of essays with a "problems" approach. Another good edited work is Grady McWhiney, ed., *Grant, Lee, Lincoln, and the Radicals* (1964). The standard study of Copperheads is Frank L. Klement, *The Copperheads in the Middle West* (1960).

The exasperating experience of the Commander-in-Chief and his generals is cataloged from the military side in Kenneth P. Williams, *Lincoln Finds a General: A Military Study of the Civil War,* 5 vols. (1949–59), and from Lincoln's point of view in T. Harry Williams, *Lincoln and His Generals* (1952). Fred A. Shannon's *The Organization and Administration of the Union Army, 1861–1865,* 2 vols. (1928), is especially helpful on the early war period. Other works on the behind-the-lines military include George W. Adams, *Doctors in Blue* (1962), and W. Q. Maxwell, *Lincoln's Fifth Wheel: The Political History of the United States Sanitation Commission* (1956).

The Northern economy is best treated in Ralph Andreano, ed., *The Economic Impact of the American Civil War* (1962), Emerson D. Fite, *Social and Industrial Conditions in the North During the Civil War* (1910), and Bray Hammond, *Sovereignty and an Empty Purse: Banks and Politics in the Civil War* (1970). A good economic overview is Thomas C. Cochran and William Miller, *The Age of Enterprise: A Social History of Industrial America,* revised edition (1961).

Perhaps the best balanced work on the topic is John Hope Franklin's monograph, *The Emancipation Proclamation* (1963). James G. Randall in Volume II of his biography *Lincoln the President* calls the Proclamation a mere "paper pronouncement." James M. McPherson emphasizes the role of the abolitionists in goading a reluctant Lincoln into action in *The Struggle for Equality: Abolitionists and the Negro in the Civil War and Reconstruction* (1964). On the white response to emancipation, V. Jacque Voegel's *Free But Not Equal: The Midwest and the Negro during the Civil War* (1967) and Forrest G. Wood's *Black Scare: The Racist Response to Emancipation and Reconstruction* (1963) are crucial works. Three other books deserve mention: Benjamin Quarles, *Lincoln and the Negro* (1962); John S. Wright, *Lincoln and the Politics of Slavery* (1970); and a collection of documents, Arthur Zilversmit, ed., *Lincoln on Black and White* (1971).

Standard works on black Americans during the war period are Benjamin Quarles, *The Negro in the Civil War* (1953), Herbert Aptheker, *The Negro in the Civil War* (1938), and James M. McPherson, ed., *The Negro's Civil War* (1865). An important biography of a white who commanded a black regiment in the war is Tilden G. Edelstein, *Strange Enthusiasm: The Life of Thomas Wentworth Higginson* (1968).

Other good books on the social and intellectual experience of the wartime North are: J. Cutler Andrews, *The North Reports the Civil War* (1955); George M. Frederickson, *The Inner Civil War: Northern Intellectuals and the Crisis of the Union* (1965); and Edward C. Kirkland, *The Peacemakers of 1864* (1927).

The Confederate South

Good general histories of the Confederacy include Frank E. Vandiver, *Their Tattered Flags: The Epic of the Confederacy* (1970); Clement Eaton, *A History of the Southern Confederacy* (1954); E. Merton Coulter, *The Confederate States of America, 1861–1865* (1950); and Charles P. Roland, *The Confederacy* (1960). Among the essay books, David Donald, ed., *Why the North Won the Civil War* (1962) is more about why the South lost. Henry Steele Commager's *The Defeat of the Confederacy* (1964) is good. Bell I. Wiley, *The Road to Appomattox*, Atheneum edition (1968), and Emory M. Thomas, *The Confederacy as a Revolutionary Experience* (1971), are extended-essay interpretations.

On Confederate polity Charles R. Lee, Jr., *The Confederate Constitutions* (1963) is the standard work on the Southern frame of government. Curtis A. Amlund's *Federalism in the Southern Confederacy* (1966) makes a case for Southern political nationalism, while May Spencer

Ringold's *The Role of State Legislatures in the Confederacy* (1966) deals with the relationship of state to central governments. In contrast to Strodes' eulogistic biography, the best work on the Davis inner circle is Rembert R. Patrick's *Jefferson Davis and His Cabinet*. On the Congress the standard study is Wilfred B. Yearns, *The Confederate Congress* (1960). A recent important supplement to this general treatment is Thomas B. Alexander and Richard E. Beringer, *The Anatomy of the Confederate Congress* (1972).

Military policy and administration are covered in Frank E. Vandiver's *Rebel Brass: The Confederate Command System* (1956), Richard D. Goff's *Confederate Supply* (1969), and Horace H. Cunningham's *Doctors in Gray: The Confederate Medical Service* (1958). Frank E. Vandiver, *Ploughshares into Swords: Josiah Gorgas and Confederate Ordnance* (1952) is a key study.

The Southern economy lacks a summary work. However, Charles W. Ramsdell, *Behind the Lines in the Southern Confederacy* (1944), Charles B. Dew, *Ironmaker to the Confederacy: Joseph R. Anderson and the Tredegar Iron Works* (1966), Paul W. Gates, *Agriculture and the Civil War* (1965), Richard C. Todd, *Confederate Finance* (1954), Robert C. Black, III, *The Railroads of the Confederacy* (1952), and Louise B. Hill, *State Socialism in the Confederate States of America* (1936) form a solid core of interpretive and specialized studies. The impact of wartime on common Confederates is dealt with in two excellent studies by Mary Elizabeth Massey, *Ersatz in the Confederacy* (1952) and *Refugee Life in the Confederacy* (1964). Bell I. Wiley's *The Plain People of the Confederacy* (1943) is a classic work on all phases of life among Southern civilians.

Bell I. Wiley's *Southern Negroes, 1861–1865* (1938) is still the major attempt of synthesis about black Confederates. Two recent studies, however, have demonstrated the exciting possibilities that exist in this area of scholarship: Robert F. Durden, *The Gray and the Black: The Confederate Debate on Emancipation* (1972), and James H. Brewer, *The Confederate Negro: Virginia's Craftsmen and Military Laborers, 1861–1865* (1969).

Works on the urban Confederacy include Gerald M. Capers, *Occupied City: New Orleans Under the Federals, 1862–1865* (1965), Kenneth Coleman, *Confederate Athens* (1968), and Emory M. Thomas, *The Confederate State of Richmond: A Biography of the Capital* (1971).

On cultural activities a sample of many books includes J. Cutler Andrews, *The South Reports the Civil War* (1970), Clement Eaton, *The Waning of the Old South Civilization* (1968), and James W. Silver, *Confederate Morale and Church Propaganda*, Norton Library edition (1967).

Turning Tides—The War in 1863

Military studies of the war in 1863 include many of the works cited for the 1862 campaigns. Works on the major field armies by Freeman, Catton, and Connelly; biographies of the principal commanders; and Catton's centennial history (*Never Call Retreat*) are especially appropriate.

On Chancellorsville see Edward J. Stackpole, *Chancellorsville: Lee's Greatest Battle* (1958), and John Bigelow, *The Campaign of Chancellorsville: A Strategic and Tactical Study* (1910), Fairfax Downey's *Clash of Cavalry* (1959) deals with the highly significant mounted action at Brandy Station. Gettysburg has had a host of students. Perhaps the best work on the entire campaign is the most recent, Edwin B. Coddington, *The Gettysburg Campaign* (1968). Others include Clifford Dowdey, *Death of a Nation* (1958); Edwin J. Stackpole, *They Met at Gettysburg* (1956); Glenn Tucker, *High Tide of Gettysburg* (1958); Wilbur S. Nye, *Here Come the Rebels* (1965); and James S. Montgomery, *The Shaping of a Battle: Gettysburg* (1959).

For the western campaigns, Earl S. Miers, *Web of Victory* (1955), and Peter F. Walker, *Vicksburg: A People at War* (1960), are good on Vicksburg. Glenn Tucker's *Chickamauga: Bloody Battle in the West* (1961) and Fairfax Downey's *Storming the Gateway: Chattanooga, 1863* (1960) cover Bragg, Rosecrans, and Grant in Tennessee. For the Trans-Mississippi theater Stephen B. Oates, *Confederate Cavalry West of the River* (1961), is good, and Robert L. Kerby, *Kirby Smith's Confederacy: The Trans-Mississippi South, 1863–1865* (1972), has filled (well) a large scholarly gap.

Biographies of commanders who emerged as important in 1863 include: Walter H. Herbert, *Fighting Joe Hooker* (1944); Donald B. Sanger and Thomas R. Hay, *James Longstreet* (1952); Hamilton J. Eckenrode and Bryan Conrad, *James Longstreet: Lee's War Horse* (1935); Freeman Cleaves, *Meade of Gettysburg* (1960); John C. Pemberton, Jr., *John C. Pemberton: Defender of Vicksburg* (1942); William M. Lamers, *The Edge of Glory: A Biography of General William S. Rosecrans, U.S.A.* (1961); Lloyd Lewis, *Sherman, Fighting Prophet* (1932); Earl S. Miers, *The General Who Marched to Hell: William Tecumseh Sherman and His March to Fame and Infamy* (1951); William T. Sherman, *Memoirs of General W. T. Sherman, Written by Himself*, 2 vols. (1887); Burke Davis, *Jeb Stuart: The Last Cavalier* (1957); John W. Thomason, Jr., *Jeb Stuart* (1930); and Grady McWhiney, *Braxton Bragg and Confederate Defeat*, 2 vols. (1969–71).

Fight to the Finish—the War in 1864–65

Activities of guerrillas during the Civil War have inspired no really comprehensive or very analytical studies. Individual raids and raiders, however, have a colorful literature. About Nathan Bedford Forrest see Robert S. Henry, *"First with the Most" Forrest* (1944), and Andrew N. Lytle, *Bedford Forrest and His Critter Company* (1931). Dee A. Brown has works on John Hunt Morgan and B. H. Grierson, *The Bold Cavaliers* (1959) and *Grierson's Raid* (1954) respectively. Richard S. Brownlee's *Gray Ghosts of the Confederacy: Guerrilla Warfare in the West, 1861–1865* (1958) is spirited and sound. Dahlgren's raid is the subject of Virgil Carrington Jones's *Eight Hours Before Richmond* (1958).

On the major campaigns of 1864 the literature is not as voluminous as the significance of these decisive encounters suggests it might be. In the East, Clifford Dowdey's *Lee's Last Campaign* (1960) is good, as is Edward Steere's *The Wilderness Campaign* (1960). Frank E. Vandiver's *Jubal's Raid* (1960) deals with Jubal Early's march on Washington, and Edward J. Stackpole's *Sheridan in the Shenandoah* covers Sheridan's march on Early.

Connelly's *Autumn of Glory* and biographies of Johnston and Sherman treat the Atlanta campaign. John Bell Hood has two standard biographies, Richard O'Connor, *Hood: Cavalier General* (1949), and John P. Dyer, *The Gallant Hood* (1950). Thomas R. Hays, *Hood's Tennessee Campaign* (1929) is standard on the subject, as is Stanley F. Horn's *The Decisive Battle of Nashville* (1956). Ludwell H. Johnson, *Red River Campaign: Politics and Cotton in the Civil War* (1958) is a classic on the abortive Federal drive up the Red River in 1864.

Three books give vivid pictures of the war's closing scenes: Rembert W. Patrick, *The Fall of Richmond* (1960); Burke Davis, *To Appomattox* (1959); and Phillip Van Doren Stern, *An End to Valor* (1958).

Restoration, Resurrection, Reconstruction

Among general histories of Reconstruction the older interpretation is best expressed in Claude G. Bowers, *The Tragic Era* (1929), William A. Dunning, *Reconstruction: Political and Economic, 1865–1877* (1907), and E. Merton Coulter, *The South During Reconstruction, 1865–1877* (1947). The best introduction to revisionist views, now accepted in some form by almost all scholars, is Kenneth M. Stampp and Leon Litwak, eds., *Reconstruction: An Anthology of Revisionist Writings* (1969). General works which reflect recent scholarship include: Rembert W. Patrick, *Recon-*

struction of the Nation (1967); John Hope Franklin, *Reconstruction after the Civil War* (1961); Kenneth M. Stampp, *The Era of Reconstruction, 1865–1877* (1965); Avery O. Craven, *Reconstruction: The Ending of the Civil War* (1969); and Allen W. Trelease, *Reconstruction: The Great Experiment* (1971). An important collection of primary sources is Walter L. Flemming, *Documentary History of Reconstruction: Political, Military, Social, Religious, Educational and Industrial, 1865 to 1906*, 2 vols., with a Foreword by David Donald (1966).

The literature on Presidential Reconstruction centers upon the character of Andrew Johnson and of his opposition in Congress. The best studies of the period 1865–1867 are: William R. Brock, *An American Crisis: Congress and Reconstruction, 1865–1867* (1963); La Wanda Cox and John H. Cox, *Politics, Principle, and Prejudice, 1865–1866* (1963); and David Donald, *The Politics of Reconstruction, 1863–1867* (1965). Important biographies of the period include: Eric L. McKitrick, *Andrew Johnson and Reconstruction* (1960); Patrick W. Riddleberger, *George Washington Julian, Radical Republican* (1966); Benjamin Quarles, *Lincoln and the Negro* (1962); Fawn M. Brodie, *Thaddeus Stevens: Scourge of the South* (1959); Richard N. Current, *Old Thad Stevens: A Story of Ambition* (1942); Ralph Korngold, *Thaddeus Stevens: A Being Darkly Wise and Rudely Great* (1955); Charles A. Jellison, *Fessenden of Maine: Civil War Senator* (1962); and David Donald's second volume on Charles Sumner *Charles Sumner and the Rights of Man*.

Some good collections of documents and essays on Reconstruction are: Harold Hyman, ed., *The Radical Republicans and Reconstruction, 1861–1870* (1967); Richard N. Current, ed., *Reconstruction, 1865–1877* (1965); Grady McWhiney, ed., *Reconstruction and the Freedmen* (1963); Harvey Wish, ed., *Reconstruction in the South, 1865–1877* (1965); Hans L. Trefousse, ed., *Background for Radical Reconstruction* (1970); Edwin Rozwenc, ed., *Reconstruction in the South* (1952); and Seth M. Scheiner, ed., *Reconstruction: A Tragic Failure?* (1968).

Congress in Command

The general histories cited above treat Congressional Reconstruction. In addition a number of topical works on the period 1868–1877 are important.

Economic questions relating to Reconstruction are the subjects of Thomas C. Cochran and William Miller, *Age of Enterprise*, revised edition (1961); Walter T. K. Nugent, *The Money Question during Reconstruction* (1967); Erwin F. Unger, *The Greenback Era: A Social and Political History of American Finance, 1865–1879* (1964); and George R.

Woolfolk, *The Cotton Regency: The Northern Merchants and Reconstruction, 1865–1880* (1959).

Constitutional issues are treated in Stanley I. Kulter's *Judicial Power and Reconstruction Politics* (1968), Harold Hyman's *Era of the Oath* (1954), and Joseph B. James's *The Framing of the Fourteenth Amendment* (1956). On race and politics see Forrest G. Wood, *Black Scare: The Racist Response to Emancipation and Reconstruction* (1970), and Vincent P. DeSantis, *Republicans Face the Southern Question* (1959).

Of course the heart and soul of Congressional Reconstruction lay in its application in the South. State studies of this process include: Thomas B. Alexander, *Political Reconstruction in Tennessee* (1950); Hamilton J. Eckenrode, *The Political History of Virginia During the Reconstruction* (1904); J. G. de Roulhae Hamilton, *Reconstruction in North Carolina* (1914); Alan Conway, *The Reconstruction of Georgia* (1966); Elizabeth Studley Nathans, *Losing the Peace: Georgia Republicans and Reconstruction, 1865–1871* (1968); Thomas S. Staples, *Reconstruction in Arkansas 1862–1874* (1923); Walter L. Fleming, *Civil War and Reconstruction in Alabama* (1950); Charles W. Ramsdell, *Reconstruction in Texas* (1910); James W. Garner, *Reconstruction in Mississippi* (1901); William C. Harris, *Presidential Reconstruction in Mississippi* (1967); William W. Davis, *The Civil War and Reconstruction in Florida* (1913); John R. Ficklen, *History of Reconstruction in Louisiana (through 1868)* (1910); Ella Lonn, *Reconstruction in Louisiana after 1868* (1918); Francis B. Simkins and Robert H. Woody, *South Carolina during Reconstruction* (1932); and Richard O. Curry, ed., *Radicalism, Racism, and Party Realignment: The Border States During Reconstruction* (1969). Some of these studies reflect the best of recent thinking; others represent the more traditional presuppositions about Reconstruction.

The best introduction to the role of black Southerners in Reconstruction is Robert Cruden's *The Negro in Reconstruction* (1969). Willie Lee Rose, *Rehearsal for Reconstruction: The Port Royal Experiment* (1964) deals with an attempt to settle blacks upon abandoned lands in coastal South Carolina. William McFeeley's *Yankee Stepfather: General O. O. Howard and the Freedmen* (1969) is a study of Howard as head of the Freedmen's Bureau. Howard A. White, *The Freedmen's Bureau in Louisiana* (1970) is a crucial case study. Otis Singletary, *Negro Militia and Reconstruction* (1957), and Samuel D. Smith, *The Negro in Congress, 1870–1901* (1966), treat specific black roles. State studies include: Joel Williamson, *After Slavery: The Negro in South Carolina During Reconstruction* (1965); Joe M. Richardson, *The Negro in the Reconstruction of Florida, 1865–1877* (1965); Vernon L. Wharton, *The Negro in Mississippi, 1865–1890* (1947); and Charles Wynes, *Race Relations in Virginia, 1870–1902* (1961).

White racism in the South is the subject of Stanley Horn, *The Invisible Empire* (1939); Allen Trelease, *White Terror* (1971); and Theodore B. Wilson, *The Black Codes of the South* (1965).

Robert V. Bruce, *1877: Year of Violence* (1959), and especially C. Vann Woodward, *Reunion and Reaction: The Compromise of 1877 and the End of Reconstruction* (1951), deal with the formal finish of Reconstruction. Finally, Paul M. Gaston's *The New South Creed: A Study in Southern Mythmaking* (1970) and C. Vann Woodward's *Origins of the New South, 1877–1913* (1951) are classic interpretations of the aftermath of Reconstruction in the South.

INDEX